Dying for a Paycheck

ALSO BY JEFFREY PFEFFER

Leadership BS: Fixing Workplaces and Careers One Truth at a Time

Power: Why Some People Have It—and Others Don't

Hard Facts, Dangerous Half-Truths, and Total Nonsense: Profiting from Evidence-Based Management (with Robert I. Sutton)

The Knowing-Doing Gap: How Smart Companies Turn Knowledge into Action (with Robert I. Sutton)

Hidden Value: How Great Companies Achieve Extraordinary Results with Ordinary People (with Charles A. O'Reilly)

The Human Equation: Building Profits by Putting People First

Competitive Advantage Through People: Unleashing the Power of the Work Force

Managing with Power: Politics and Influence in Organizations

Organizations and Organization Theory

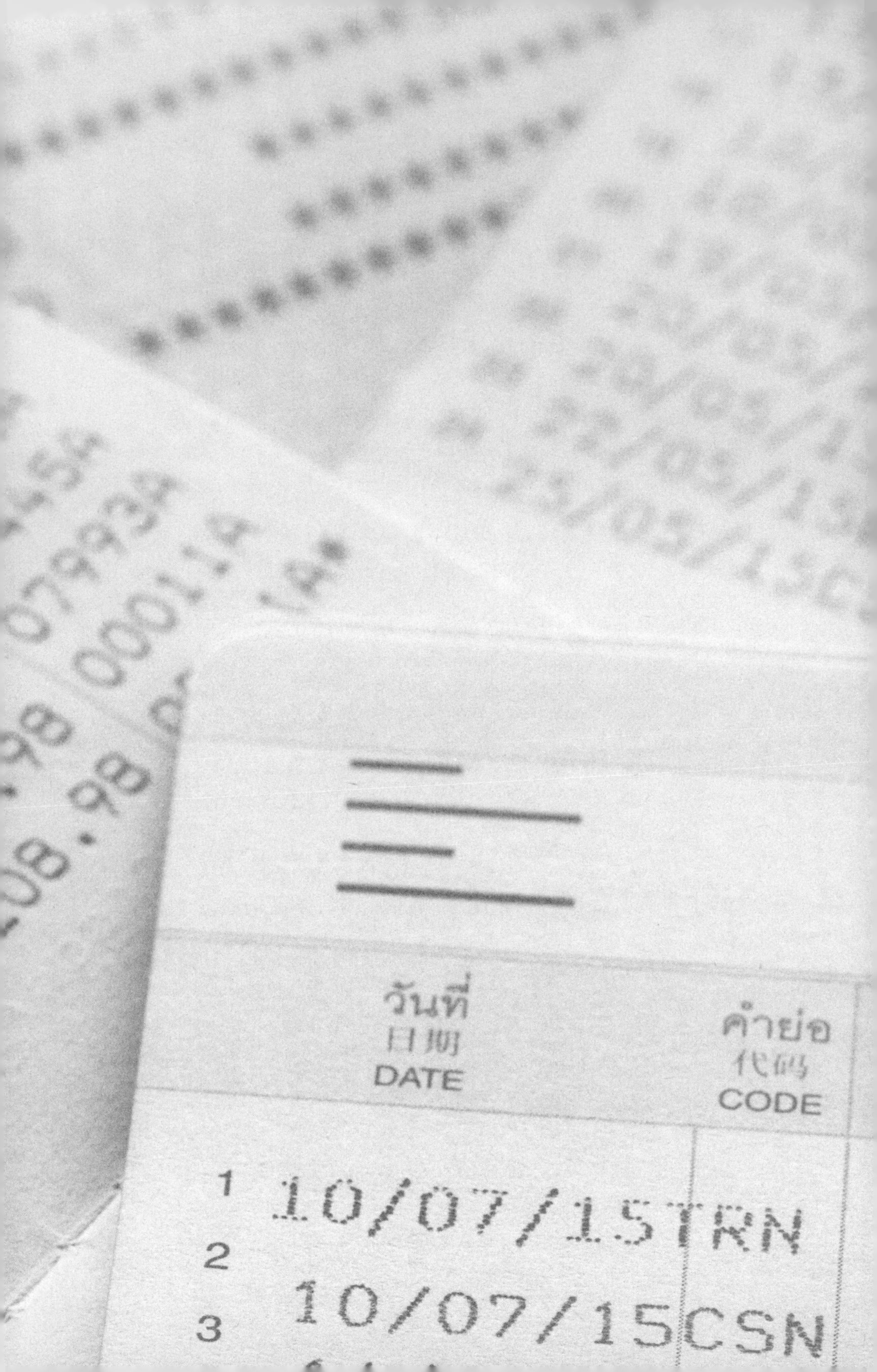

	วันที่ 日期 DATE	คำย่อ 代码 CODE
1	10/07/15	TRN
2		
3	10/07/15	CSN

Dying for a Paycheck

HOW MODERN MANAGEMENT HARMS EMPLOYEE HEALTH AND COMPANY PERFORMANCE—AND WHAT WE CAN DO ABOUT IT

JEFFREY PFEFFER

An Imprint of HarperCollins*Publishers*

HarperCollins books may be purchased for educational, business, or sales promotional use. For information, please email the Special Markets Department at SPsales@harpercollins.com.

FIRST EDITION

Frontispiece: Photograph by Arisara T/Shutterstock

Library of Congress Cataloging-in-Publication Data has been applied for.

ISBN 978-0-06-280092-3

18 19 20 21 22 LSC 10 9 8 7 6 5 4 3 2 1

To the Amazing Kathleen,

who was, is, and always will be

the love of my life.

Contents

Dying for a Paycheck

Introduction

YOU DON'T HAVE TO work in a coal mine, on an oil rig, in a chemical plant, or in construction to face a possibly toxic, health-destroying workplace. In today's work world, white-collar jobs are often as stressful and unhealthful as manual labor or blue-collar work—frequently more so. That's because physical dangers at work have been largely eliminated by the Occupational Safety and Health Administration (OSHA) in the United States and comparable agencies in other countries. Reprising a lesson from the quality movement that what gets inspected—and measured and reported—gets affected, countries pay attention to workplace fatalities and incidents, such as falls or chemical spills, where bodily harm can be readily ascertained. The result: the rate of workplace deaths in the United States decreased 65 percent just between 1970 and 2015, while the rate of workplace injuries fell some 72 percent over that same time.[1]

Meanwhile, stress at work, not subject to OSHA reporting or intervention, and seemingly invisible and accepted as an inevitable part of contemporary workplaces, just keeps getting worse for almost all jobs, resulting in an ever-higher physical and psychological toll. For instance, the health website WebMD reported that work was the number one source of stress,[2] and the American Psychological Association's 2015 report *Stress in America*[3] noted that the top two sources of stress were money and work, with almost one-quarter of all adults reporting extreme levels of stress. Another poll of almost three thousand people reported that nearly half of employees reported missing time at work from work-related stress, 61 percent said that workplace stress had made them physically sick, and 7 percent said they had been hospitalized because of workplace stress and its physiological effects.[4]

If the aggregate statistics are disturbing, the individual stories are truly horrifying. Talk to the person in a senior finance role working in a rapidly growing medical services provider. Confronting almost impossible work demands that required frequent all-nighters, she began taking stimulants, moved on to the exceedingly available cocaine, and numbed the constant workplace stress and abusive supervision with alcohol. Her (ultimately successful) detox process from workplace-induced alcohol and drug addiction required enormous amounts of psychological and financial resources—and, of course, leaving her toxic place of employment.

Or interview the television news producer who demonstrated organizational loyalty and commitment by being willing to go anywhere in the world at any time on almost no notice to help get the story. That person gained sixty pounds in a short period from not having the time to eat properly, let alone exercise. The unrelenting job demands jeopardized the person's marriage and the relationship with their child as well as their physical and mental health.

Or converse with the person receiving workers' compensation while on disability leave after being diagnosed with post-traumatic stress disorder caused by their job at the electric utility Southern California Edison. The PTSD came from excessive work demands—too much work given, too lean staffing levels, and the unrelenting pressure from supervisors to complete the impossible workload.

The stories are almost endless and the costs, to people, their employers, and the larger society, are enormous. For example, the American Institute of Stress maintains that job stress costs US employers more than $300 billion annually.[5] The ill-health from workplace stress adversely affects productivity and drives up voluntary turnover. One poll found that nearly 50 percent of the respondents reported "having changed jobs to escape the stress."[6] As we will see in Chapter 2, on the toll of unhealthy workplace practices, the costs to just the US health-care system approach $200 billion a year, and may be more.

Unfortunately, the problems from what IESE Business School professor Nuria Chinchilla once aptly called *social pollution* seem to be getting worse, not better. Possibly the saddest part of the tale: even as organizations of all kinds regularly permit, if not encourage, management practices that literally sicken and kill their employees, these same employers *also* suffer because toxic management practices and unhealthy workplaces do *not* improve organizational profitability or performance. On the contrary, unhealthy workplaces diminish employee engagement, increase turnover, and reduce job performance, even as they drive up health insurance and health-care costs. All too many workplaces have management practices that serve *neither* the interests of employees nor their employers, truly a lose-lose situation.

People's needless harm and suffering occur even as companies tout their environmental bona fides. Ironically, companies have developed elaborate measures to track their progress on environmental sustainability with little thought given to the companies' effects on *human* sustainability. Although environmental sustainability obviously is essential, so is human sustainability—creating workplaces where people can thrive and experience physical and mental health, where they can work for years without facing burnout or illness from management practices in the workplace. We should care about people, not just endangered species or photogenic polar bears, as we think about the impact of corporate activity on our environments. And as companies obsess over their carbon footprint, they would do well to consider their effects—their footprints—on the human beings, a carbon-based life-form, who work for them.

As we will see in the pages that follow, if anything is going to change with respect to workplace well-being and employee physical and mental health, some or a combination of the following things will need to occur. First, current and prospective employees must understand what constitutes health risks in their work environments, and that includes the psychosocial risks that are today more omnipresent and dangerous than the risks of physical injury. Armed with that information, people must then begin to select and deselect their employers at least partly based on stress-related dimensions of work that profoundly influence their physical and mental health.

Second, employers will need to understand and measure what their toxic management practices are costing them, both in direct medical costs and more indirectly in lost productivity and increased turnover. That understanding and quantification of the costs of toxic work environments seems like a necessary first step toward change.

Third, governments at all levels will need to first acknowledge—and measure—and then do something about the externalities created as employers offload people who were physically and psychologically damaged at work onto various parts of the public health and welfare system. The public costs of privately created workplace stress and unhealthy workplaces have already prompted policy attention and action in the United Kingdom and in many Scandinavian countries, in part because with government-funded health care, it is in the economic interests of public agencies to reduce unnecessary health-care costs, including preventable costs from workplace stress.

And fourth, societies will need social movements, or maybe several social movements, that make human sustainability and people's work environments as important as environmental sustainability and the physical environment have become. Decades ago, companies regularly dumped pollutants into the air, water, and ground. Then people decided that preserving the physical environment and having businesses pay for the external harm they were causing were worthy social goals. Because of the environmental movement, publicity, and political pressure, governments all over the world passed laws and nations developed norms that curtailed many actions that polluted the physical environment. In a similar fashion, societies would benefit from movements that resolutely take the importance and sanctity of human life and people's physical and psychological well-being more seriously—not just at life's very, very beginning or at its very, very end, but throughout people's lives, including their lives at work.

ANOTHER INCONVENIENT TRUTH

Several distinct but interrelated events caused me to delve into the topic of work organizations and their effects on human health, while undertaking the research that resulted in this book.

First, many decades of research and teaching by both myself and colleagues around the effect of high-commitment or high-performance work practices on productivity and other dimensions of organizational performance[7] had resulted in little to no positive change. Notwithstanding the publication of numerous books, including some of my own,[8] on this topic, workplaces were, if anything, getting worse with less employee engagement and satisfaction and diminished trust in institutional leadership.[9] Books, articles, and talks on the connections between people and profits seemingly weren't going to change management decisions or organizational practices. What might?

As I participated in meetings of the Hewitt Human Capital Leadership Council (prior to Hewitt's merger with Aon), a group of senior human resource leaders from large corporations, and as I served on the Stanford Committee for Faculty and Staff Human Resources, I couldn't help noticing something. The conversations often focused on health-care costs. Employers seemed obsessed with and relentlessly focused on reducing these costs. The thought crossed my mind that many of the management practices that produced higher levels of employee loyalty, engagement, and performance—things such as job security and decision-making discretion—might also produce healthier workplaces. If that were the case, perhaps employee health and health-care costs could become the lever to increase the adoption of high-commitment work arrangements, management practices that had been advocated for so long but were so infrequently embraced and quickly abandoned in times of economic stringency. If companies and countries were going to "bend the cost curve" of health, to use an oft-heard phrase, changing work environments just might be one of the best places to focus efforts and attention.

Second, as I sat on the various committees just mentioned, I was struck by how everything was always about "costs" and "resources," particularly when it came to people. To take just one example, because of the recession that began in 2007 to 2008, Stanford University laid off between four hundred and five hundred people[10] and, earlier in the decade, had instituted a wage freeze in the face of a budget shortfall,[11] notwithstanding the university's enormous endowment. During that time, as I drove through the campus one day, I noticed enormous specimen trees sitting in planter boxes awaiting planting in the ground. About a decade earlier, there had been much publicity about the demise of a three-hundred-year-old large heritage oak near the Stanford Family Mausoleum on campus. This tree had "been the object of much care and affection" and had received heroic efforts to save its life.[12] Some years later, a Palo Alto news article remarked on the apparently newsworthy event of the cutting down of an oak tree near the soccer stadium because it could not be saved—but it would be replaced by six new trees.[13] Observing all this, I commented to several people that at Stanford, you were better off being a tree than an employee. At too many workplaces, trees—or maybe landscaping—fare better than people.

Language, the terms people use to describe the world, tells a lot. When we talk about people at business, we often use terms such as *human resources* and *human capital*. When people describe wages and health benefits, *employee* or *health care* is often followed by the word *costs*. Years ago, independent power producer AES's cofounder, Dennis Bakke, told me that he objected to one of my book subtitles that read "building profits by putting people first."[14] Bakke said that putting people first should not be solely or maybe even at all in the interests of profits, or costs. Instead, Bakke argued, people, as human beings, as living creatures, deserved to have their welfare and well-being receive some priority in management decision making, independent of the effect of that prioritization on costs or profits.

We need to change the language routinely used in business.

Well-being and physical and mental health need to become much more focal in conversations and policies. As Bob Chapman, CEO of the privately owned $2.5 billion manufacturing company Barry-Wehmiller, likes to say, corporate leaders have a responsibility to steward the lives of the employees who are in their hands. The people who come to work are the husbands and wives and sons and daughters of family members who love them. Leaders should ensure that at the end of the day, their employees return home in good shape, prepared to live fulfilled lives outside of work.

Third, in political discourse in the United States and some other countries, there is vigorous, ongoing discussion of "pro-life" policies. But such debates and the laws, appropriations, and regulations that accompany them seldom consider what happens to people during most of their lives, when they are working. If we take seriously the fundamental sanctity and importance of human life and well-being, I concluded that there is a moral, ethical reason to be concerned about human health and well-being in the workplace. And if I was concerned about people's welfare and how that was affected by work environments, I ought to understand the magnitude and dimensions of the issue.

I had these ideas already in mind when IESE professor Nuria Chinchilla asked me to participate in a conference she was organizing on the general theme of work and family. Chinchilla had talked to me about social pollution and had commented that the real "inconvenient truth"[15] was not just the destruction of the physical environment but also the degradation of the social environment, in part through how employers operated. The conference never occurred, but that paper, which began my exploration of the issue of the workplace and human health, appeared in a refereed journal and laid out some of the first ideas on the topic of human sustainability.[16] From that point on, I have gathered information from interviews and epidemiological data, and elicited the collaboration of outstanding operations-research colleagues to help estimate the aggregate effects of harmful workplace exposures. This book represents what I have learned from these efforts.

I can summarize this learning in a few short sentences. The workplace profoundly affects human health and mortality, and too many workplaces are harmful to people's health—people are literally dying for a paycheck. Most important, the situation is worse than I had imagined, affecting people in numerous occupations, industries, and geographies, and cutting across people of various ages and levels of education. What I learned and the people I encountered in my research have fueled my passion and commitment to bring both the data and the stories to light. I do this in the hope that the information will stimulate the many important but attainable changes required to stop the unnecessary psychological and physical carnage occurring in workplaces all over the world.

Simply stated, work environments matter. We know they matter for people's engagement, satisfaction, turnover intentions, and performance—findings that constitute a vast research literature in the domain of organizational behavior. Work environments matter also for people's physical and mental health, and well-being. It follows that concern for life and human sustainability, as well as a focus on costs and productivity, needs to include a focus on the workplace and its effects.

Chapter 1

Management Decisions and Human Sustainability

"According to the Mayo Clinic, the person you report to at work is more important for your health than your family doctor."

—BOB CHAPMAN, CEO of Barry-Wehmiller and author of *Everybody Matters*

THE HEADLINES—AND THE DATA—TELL the tale. An Uber software engineer making $170,000 a year, Joseph Thomas, committed suicide in August 2016, by shooting himself. His father and his wife blamed workplace stress. "He worked long hours . . . he felt immense pressure and stress at work, and was scared he'd lose his job. . . . He became someone with very little confidence in himself. . . . He was saying he couldn't do anything right."[1] Mr. Thomas was not an isolated case, with Uber employees attributing "panic attacks, substance abuse, depression, and hospitalizations to the stress of the job."[2]

Workplace stress and its health consequences affect people everywhere. Between January 2008 and the spring of 2010, at least forty-six employees of France Telecom committed suicide, with observers pointing to cost-cutting and reorganizations as the cause.[3] In just the four months between January and May 2010, nine employees at Foxconn, the large electronics manufacturer in China that supplies Apple and HP, among many others, killed themselves, and two other workers were injured in suicide attempts.[4] The presumptive cause, according to employees, was the working conditions at Foxconn.

Moritz Erhardt, a twenty-one-year-old Merrill Lynch (part of Bank of America) intern, collapsed and died in London after working for seventy-two hours—three days—straight. The coroner's report said that Erhardt died "as the result of an epileptic fit that may have been triggered by stress and fatigue."[5] Watami Food Service in Japan was "accused of driving a new female employee to suicide just two months after joining the company . . . the woman's monthly overtime work exceeded 140 hours."[6] Severe economic problems in the agricultural industry in India resulted in almost two hundred thousand farmers committing suicide between 2007 and 2009 because of "rising debt and resulting economic and existential despair."[7]

The consequences of workplace stress cut across countries, specific jobs, and organizational levels. A Chicago commuter train director being investigated for an unauthorized vacation payout stepped in front of a train and killed himself. A Maryland lawyer who discovered he was about to lose his job died from a self-inflicted gunshot wound. In 2008, as employment insecurity and stress from the severe recession increased, US workplace suicides reached their highest level ever.[8]

Some of the most problematic, stress-causing aspects of work environments include low wages, shift work, and the absence of job control. For example, low wages produce stress from having to survive with little income, and inadequate income impairs access to healthcare services. Not surprisingly, a number of research studies find that low wages predict obesity, anxiety and depression, low birth weights, and hypertension.[9]

Many of these problematic job attributes affect primarily lower-level employees. However, professional and C-Suite executives are scarcely immune to the effects of poor working conditions on their health and well-being. For instance, "Swisscom CEO Carsten Schloter, 49, had trouble with being on call 24-7. Pierre Wauthier, 53, CFO at Zurich Insurance Group, was in the middle of a horrendous conflict with his CEO." Both men committed suicide in 2013.[10]

Some people facing difficult workplace conditions get sick or die. Some people confronting toxic workplaces kill themselves. Some individuals facing intolerable workplace stress kill others. In June 2017, a former employee who had been fired from his job at Fiamma, a business that makes awnings and other accessories for recreational vehicles, arrived at his former employer and systematically tracked down and killed five people before he committed suicide.[11] Such instances are all too common. In 1986, a mail carrier murdered fourteen coworkers and wounded six others—thereby prompting the phrase "going postal."[12]

In 2013, 397 people were murdered at work in the United States. The presumably good news: that number was down from the 475 work-related homicides reported in 2012. Between 1992 and 2010, there were almost *fourteen thousand* workplace homicide victims.[13] The number of people killed in work-related violence while at the workplace is "more than were killed by fires and explosions, getting caught in equipment or machinery and exposure to harmful substances *combined*."[14] Of course, killings are the most severe and dramatic form of workplace violence. The Occupational Safety and Health Administration estimates that some *two million* employees per year are victims of workplace violence, with many instances going unreported. Clearly, workplace violence is a serious health risk.

People, particularly educated, skilled people, often surprise themselves by their reactions to stressful work environments. A self-described "recovering banker" in South Africa wrote to me about "falling off the corporate hamster wheel" and slipping into a severe clinical depression, something that two business school degrees and numerous leadership training programs had scarcely prepared him for. The whole experience took him by surprise:

> I ignorantly and arrogantly thought that depression didn't happen to people who were "successful," with a good job, house in the suburbs, station wagon, and so on. I never returned to work after my breakdown, but as part of my recovery process, embarked on a master's degree in Applied Psychology, developed a stress symptom survey, and wrote a book about my

> experience. Data from some 2,500 white-collar employees uncovered that *all* organizations we have surveyed are displaying worrying levels of symptomology that is impacting all key business areas.

Similarly, a Salesforce.com employee in San Francisco, someone with a business degree from a very prestigious school, told me that when she joined the organization in a management role, she almost immediately had to go on antidepressants to cope with the work environment. Over the years, she has relied on psychotherapy, a career coach, occasional weekends away, a supportive spouse, and massages among other things to help her handle a workplace in which the demands from her various bosses, long working hours, and the threat of being fired at any moment for any performance slipup or political miscue are omnipresent.

Like many "successful" people working in high technology, she doesn't have that much control over her job and her life. Many months pregnant with her first child, she learned on a Thursday that she needed to miss a social engagement on that Saturday so she could be on a flight to Paris to arrive on Sunday for a Monday meeting. This is just one example of an ever-changing schedule and job demands that leave her feeling not in control of her environment. Her coping strategies, all of which are expensive—the total cost for the therapists, the personal trainer, and others undoubtedly exceeds $2,000 a month—are possible only because she and her spouse have excellent educations and good jobs. How do the majority of workers, whose salaries don't top the charts, cope with similar workplace stress?

Her experience is scarcely unique, even within Salesforce, a company currently on *Fortune*'s Best Places to Work list. A colleague of hers who had recently delivered a child and was ostensibly on maternity leave felt pressured to return to work less than two weeks after giving birth so she could present a keynote speech at a major Salesforce event. Naturally enough, the request to come back into work was posed as a compliment: "You have this big role at this important, high-visibility meeting, so you should be flattered to be invited and certainly not miss the opportunity to shine in front of the Salesforce brass and the many attendees." The not-so-implicit message: What's wrong with you that your job doesn't come before even your newborn?

Both individuals have contemplated leaving their jobs. That fact demonstrates that difficult bosses and stressful work environments harm not only people's health: toxic workplaces are also an important cause of turnover, job dissatisfaction, and other forms of productivity loss for organizations.

Systematic data buttress the scores of case examples I uncovered in my research. There is the so-called Black Monday Syndrome, the fact that more people have heart attacks on Monday morning than at other times during the week, maybe because they are back at work after the weekend. The prevalence of heart attacks on Monday morning has caused hospitals to staff emergency rooms to correspond to the increased risk.[15]

The aptly named American Institute of Stress has collated numerous studies of stress. Some highlights from these data:

- "Job stress is far and away the major source of stress for American adults and . . . it has escalated progressively over the past few decades."
- 80 percent of workers in the Attitudes in the American Workplace survey reported feeling stress on the job.
- Two separate studies reported that about 10 percent of employees said that there was physical violence or an assault in the workplace because of job stress.[16]

One report by the National Institute for Occupational Safety and Health "included data showing that one-quarter of employees view their jobs as the major stressor in their lives and that problems at work are more strongly associated with health complaints than any other stressor, including financial or family problems."[17]

Work environments are for the most part the same in other countries—also frequently too stress-inducing. An annual national survey measuring stress in Australia found that in 2014, 45 percent of Australians "reported being stressed out about work," that in 2013, stress was having at least some impact on the physical health of about *three-quarters* of Australians, and that workplace stress was at a two-year high.[18] A 2012 Statistics Canada survey showed that 28.4 percent of Canadians found most work days to be either quite a bit or extremely stressful.[19] And a report in the United Kingdom concluded: "The evidence is overwhelming that work-related mental ill-health is a major problem in our society with substantial economic, commercial, and human costs."[20]

The Gig Economy and Workplace Stress

The evidence suggests that the adverse effects of work environments on people's health may be getting worse. One reason is the changing nature of work and specifically the rising prevalence of precarious employment—the contract and freelance work of the so-called gig economy. Some forecasts predict that by 2020, "40 percent of the US workforce will be so-called contingent workers."[21] In 2015, the Freelancers Union noted that one-third of working Americans had engaged in some freelance work during the past year.

People working on short-term contracts confront more economic uncertainty and insecurity, and they seldom receive paid time off or other benefits, including training. While many people who perform "gigs" are doing it to supplement their income, data suggest that sharing economy workers don't make very much money. A chart in *Fortune* reported that the average monthly income was $229 for people working for DoorDash, $364 for Uber drivers, $377 for Lyft, and

$380 for TaskRabbit. People working for Fiverr made on average just $103 in a month and $98 for Getaround.[22]

A *New Yorker* article quoted platform economy companies' own websites and blogs to make the point of how stressful and difficult such working arrangements are. One Lyft driver in Chicago was praised for picking up a passenger while nine months pregnant and finishing the trip as she went into labor. Lyft drivers net about eleven dollars per trip, so "maybe Mary kept accepting riders because the gig economy has further normalized the circumstances in which earning an extra eleven dollars can feel more important than seeking out the urgent medical care that these quasi-employers do not sponsor." Fiverr, which touts itself as the freelance marketplace for the lean entrepreneur, apparently had an ad campaign on New York City subway cars that advocated eating coffee for lunch and noting that "sleep deprivation is your drug of choice" if you are a "doer." A Fiverr video recommended answering "a call from a client while having sex."[23]

Beyond the horrific stories, there is ample systematic evidence showing the adverse effects of insecure, often contingent employment on people's health and well-being. For instance, one review of *ninety-three* studies of precarious employment in industrialized countries "found precarious employment was associated with a deterioration in occupational health and safety . . . in terms of injury rates, disease risk, hazard exposures, or worker (and manager) knowledge of OHS [occupational health and safety] regulatory responsibilities."[24]

Management and Government Neglect of Workplace Stress and Its Costs

Notwithstanding the prevalence of workplace stress and its documented ill-effects on physical and mental health, strangely—and unfortunately—the workplace and its effects on social sustainability and health remain mostly under the radar. Workplace stress is largely ignored by employers, governments, and, yes, business schools, too, notwithstanding an enormous epidemiological literature on the effects of workplace conditions on physical and mental health[25] with an enormous toll in both health-care costs and population mortality that I describe in Chapter 2. Chris Till, the former chief executive of the Human Resources Institute of New Zealand, told me that when he talked to the New Zealand government about the connection between workplace conditions and population health, the response was, "Stress is just a normal part of work," with the implication being that nothing could or would be done. Till noted that the government has not yet figured out that workplace injury consisted of more than dramatic physical injuries or accidents—that chronic stress and exposure to management practices that adversely affect health causes both physical and mental health problems and imposes costs borne by business and society.

Dame Carol Black, a principal in Newnham College at Cambridge University, told me that in 2011, she and Professor Sir Cary Cooper, a noted organizational psychologist, conducted a quick survey of more than one hundred UK business schools to assess whether they included teaching on health, employee engagement, and well-being in *any* of their courses. They found that the answer to this question was "a resounding no."[26] Nor is the situation much different inside employers, with a very small fraction of organizations measuring workplace-related stress and an even tinier proportion trying to address the problem.

Christy Johnson, a Stanford MBA graduate who is the founder and CEO of strategy consulting firm Artemis Connection, has been interested in the people aspect of strategy implementation. She commented to me on "the striking resistance to getting people to be honest about what's going on with their workforce." When I pushed back on that comment and asked her about the activities of HR departments and the employee surveys that many places conducted, her response was that these activities were mostly about compliance with rules and legal regulations and risk management—not getting sued—and that many places did not do much with the survey data they collected.

One notable exception to the neglect of systematically measuring workplace-induced health and well-being is the Gallup-Healthways national surveys of well-being, data that, along with Gallup's research expertise, has brought attention to well-being, employee health, engagement, and company performance. But note that Gallup's results are reported by geographic area, not by specific company—so there is no spotlight on specific workplaces that are doing particularly well or poorly. Moreover, Gallup reported that "only 12 percent of employees strongly agree that they have substantially higher overall well-being because of their employer."[27]

It Doesn't Have to Be This Way

Of course there are exceptions, albeit not enough of them. Some companies demonstrate that it is both possible and profitable to care for people's physical and mental health and overall well-being.

In 2004, Mark Bertolini, currently the CEO of health insurance company Aetna, suffered a severe skiing accident that almost killed him and left his left arm in constant agonizing pain. That, plus a son dealing with a rare cancer, caused him to get more interested in health as well as in alternative therapies. Aetna has made employee health a priority, with a focus on physical, mental, social, and financial health.[28] In 2015, Aetna increased its internal minimum wage to sixteen dollars per hour, which was a 33 percent increase for the company's lowest paid employees. About 5,700 people saw their wages increase. The company also changed its health benefits to reduce employees' out-of-pocket expenses. The company offers free yoga and meditation classes that about one-quarter of the workforce has participated in. People who have taken at least one class "report, on average, a 28 percent reduction in their stress levels, a 20 percent improvement in sleep quality, and a 19 percent reduction in pain. They also become more effective on the job."[29] The company also offers a weight loss program and health screenings for its employees. In 2016, Aetna launched a student loan repayment program under which it will make matching loan payment contributions up to $2,000 per year. At Aetna, health-care costs have either gone down or, some years, gone up less than the national average—possibly because of the company's focus on employee well-being.

Bob Chapman is the CEO of Barry-Wehmiller, a $2.5 billion manufacturing company with about twelve thousand people working in plants all over the world. One day a number of years ago, Chapman had an insight that he explained to me: "We became aware that all twelve thousand people who work for us are somebody's precious child, and we know that the way we treat them will have a material impact on their life." Chapman decided that the goal of the company should be to send people home fulfilled at the end of the workday. When the company began seeing employees not as objects but as people who are precious to others, they built a culture in which people cared for one another. One consequence: a much higher level of altruism "where people genuinely offered to do things for others without expecting anything in return." The company has been quite financially successful, with a compound growth rate in earnings of about 16 percent per year, even though it operates in very difficult manufacturing industry segments.

Chapman is now an evangelist for this way of thinking, having written a book, *Everybody Matters*,[30] and going around giving talks about the Barry-Wehmiller approach and its journey to building a culture focused on employee well-being. He commented, "Eighty-eight percent of all people in this country feel they work for an organization that does not care about them. Three out of four people are disengaged. We know for a fact that when people do not feel valued, when they do not feel like they work in a good environment, there are consequences. I think there's something like a 40 percent reduction in health-related issues when people feel happy in their work compared to feeling stressed."

In this book, we will meet some of the companies that do care about their people's well-being, and we will also review numerous research studies (and books) that speak to the economic and social rationales for taking care of employees.[31] It *is* possible to do well and to do good at the same time. But the data on work stress, employee health, and employee engagement suggest that many more company leaders need to get—and heed—the message.

WHERE ARE THE PEOPLE IN THE SUSTAINABILITY MOVEMENT?

Sometimes even the most mundane actions and decisions reveal a lot about existing social values and priorities. So while economic development and land use decisions have many—some argue too many and too onerous—requirements for preserving the physical environment, such regulatory oversight invariably mostly ignores the well-being of the employees who may be affected.

A simple example. When in 2010, Safeway, the large grocery store chain, sought to expand its store in Burlingame, California, near where I live, the company filed an environmental impact report open to the public's inspection. EIRs are of course required for any significant building or redevelopment projects. The report detailed the effects of the store expansion and construction on traffic patterns and congestion, outlined the landscaping and signage plans to preserve as much aesthetics as possible, and highlighted the many things that the company and its contractors would do, such as recycling waste from the demolition of the old structure, to minimize the environmental impact of the project.

There was, of course, nothing unusual about this report—one of hundreds of thousands filed each year. The fundamental premise behind such environmental reviews is simple: building anything invariably disturbs aspects of the physical environment, and good stewardship requires that companies take care to minimize the physical disruption and conserve and preserve as much as possible of the natural environment while still permitting economic progress and development to occur. Should such building or remodeling entail the significant modification or destruction of structures deemed to be of historical significance, the burdens placed on the project are correspondingly higher and the requirements for preservation all the greater. In addition, filing such reports and going through environmental reviews *prior* to construction recognizes the fact that it is easier to prevent harm than it is to subsequently remedy possible adverse impacts to the physical environment or historically significant buildings or gardens once damage has occurred.

It has become taken for granted that in the case of the physical environment, we are concerned about sustainability and environmental degradation. Laws and regulations preclude and punish activities that foul the air or dirty the water. Many companies trumpet their "green" credentials in their advertising, annual reports, and other messaging. They detail their actions to offset carbon emissions and mitigate other forms of environmental danger. These practices have become such a part of everyday business conduct that people often forget there was a time not that long ago when environmental regulations were vigorously opposed and many fewer businesses had made environmental sustainability an important part of their branding, targeted at both their customers and employees.

At first glance, nothing seems missing from the Safeway EIR, which is, because of the limited scope of the project—just replacing some existing buildings in an already developed commercial area—quite boring to read. But something *is* missing from consideration of the store remodeling's impact. The store would be closed slightly more than a year during its reconstruction. The existing store had scores of employees. This store closing occurred in 2010, during a time of economic stringency as the US job market slowly recovered from a severe recession. So while Safeway would remove trees and temporarily disrupt traffic and parking during construction, all factors addressed in its EIR, the company's actions would also affect the economic well-being and lives of its employees, something not discussed anywhere in its environmental impact statement. Although as it turned out Safeway did offer transfers to nearby stores to at least some of its employees, there is no mention of this in the EIR, no mention of what would happen to the other employees, no mention, in short, of the *human* impact of this relatively routine act of economic development.

Nor is this case unusual. The European Union risked a trade war with the United States by seeking to force airlines, including those from countries outside the European Union, to pay for the carbon pollution created by flights into and within Europe.[32] Meanwhile, the European Union apparently was unconcerned about whether or not those same airlines, such as United, Delta, and American, had already reduced and continued to cut wages, jobs, and pensions, thereby negatively affecting the human environment and the psychological and physical well-being of their employees.

Want more evidence of this neglect of people in the sustainability reporting movement? If you go to the website where automobile manufacturer General Motors presents its sustainability bona fides, you can learn that GM is number one in clean energy patents, is among the top five in the world in the number of solar arrays hosted, has eleven landfill-free sites, and operates in twenty-six sites certified by the Wildlife Habitat Council.[33] What you won't learn is the number of jobs the company has cut over the past decade, what GM has done to reduce wages and benefits for new and experienced employees, and how the company manages its office and plant work environments in ways that affect people's well-being. Nor does General Motors in its sustainability reporting present data on the aggregate physical and mental health of its current or former employees.

Similarly, Walmart, the largest employer in the United States with more than one million employees, has three environmental sustainability goals that cover energy, waste, and products.[34] The company's global responsibility reporting emphasizes renewable energy and emergency preparedness, among other things. When the report speaks to measures pertaining to people, the focus is on the number of associates promoted, the proportion of new hires that were women and people of color, and the company's record of hiring veterans.[35] No mention of providing wages that people can live on, health insurance so they can access health care, or work-family policies such as scheduling regular hours so associates can meet their nonwork obligations.

For all the laudable advances made in reporting about and to various stakeholders, we have not begun to scratch the surface when it comes to reporting on and promoting human sustainability. It remains the case that "the study and reporting of human rights and labor issues linked to sustainability risks are far less advanced than environmental and governmental ones."[36]

These examples are not to single out Safeway, GM, Walmart, or any other specific company for its reporting or lack thereof about the human consequences of its management practices. Reporting on initiatives to reduce waste, conserve energy, recycle, and generally protect the physical environment is rapidly becoming the norm among a growing number of particularly larger companies that are increasingly embracing evermore comprehensive sustainability reporting. Reporting on employee well-being, when it occurs at all, is frequently limited to data on time lost from accidents and other very limited indicators that fail to adequately assess social sustainability.

Of course, there are exceptions, and some companies have adopted, and report on, a more comprehensive perspective on employee well-being. Other companies could learn from these cases. For example, in 2012, BT (British Telecom) revised their health and safety policy to include employee health and well-being as key components of the company's people strategy. The company reports on lost time because of illness as well as accidents. Promoting good health is the first item listed in BT's health and well-being strategy. The company provides support for people who become ill or disabled to be able to transition to different jobs so that they do not have to leave the workforce. BT has developed a "mental health toolkit" and a "stress risk assessment and management tool" and trained almost "5,000 people managers in mental health support since 2008." Most important, BT's management system and philosophy begins with: "The first and foremost principle for any organization should be to avoid doing harm to its people."[37] If more companies took employee health this seriously in both goals and training, companies and people would benefit.

The simple fact that as a society we are apparently profoundly concerned about the physical environment and largely indifferent to what companies do to the social environment, to the human beings who work for them, has important implications for understanding the contemporary world. It helps explain why jobs, particularly good jobs, are disappearing and why many employees, in numerous countries, report increasing levels of stress and psychological and physical distress. The world of work provides a daily manifestation of the simple truism: out of sight, out of mind, or its corollary from the quality movement, what gets inspected gets affected, and what does not get measured, doesn't change or even degrades. With no measurement, no reporting, no requirements for considering the consequences of creating social pollution, as distinguished from environmental pollution, work organizations continue to use decision logics that leave them blissfully—perhaps even willfully—unaware of what they are doing to their employees.

People Are Missing in Public Policy, Too

The emphasis on the physical over the social environment holds not just for companies and their reporting but for public policy as well. At both local and national levels, environmental regulations, for instance, limit waste discharges and carbon dioxide emissions and mandate automobile mileage standards. There are best practices, policies, and regulations for corporate governance, such as requiring outside directors on certain board of director committees, and efforts to measure, disclose, and limit environmental and governance risks. These activities are much more extensive than are comparable efforts focused on employee well-being. Monitoring the most basic aspects of physical safety such as workplace accidents and deaths has, over time, driven down workplace fatalities and injuries substantially, and some aspects of chemical exposure have been regulated. But otherwise employers in the United States and elsewhere are mostly free to impose layoffs, require flexible hours and shift work, and inflict other hardships that have important consequences for human health without considering the effects of these decisions.

It is true that there has been some, albeit limited, policy focus on the effects of workplace conditions on employee health and well-being, and such an emphasis is growing. The World Health Organization, recognizing that health is a human right and that population health confers many benefits, has acknowledged the psychosocial causes of ill-health, including such causes located in the workplace.[38]

In the United States, for decades the National Institute for Occupational Safety and Health (NIOSH) has recognized that the work environment can be a threat or risk factor for people's physical and mental health. The agency has sought not only to assess the magnitude of the health risks at work but also to have employers remediate unhealthful conditions in workplaces to reduce the enormous human toll.[39] However, it was only in June 2011 that "NIOSH launched the Total Worker Health Program . . . as a strategy of integrating occupational safety and health protection with health promotion to prevent worker injury and illness,"[40] and around the same time, the US Department of Health and Human Services announced Healthy People 2020, with the goal of increasing access to programs to reduce employee stress.[41] But for the most part, the emphasis remains on preventing occupational injuries and exposure to hazardous physical conditions coupled with encouraging health promotion programs, with comparatively limited attention focused on changing the psychosocial dimensions of work that have profound effects on health.

There has been somewhat more policy attention to the connection between work and health in the United Kingdom. Possibly because of more and better measurement, and partly because health costs created by harmful workplace practices affect governmental budgets because of how health care is delivered and paid for, the United Kingdom has focused somewhat more public policy attention on this issue. Dame Carol Black, a principal at Cambridge University, noted in a personal communication to me that "The British Government (of whatever political persuasion) has been increasingly interested in this agenda since 2005 when they produced the report '*The Health, Work and Well-Being Strategy—the Vision*'. . . . We still have a long way to go, but the effect of poor work, poor workplaces, poor leadership, and inadequate, poorly trained managers is now gaining traction."[42]

Policy attention and reporting permits public entities to estimate the costs of harmful work environments, and that measurement, in turn, spurs action. So, in the United Kingdom, "between 2007 and 2008 an estimated 13.5 million working days were lost to stress-related absence."[43] And "an estimated 1.1 million people who worked in 2011 to 2012 were suffering from a work-related illness."[44] Because of the enormous economic costs of workplace-induced stress, the UK Health and Safety Executive agency has promulgated management standards to try to reduce the incidence—and therefore the costs—of work-related health problems. Nevertheless, the UK guidelines and the NIOSH initiatives rely more on voluntary implementation by companies than do comparable policies instituted by other agencies that are focused on the physical environment and that have more substantial fines and regulatory enforcement resources behind them.

The implication: if we truly care about human beings and their lives, including how long people live—if we are concerned with social sustainability and not solely environmental sustainability—we need to first understand and then alter those workplace conditions that sicken and kill people.

HEALTH AS A MEASURE OF WELL-BEING AND SOCIAL SYSTEM EFFECTIVENESS

We should care about mortality and human well-being for several reasons. In the first place, international human rights laws and conventions, such as the Universal Declaration of Human Rights and the International Covenant on Economic, Social, and Cultural Rights, consider workplace health and safety issues to be fundamental human rights.[45] The moral and social justice foundations for considering human health abound.

Second, health status is one important indicator of organizational or any other social system's performance. As British epidemiologist and expert on health policy Sir Michael Marmot wrote, "Health functions as a kind of social accountant. If health suffers, it tells us that human needs are not being met."[46] He quoted Nobel Prize–winning economist Amartya Sen: "The success of an economy and of a society cannot be separated from the lives that members of the society are able to lead."[47] Health status and well-being—self-reported physical and mental health—and other indicators such as infant mortality and people's life expectancy, are all good barometers of how well any social system, be it a country, city, or work organization, is functioning.

In well-functioning systems, people are well and live long. When systems break down or suffer dysfunction, people get sick and die. This general principle is nicely illustrated by analyses of the missing men of Russia and Eastern Europe. The dissolution of the Soviet Union and the freeing of the Soviet-dominated or occupied countries of Eastern Europe would eventually lead to economic growth and improving health. But in the transition, access to formerly state-provided health services declined, unemployment and economic inequality and insecurity all increased and social problems including alcohol abuse soared. During this turbulent time, there were dramatic declines in life expectancy in much of Eastern Europe and a decrease in average male longevity of seven years in Russia following 1989.[48] Put another way, "in the decade following the collapse of Communism . . . there were an estimated 4 million excess deaths . . . over and above what would have been expected from the historical trend."[49] Declining health and increased mortality mirrored and reflected the economic insecurity and breakdown of social support systems as Eastern European countries transitioned to new governments and social arrangements.

Another oft-used indicator of social system functioning is life satisfaction or subjective well-being, and economists as well as other social scientists are increasingly interested in understanding the determinants of happiness as well as how to best measure the construct.[50] Not surprisingly, happiness and health status are positively related. A study of 151 early adolescents reported a positive correlation between health and happiness,[51] with a similar positive relationship between health and happiness observed in a sample of 383 older adults.[52] A study of the relationship between happiness and health in forty-six countries found a strong relationship between the two,[53] and the World Database of Happiness summarized numerous studies from multiple countries evidencing strong correlations between health status and happiness.[54] These results make sense because it is harder to be happy if a person is ill. The relationship between health status and measures of subjective well-being further make the case that the health of an organization's employees is a useful and important measure of one dimension of organizational effectiveness.

In addition to the moral importance of human life and the role of health as an indicator of system functioning, there is also a strong economic rationale for a greater focus on the effect of the workplace on employee well-being. It should not be news that health-care costs are soaring all over the world, in part because of aging populations—birth rates have declined, which means that average population ages have increased—but also because of ever-eroding employment circumstances. One study linking working conditions to mental health noted that "available evidence provides support for the idea that job quality in most European countries has progressively deteriorated,"[55] and what is true for Europe holds also in the United States with its more laissez-faire approach to labor market protections.

Much if not most of the increase in health-care costs faced by countries around the world arises from chronic (and somewhat preventable) diseases such as cardiovascular disease and diabetes. A World Economic Forum (WEF) report noted that in the United States, 75 percent of the more than two trillion dollar annual health-care spending was accounted for by people with chronic diseases. And these chronic conditions such as diabetes and circulatory problems are spreading throughout the developing world, including to countries such as China, Russia, India, and Brazil.[56] Ill-health exacts a huge toll on productivity at both the societal and individual company levels of analysis. That same WEF report stated that the productivity losses from employees with chronic disease were as much as *four times* the already-large direct costs of treating those diseases.

HEALTHY PERSONAL BEHAVIORS COME FROM HEALTHY WORKPLACES

Because of ever-increasing health-care costs, the productivity loss arising from sickness, and the costs coming from having to replace employees who left the labor force because they were too ill to work, employers and governments around the world have instituted programs to enhance employee health and well-being. Such initiatives, however, focus almost exclusively on influencing *individual* decisions such as those concerning diet, exercise, smoking, and alcohol and substance abuse, leaving the context—the work environment—that affects people's stress levels, and consequently their behavior, largely untouched.

Such health improvement programs are particularly common in the United States, where employers have traditionally been more directly responsible for paying for employee health insurance and, thus, indirectly employees' health-care costs. A RAND Corporation report evaluating employee wellness programs noted that almost 50 percent of the employers in the United States with more than fifty employees and 92 percent with more than two hundred employees offered some sort of wellness promotion program in 2009.[57] These programs encourage employees and their families to exercise, give up smoking, eat a healthier diet, restrict their alcohol intake, and monitor various biomarkers such as blood pressure and cholesterol to keep them at healthy levels. A survey of some eight hundred large and midsize employers by the consulting firm Aon Hewitt reported that 79 percent used rewards such as lower insurance premiums to try to get people to improve their health. Increasingly, Aon Hewitt found, companies were also imposing penalties for employees who did not improve on various biometric and lifestyle measures.[58]

Although employers are obviously concerned about health insurance costs and also employee absence, turnover, and productivity, and therefore attempt to improve these outcomes as they are affected by individual health, the focus of most wellness programs is too narrow to accomplish much. Employer interventions such as nutritional and stress counseling and exercise classes and the modest financial incentives offered to workers to induce them to participate in wellness screenings, and even public policy interventions such as cigarette taxes, focus almost exclusively on getting individuals to make decisions to engage in lifestyle changes.

As one example, the large grocery store chain Safeway has received much attention for its Healthy Measures program. That CEO-inspired initiative offered employees reductions in their health insurance premium contributions if they stayed within certain predetermined limits on smoking, obesity, blood pressure, and cholesterol.[59] The assumption of this and similar programs is that if you improve people's knowledge about nutrition and exercise, offer them exercise and stress-reduction opportunities, measure their health status, and possibly offer some financial inducements for participating, these interventions will be sufficient to get behavioral change. The problem is that employers seldom consider the workplace itself and what occurs there as important causal factors affecting individual behavior.

Such neglect is unfortunate because extensive research shows that individual health-relevant decisions such as drinking, smoking, drug abuse, and overeating are profoundly affected by job-related conditions.[60] For instance, we know that work hours are long in many law firms that are also often characterized by very interpersonally competitive cultures. A *New York Times* article reported that "21 percent of lawyers qualify as problem drinkers while 28 percent struggle with mild or more serious depression and 19 percent with anxiety."[61] Moreover, as that article noted, many lawyers apparently have serious drug addiction issues that start by using stimulants to help them maintain their demanding schedules.

The work environment affects how people think about their lives and also their level of psychological well-being. Not surprisingly, people who do not like their lives are less likely to take good care of themselves. As psychiatrist Richard Friedman, explaining addiction, wrote:

> No one will be shocked to learn that stress makes people more likely to search for solace in drugs or food (it's called "comfort food" for a reason). . . . Now we have a body of research that makes the connection between stress and addiction definitive. More surprising, it shows we can change the path to addiction by changing our environment.[62]

Companies know about these work-environment effects, but nonetheless fail to act. For instance, a 2008 study by human resource consulting firm Watson Wyatt (now Towers Watson) found that 48 percent of organizations said that job-related stress, caused by long work hours and lean staffing policies that resulted in fewer people doing more work, affected business performance. However, only 5 percent of the employers said they were doing anything to address these health- and performance-related issues.[63]

Because the job conditions that affect health are not the primary focus of most employer wellness interventions, not surprisingly, workplace wellness programs often don't work very well, although the evidence on their success is mixed. The first important fact about wellness programs is that only a tiny fraction of these interventions have been evaluated at all. Second, an important issue with workplace wellness programs is employee participation. For instance, supermarket chain H-E-B found that annual health-care claims were about $1,500 less for participants in its workplace wellness program.[64] But a RAND study reported that employee participation rates frequently were not that high, with fewer than half of employees in workplaces offering wellness programs participating. A Gallup survey found that "only 24 percent of employees at companies that offer a wellness program actively participate in it."[65] Even at Stanford University, which has a long-running, well-administered, comprehensive, leadership-supported program with financial incentives for participation, a significant fraction of employees—more than 35 percent—do not avail themselves of the program.

One meta-analysis of thirty-two published studies concluded that "medical costs fall by about $3.27 for every dollar spent on wellness programs and that absenteeism costs fall by about $2.73 for every dollar spent."[66] However, a more recent, comprehensive analysis concluded that "wellness programs produce a return-on-investment . . . of less than 1-to-1 savings to cost."[67] And a study of PepsiCo's wellness program, Healthy Living, found that "seven years of continuous participation in one or both components [of the program] was associated with an average reduction of $30 in health care cost per member per month," with the disease management component accounting for the lower costs while the lifestyle-altering component had no effect.[68] The RAND report found that wellness programs had some effect on lifestyle choices such as diet and exercise, but an analysis of more than 360 thousand employees from five employers noted that the difference in health-care costs between people who participated in wellness programs and those who did not was just $157 annually, an amount that is neither statistically nor substantively significant.[69] You can't expect people to adopt healthy lifestyles when their work environments reinforce or even cause poor habits.

Separate from debates about the *effectiveness* of employer-initiated workplace wellness programs, it is quite instructive to think about the *criteria* most often used to evaluate these wellness interventions. Evaluations focus almost exclusively on health-care *costs*. Costs obviously are important. But maybe, just maybe, assessments of employee *wellness* programs should also focus on employees' *wellness and well-being*—their health, both physical and mental, and even their mortality and morbidity. Health status is not perfectly correlated with costs. After all, if a person drops dead, health-care spending stops. Privileging economic costs over human well-being shouldn't occur as thoughtlessly as it now does, and costs certainly should not be the sole criterion used in assessing whether wellness programs worked or did not.

EMPLOYER CHOICES AND HEALTH-CARE SYSTEM PERFORMANCE

Discussions of health and health-care costs often begin, as I have noted, by focusing on individual choices. One analysis estimated that poor individual decisions concerning diet, exercise, and substance abuse contributed to more than 1 million of the 2.4 million annual deaths in the United States.[70]

In addition to individual decisions, much public policy discussion and empirical research focuses on two other possible causes of the underperformance of the US health-care system, where underperformance means spending a large amount of money without obtaining better health outcomes. To be clear, the United States, despite being a leading source of drug and medical device innovation and despite enormous investments in technology and health infrastructure, clearly underperforms. According to the OECD, the United States spends $7,662 per person (adjusted for purchasing power parity) on health care, which is 2.6 times the OECD average and is the highest amount in the world. America devotes 16.9 percent of its GDP to health care, 1.8 times the OECD average, and again has the highest proportion in the world. Nonetheless, the United States ranks just twenty-seventh for life expectancy at birth, fifty-third in deaths per one thousand live births—a measure of infant mortality—and twenty-third in life expectancy for men aged sixty-five.[71]

One focus for reducing health costs and improving health system performance has been on societal-level choices such as the way the health-care system is organized and paid for and the administrative cost burden thereby created.[72] Because the administration of much health-care reimbursement in the United States has been left to insurance companies, the evidence suggests that the United States confronts a particularly large administrative overhead expense of about 30 percent. Such expense is an almost inevitable result of health-care providers having to deal with a multitude of insurance companies and insurance companies transacting with numerous providers. A related more macro-level focus has been on what insurance should and should not be required to cover (for example, preexisting conditions, birth control, and alternative health therapies). Yet another macro-level focus has been how to pay for the medical costs of the aging populations that most advanced industrialized countries confront, and particularly how the cost burden should be shared between individuals and the larger society.

A second focus on the determinants of health system performance has been on the internal administrative dynamics of health-care organizations that actually deliver care, including how to ensure that the incentives providers face work to ensure cost-effective care. For example, there have been studies of the effectiveness of incentive pay and also analyses of practices that encourage learning and continuous improvement in health-care organizations.[73]

These are important factors to consider, of course, but ignoring the effects of employer actions that determine workplace conditions seems singularly unwise. Looking at what employers do daily to create healthy or harmful workplaces is a crucial missing piece of the story of human well-being, health, and health-care costs.

Consider as just one example the effects of employer decisions about wages. Although wages are partly determined by labor market conditions, there are low-wage and higher-wage employers in the same industry—Costco and Walmart being one example of such differences. And the evidence is clear: wages affect health. For instance, a study of more than seventeen thousand people using Panel Study of Income Dynamics data reported a negative and strongly statistically significant correlation between wages and the self-reported (based on a physician's diagnosis) incidence of hypertension. The data show that the higher the wages earned, the lower the likelihood of reporting high blood pressure. The effect of wages on health was greater for women and for younger working people between twenty-five and forty-four years old. This was a prospective, longitudinal study, so that wages in an earlier wave of the study were used to predict newly diagnosed high blood pressure, thereby helping to establish the direction of the causal relationship. The evidence showed that a doubling of wages was related to a 25 to 30 percent diminished risk of hypertension.[74] Many other employer decisions affecting work hours and work-family conflict also affect health, as we will see throughout this book.

My fundamental message is simple: employers have a choice. They can implement practices that enhance human well-being—physical and mental health—thereby reducing their own costs from employee medical expenses, absenteeism, workers' compensation insurance costs, and the productivity loss from having employees who are physically at work but not "really there" (a problem called *presentism* in the research literature). Such employer actions will also reduce the costs to society from people's poor physical and mental health and the harm done to individuals. Simply put, employers can make decisions to improve people's lives in fundamentally important ways. Or, alternatively, employers can, either intentionally or through ignorance and neglect, create workplaces that literally sicken and kill people.

If we want to build a healthier society, develop policies that promote social sustainability and healthy workplaces, and cut unnecessary health-care costs and sickness and death, one important place to focus is on workplace-specific interventions that enhance people's health and the social sustainability of work organizations.

Chapter 2

The Enormous Toll of Toxic Workplaces

WORKPLACES CAN BE HAZARDOUS to your health, even at a for-profit employer of primary-care doctors. A now-former employee, let's call her Susan, described the toll of too much work on her and some of her colleagues and a CEO who "freaked out if things didn't get done":

> I was just talking to one of our VPs the other day. She was breaking out in shingles because of the stress. . . . This past summer, I had a panic attack, and that had never happened to me before. I got to the point where I was so unhappy I was in tears every day. Hating what I was doing. . . . Just as office manager, I was juggling a job that should have been for two people, if not two and a half.

In my research, I heard a plethora of stories and anecdotes, and I came across many articles and much data about workplace stress and its consequences. The challenge: to find the data and do the analyses that would, with reasonable accuracy, estimate the economic and human toll of harmful management practices. That is the subject of this chapter.

For almost a decade, I have believed that harmful workplaces adversely affect physical and mental health and exact a tremendous economic and human cost. Moreover, it is management decisions that create toxic work environments, and it is management decisions that could, and in too few cases do, fix them. But if people are literally dying for a paycheck, if harmful work practices exact enormous costs, then it seems to me that we ought to address at least four questions that would help define the scope of the problem:

- How truly harmful, how bad, are a set of identifiable and reasonably common dimensions of contemporary work environments?
- What is the aggregate toll, both in lives and dollars, of these workplace exposures in the United States?
- To what extent might the differential exposure to harmful work environments explain the ever-growing inequalities in health outcomes such as life spans?
- And, most important, how much of the human and economic toll might be preventable, given the facts of economic competition and technological change that make the goal of creating no workplace stress seemingly impossible?

Addressing these questions required analytic and modeling skills far beyond my capabilities. I was fortunate to be able to induce Joel Goh, at the time a doctoral student at the Stanford Graduate School of Business and now a professor at the National University of Singapore, and Stefanos Zenios, a chaired professor in our operations and information technology group, to help me answer these four questions. This chapter describes what we learned and highlights the work of other researchers and countries that also sheds light on these topics as well as other dimensions of the toll bad workplaces are exacting. For those not interested in the details, such as which workplace exposures are the most harmful and how we went about putting together our analyses, here are our best estimates of the answers to each of the questions we posed:

- The ten workplace exposures we identified and studied are, with almost no exceptions, as harmful to health, including mortality and having a physician-diagnosed illness, as exposure to secondhand smoke, a known and regulated carcinogen.

- In total, workplace environments in the United States may be responsible for 120 thousand excess deaths per year—which would make workplaces the fifth leading cause of death—and account for about $180 billion in additional health-care expenditures, approximately 8 percent of the total health-care spending.
- Differential exposure to harmful workplace environments, largely affected by people's level of education (and to a much, much smaller extent by race and gender), account for somewhere between 10 and 38 percent of the (growing) inequality in life spans.
- By comparing the United States to a set of twenty-seven countries in Europe, we estimate that about sixty thousand, or half of the deaths, and about $63 billion, or one-third of the excess costs, might be preventable.

Other research also points to a high human-and-economic toll. One empirical approach focuses on the percentage of specific diseases that are attributable to workplace conditions—so-called Attributable Fractions (AF). Using that method, a UC Davis researcher estimated that in 2007, there were 5,600 fatal injuries and 53,000 fatal illnesses attributable to workplace conditions, with a cost "at least as large as the cost of cancer."[1] Another study, employing the same methodology and using 1997 data, estimated forty-nine thousand deaths, which would make occupational death the eighth leading cause of death in the United States.[2]

In Australia, workplace stress costs the economy about $14.8 billion a year according to one estimate, with work pressure, harassment, and bullying comprising some 75 percent of psychological injury claims.[3] Moreover, the executive director of the Australian Psychological Society reported that a stress and well-being survey revealed "a downward trend in psychological health and well-being,"[4] a pattern observed in the United States as well. A survey of methods designed to measure health-related productivity losses reported that in the United States, "approximately $260 billion in output is lost each year . . . because of health-related problems."[5]

A study reported in a Chinese journal in 2006 estimated that "at least one million people in China currently die from overwork each year." A report from the Shanghai Academy of Science and Technology reported that "as many as 70 percent of China's intellectuals [mostly university professors] faced, to a greater or lesser degree, the risk of premature death from exhaustion."[6] And an analysis using World Health Organization comparative risk assessment methods to calculate the burden of occupational hazards estimated that there were 850,000 deaths worldwide and a loss of twenty-four million years of healthy life.[7] The European Agency for Safety and Health at Work estimated that stress accounted for 60 percent of all lost days in the workplace.[8] These estimates all speak to a staggering human and economic toll from harmful workplace practices.

OTHER CAUSES OF PEOPLE'S HEALTH

One might wonder whether other factors might explain health-care costs and mortality. Although the workplace is an important environment for people, it is obviously not the only setting or the only cause of health issues. For instance, the family has an important effect on health. As one early analysis noted, "The family constitutes perhaps the most important social context within which illness occurs and is resolved. It consequently serves as a primary unit in health and medical care."[9]

A large and growing research literature also demonstrates the importance of the community where one lives on people's health and well-being. A study in Hamilton, Ontario, Canada, found that the socioeconomic composition of neighborhoods affected health status and the strength of the relationship between smoking and health.[10] Another analysis using data from Chicago examined the role of residential instability, immigrant concentration, and socioeconomic status on health.[11] Communities matter for health because of the social and material resources, including the availability of health-care resources that vary by community.

Social networks and interpersonal relationships also affect health. The effects of social relations on health derive from many pathways, including the effects of people's connections on their individual behaviors. Consider some examples of this effect. One study found that being overweight moved through social networks in a process of social contagion. An individual's chances of becoming obese increased by some 57 percent if that individual had a friend who became obese in a given time period.[12] A review of the research literature concerning social effects on alcohol use described three mechanisms that helped explain peer influence on drinking: peers actually offering or supplying alcohol, peers modeling alcohol consumption, and peer behavior that helps determine social norms and expectations about what is appropriate alcohol consumption.[13] Studies of drug use consistently concluded that "the social environment plays a critical role in determining the likelihood that an individual will use drugs or will develop a drug use disorder."[14] In many important ways, people are influenced by their peers, and this effect occurs for health-relevant behaviors as well.

This powerful influence of peers on behavior is one reason that substance abuse programs typically provide mentors and social support for people to call when they need help modifying their behavior. And such programs frequently incorporate efforts to change with whom people associate so that they remove themselves from the influence of others who are engaging in self-harming behaviors. Moreover, social relationships also can provide friendship and emotional support, people to talk to, which can reduce the harmful effects of stress.

Other factors, too, influence health and longevity. For instance, genetics and random chance, such as being in an automobile accident or inadvertently purchasing a car with mechanical issues, affect people's health and mortality. As one medical article noted, "Genes affect virtually every human characteristic and disease."[15]

Thus, not all disease or ill-health is controllable by what individuals do. Nor is all disease and death the result of what happens to people in the workplace. However, the workplace has very important effects on health.

ESTIMATING THE HEALTH EFFECTS OF WORKPLACE EXPOSURES

The job is where working people spend time, where they earn their income, where they attain—or not—social status and prestige. In the United States, a job is where employers decided, at least prior to the passage of the Affordable Care Act and to some extent even after that law was passed, if, and what kind of, health insurance and therefore what kind of health-care access, employees would have. Workplaces can be stress-filled or not. Extensive research, published over decades, consistently shows the adverse health effects of stress[16] and even some of the causal pathways, for instance by inducing unhealthy individual choices.[17]

Any workplace practice that increases stress makes human well-being worse and health-care costs higher, while any management practice that either directly mitigates stress or provides ways of coping with it increases well-being and reduces health-care costs correspondingly. And because health and longevity are directly related to being able to access health care, workplace policies such as the provision of health insurance and the cost of accessing health care through that insurance also have consequences for both people's physical and psychological well-being and their economic security.

It ought to be straightforward to estimate the effects of workplace practices on health and the associated costs, but it is not because no longitudinal data provide measures of both people's work environments and their health over time. Thus, Goh, Zenios, and I had to use indirect estimation methods and data from numerous sources in a model to calculate the physical and economic costs of harmful management practices. Readers interested in the methods and the sensitivity analyses we used to ensure that the numbers were robust should consult the technical details available in peer-reviewed published articles.[18]

We used a straightforward and logical analytical process. First, we assessed the prevalence of employer practices and workplace conditions (which we called work exposures) that reasonably would be expected to adversely or positively affect employee health. We used data from several waves of the General Social Survey, a national random sample that measures attitudes and conditions that people experience in their lives, to estimate the extent to which the population was exposed to various workplace conditions.

Then we used meta-analysis, a procedure for combining the results from multiple studies, to estimate the magnitude of the effects of the workplace exposures on mortality and morbidity above what would be expected for people who did not confront these workplace circumstances.[19] Finally, we estimated the costs of these adverse health outcomes using national data on medical costs for people with different levels of health. Throughout this process, we employed a variety of techniques to guard against double-counting the effects of multiple workplace exposures or, for that matter, multiple negative health outcomes that might result.

Our review of the epidemiological literature uncovered ten prominent workplace exposures related to employer decisions that affect human health and longevity:

1. Being unemployed (sometimes, although not invariably, a consequence of being laid off);
2. Not having health insurance;
3. Working shifts (as opposed to customary daytime workdays) and also working longer periods, such as ten- or twelve-hour shifts as contrasted with the more customary eight hours;
4. Working long hours in a week (e.g., more than forty hours);
5. Confronting job insecurity (for example, because colleagues had been laid off or fired);
6. Facing family-to-work and work-to-family conflicts;
7. Having relatively low control over one's job and job environment, including having relatively little freedom and decision discretion at work;
8. Facing high job demands such as pressure to work fast;
9. Being in a work environment that offered low levels of social support (for instance, not having close relationships with coworkers that provide social support to mitigate the effects of work stress); and
10. Working in a setting in which job- and employment-related decisions seemed unfair.

For most of these measures, we used data from several of the most recent waves of the General Social Survey to estimate the frequency of occurrence of these conditions in US workplaces.

Then we did a search of the online database MEDLINE for articles that contained terms corresponding to these workplace conditions and health status. Our initial search uncovered almost three thousand articles. This large number of studies suggests that a) there is a large epidemiological literature relating elements of the work environment to health, and b) the work environment dimensions we started with were a reasonable place to begin to estimate the effects of job circumstances on health. To make the meta-analysis task manageable, we used only those articles that employed relatively large samples (more than one thousand people) and articles that utilized the most advanced and appropriate statistical methods. In the end, we incorporated the results of more than two hundred studies for our meta-analyses of the mortality effects of workplace practices. We used these studies to derive estimates of the magnitude of the health effects of the various workplace exposures, which, of course, vary in the severity of their consequences for people's well-being.

While there have been other prior reviews and meta-analyses of the effects of workplace conditions on health, many of these have focused on single workplace stressors such as job insecurity,[20] work hours,[21] the absence of social support in the workplace,[22] and psychological demands and job discretion.[23] What our empirical estimates add to the existing research literature is that our results incorporate the most recent empirical findings and employ common methods and criteria to investigate the effects of *ten* workplace dimensions on *four* health outcomes.

The four health outcomes we considered are: mortality, presence of a physician-diagnosed illness or medical condition, self-reported mental health, and self-reported physical health. The research literature typically identifies health problems (and mortality) as either present or absent, a convention that we also followed.

It is important to note that self-reported physical health, whether measured by a single item or a scale, has been shown to be a significant predictor of subsequent mortality and morbidity, even after statistically controlling for other health-relevant factors.[24] Moreover, this prospective ability of self-reported health to predict subsequent illness and death holds across different ethnicities and ages, so the value of self-reported health as a measure apparently is quite general.[25]

MANY WORKPLACE PRACTICES ARE AS HARMFUL AS SECONDHAND SMOKE

In the medical literature, health effects are typically reported as odds ratios, a practice my colleagues and I followed when we did the meta-analyses. An odds ratio of 2, for instance, would mean that someone exposed to a particular workplace stressor would have twice the odds of experiencing a particular health outcome, such as mortality or a physician-diagnosed condition, as someone not so exposed.[26] To nonscientists, interpreting an odds ratio—how substantively important is the effect?—is often difficult. Therefore, to provide some context for ascertaining the practical importance of the results of our analyses summarizing the effects of workplace stressors on health, we compared our effect sizes with the health effects of exposure to secondhand smoke. Secondhand smoke is a known environmental carcinogen. More important, because of the recognized adverse health effects of exposure to secondhand smoke, public policy in the United States and increasingly throughout most of the world has focused on implementing regulations that reduce the chances of exposure to this hazard. Consequently, smoking is no longer permitted on public transportation such as airplanes, trains, or buses, or in offices, restaurants, theaters, and many other public places.

Figure 1, *A* to *D*, below graphically presents the odds ratios from our meta-analyses for the effects of various workplace exposures on the four health outcomes, reported in a paper published in a peer-reviewed journal,[27] along with the size of the health effects of secondhand smoke on these same outcomes as reported in the medical literature. The inescapable conclusion: most of the workplace exposures have health effects comparable to or even greater than exposure to secondhand smoke. These results suggest that the work exposures, considered one at a time, pose significant health risks for employees.

Odds ratios higher than 1 indicate that the exposures listed here increased the odds of negative health outcomes. No health insurance,

FIGURE 1.
Comparing Health Effects from Work Stressors to Secondhand Smoke Exposure

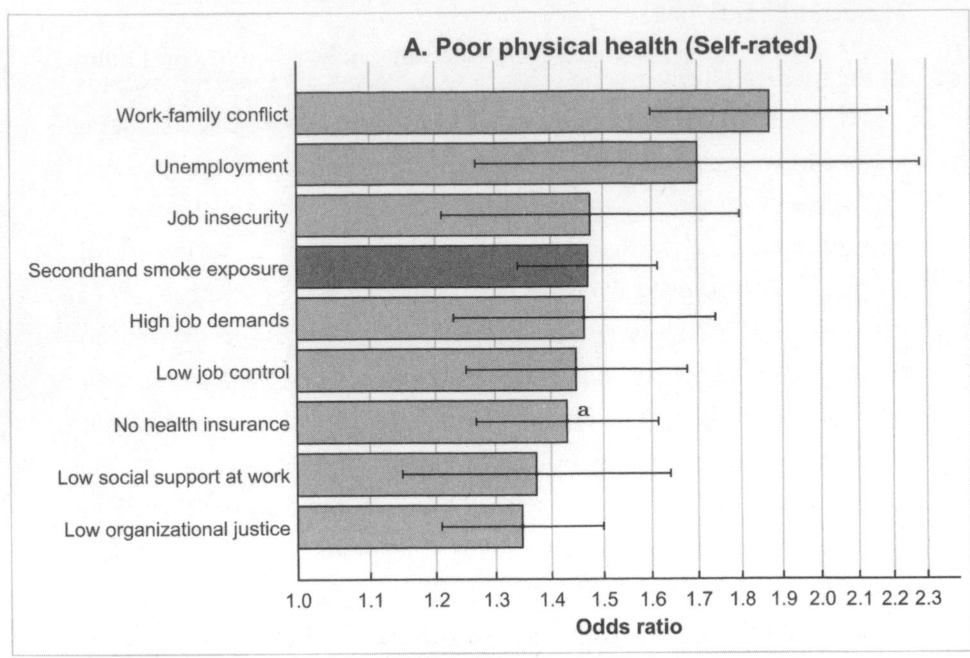

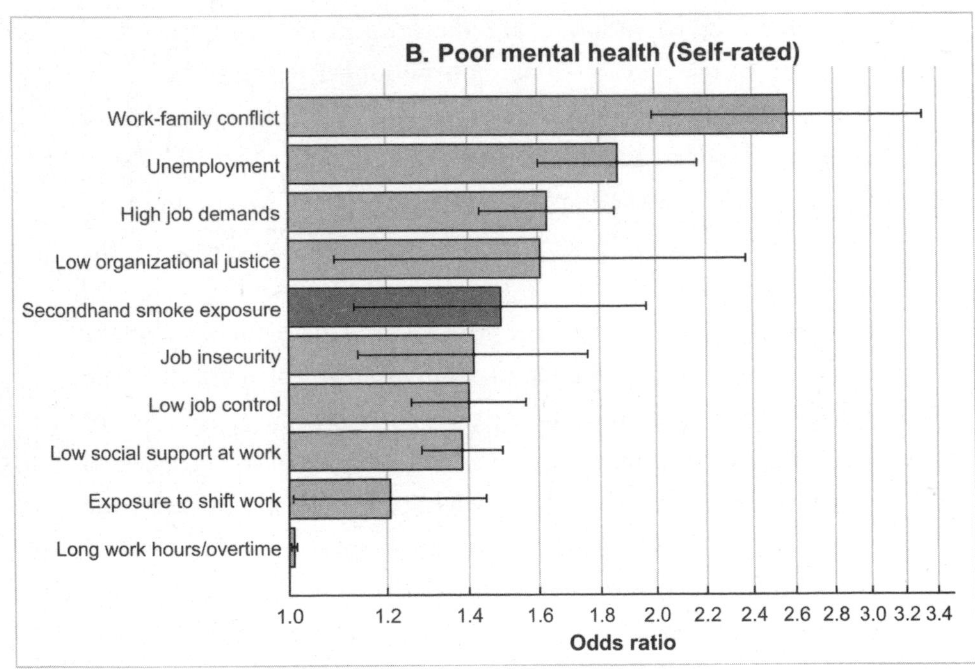

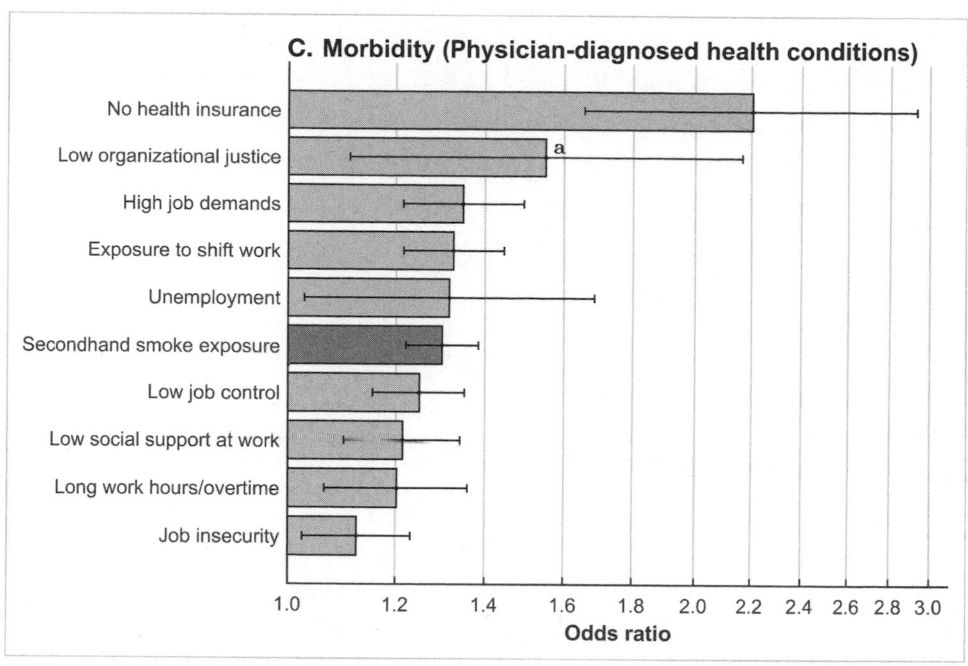
C. Morbidity (Physician-diagnosed health conditions)
No health insurance
Low organizational justice
a
High job demands
Exposure to shift work
Unemployment
Secondhand smoke exposure
Low job control
Low social support at work
Long work hours/overtime
Job insecurity
1.0
1.2
1.4
1.6
1.8
2.0
2.2
2.4
2.6
2.8
3.0
Odds ratio

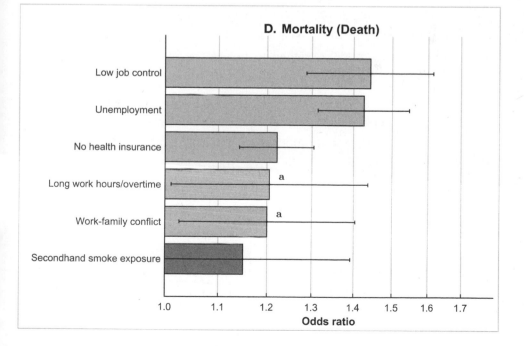

D. Mortality (Death)
Low job control
Unemployment
No health insurance
Long work hours/overtime
a
Work-family conflict
a
Secondhand smoke exposure
1.0
1.1
1.2
1.3
1.4
1.5
1.6
1.7
Odds ratio

for instance, increased the odds of a physician-diagnosed health condition by more than 100 percent. Odds ratios for exposures marked with an *a* were calculated with two or fewer studies and may be less reliable. Error bars are included to indicate standard errors. These bars indicate how much variation exists among data from each group. If two error bars are separated by at least half the width of the bars, this indicates less than a 5 percent probability that a difference was observed by chance (i.e., statistical significance at $p < .05$).

ESTIMATING THE AGGREGATE HEALTH EFFECTS OF WORKPLACE EXPOSURES ON MORTALITY

An adverse health effect of a workplace exposure that occurs infrequently is not something that would prompt organizational or public policy interventions. Health outcomes are determined both by the extent to which some exposure leads to adverse health consequences and also the prevalence of that exposure. The next task my colleagues and I undertook was to estimate the aggregate health effects of all ten exposures on two outcomes of great interest: mortality and health-care costs. I present the results for the analysis of mortality first.

Employing a model designed to reduce the likelihood of double-counting, Goh, Zenios, and I estimated that the number of total excess deaths each year attributable to the ten workplace conditions was about 120,000 people. To put this number in perspective, this is more deaths coming from poor, unhealthful, stressful workplace conditions than the number of deaths resulting from diabetes, Alzheimer's, influenza, or kidney disease and about as many deaths as were reported in 2010 from both accidents and strokes. The data on deaths by cause come from the Centers for Disease Control.[28]

We also estimated the marginal contribution of each workplace condition to mortality, and I present these results in Table 1. Note that for various statistical reasons, the numbers in the table do not add up to the number estimated overall.

TABLE 1. Workplace Exposures and Excess Mortality

WORKPLACE CONDITION	ANNUAL EXCESS DEATHS
Unemployment	35,000
No insurance	50,000
Shift work	13,000
Long work hours	0
Job insecurity	29,000
Work-family conflict	0
Low job control	17,000
Low social support	3,000
Low fairness	–
High job demands	8,000

The absence of health insurance is the employment condition leading to the greatest number of excess deaths, followed by being unemployed and then by job insecurity. Shift work is associated with thirteen thousand excess deaths. An absence of job control and discretion at work is also an important contributor to excess mortality, causing some seventeen thousand excess deaths each year. Previous research has identified job control as an important factor predicting cardiovascular incidence and mortality.[29] Our research is consistent with that finding and also supports previously reported studies that demonstrate the impact of not having health insurance on mortality.[30] Some factors that, as shown below, do contribute to increased costs, do not increase mortality in our data. They make people sick but don't kill them.

It is important to note that psychosocial aspects of work such as insecurity, low social support, and not having control over the conditions of one's work have important effects on excess deaths.

Is this estimate reasonable?

The figure of 120,000 deaths per year makes workplace management practices the fifth leading cause of death in the United States. Is the workplace really that important for human health and well-being? Without excessively belaboring the point, here are some reasons why I believe this estimate is, as it was designed to be, conservative in its assessment of the toll of the workplace on mortality.

Implications from a Study of the Effects of Individual Choices on Health

About a decade ago, Ralph Keeney of the Fuqua School of Business at Duke University published a paper in which he argued, using a mathematical modeling approach and existing data, that of the 2.4 million deaths that occurred in 2000, 1 million were the result of personal decisions. He also showed that 55 percent of the deaths for people between the ages of fifteen and sixty-four were the result of personal decisions.[31] Keeney's conclusion: individual choices concerning behaviors such as smoking, eating (obesity), exercise, and alcohol abuse were a substantial cause of death.

Keeney argued that these personal choices about health-relevant behaviors could be changed to reduce the mortality rate in the United States. Keeney's conclusion is, in its tone, no different from the assumption underlying many organizationally sponsored health improvement efforts: that intervening to affect individual behaviors and decisions can affect population health to lower health-care costs. But what Keeney and many health improvement efforts overlook is that studies consistently demonstrate the connection between stress, including workplace-induced stress, and unhealthy individual behaviors such as overeating.[32] Other empirical research demonstrates the effects of stress on individual behaviors such as alcohol consumption,[33] cigarette smoking,[34] and drug abuse.[35] These are precisely the types of personal decisions that Keeney implicated in his analysis of the toll of personal choices on mortality.

There is no reason to believe that the effects of workplace stress on these unhealthy behaviors would be different from any other source of stress. Individuals respond to stress, as many examples in this book illustrate, by self-medicating with drugs or alcohol to numb the psychological pain of an unhealthy workplace. People compensate for the psychological depletion of energy from a stressful work environment by overeating. Keeney's analysis suggested there are one million excess deaths from individual choices. We know that stress affects these individual choices to eat too much, not exercise, take drugs, and abuse alcohol and smoke. We further know that the workplace is an important, if not one of the most important, causes of stress. Consequently, attributing only about 12 percent of the total toll from individual choices on mortality to workplace-induced stress seems quite reasonable, if not conservative.

The Physiological Mechanisms Linking Stress to Health

We don't just observe an empirical relationship between the presence of stress and health outcomes. Over time, we have learned more precisely how harmful stress is and the ways in which stress produces adverse physiological responses. Research increasingly demonstrates the effects of stress on disease. For instance, "For men, prolonged exposure to work-related stress has been linked to an increased likelihood of lung, colon, rectal, and stomach cancer and non-Hodgkin lymphoma."[36] Moreover, we are increasingly understanding the mechanisms linking stress to disease.

Our evolutionary ancestors faced a world filled with threats. When confronted with some physical threat, organisms that could either outfight or outrun the threat had a survival advantage. Therefore, it was adaptive, in the presence of a stressor—a threat—to exhibit an elevated heart rate that would move blood and oxygen more efficiently through the body to muscles that would be useful for escape or conflict, to have heightened awareness and sensitivity to better apprehend one's surroundings and to react more quickly to a perceived threat. However, what is adaptive in response to episodic, short-term threats—a metabolic response that raises the pulse rate—is unhealthy in the presence of chronic stress.

As I noted in a paper with Berkeley social psychologist Dana Carney:

> When a person perceives the demands of a situation to exceed his or her own . . . resources, the mind makes sense of this discrepancy by appraising it as a threat. . . . If the stress response is strong enough, the result is elevated cortisol levels. . . . Cortisol is a catabolic (i.e., cell "breaking down") hormone with links to chronic stress, systemic inflammation, accelerated cellular death, and generally poor health.[37]

Evidence shows that although elevated cortisol is adaptive in the face of a short-term, immediate threat, constantly elevated cortisol and other hormones produced in response to stress adversely affect health.[38] These physiological pathways from stress to ill-health provide causal explanations of how workplace stress can lead to sickness and death.

The Importance of the Workplace as a Source of Stress

In addition, the available evidence consistently indicates that the workplace is an important source of stress and that many if not most of the causes of workplace stress are getting worse. For instance, economic insecurity has increased as the frequency of layoffs has grown and more people work in increasingly transitory, contingent work arrangements. Fewer companies offer health insurance as a benefit, and many of the costs of health care have been shifted to employees with ever-increasing deductibles and co-payments, a topic I examine in Chapter 4. Job control and job autonomy have diminished with the increasing availability and use of computer-based monitoring of work and work processes. Work hours have increased as global competition has intensified work, a topic explored in more detail in Chapter 5, where I consider the effects of work hours on health. Work-family conflict has grown with the availability of technologies that keep people always connected to their workplace and with the rise in working hours. Shift work and irregular work hours are more common as the hours of operation of establishments ranging from airports to food services have increased to be able to meet consumer demands whenever they occur. Fewer countries require stores to close on Sunday. To take a simple example, when I first began going to Barcelona in 2006, few stores were open on Sunday. Now, many more are—a trend occurring in many countries as the hours of operation of all sorts of business have expanded.

In short, although some workplaces have tried to do things to enhance employee health and well-being, for the most part, workplace stressors have grown in frequency and importance over time. Thus, it is completely reasonable to presume that the health effects of workplace stress are large and increasing.

THE EFFECTS OF WORKPLACE PRACTICES ON HEALTH-CARE COSTS

As I argued in Chapter 1, health-care costs bedevil both employers and governments, not just in the United States but all over the world. This focus on curtailing health-care costs raises this important question: How much do the ten workplace exposures we have identified cost, just in direct health-care costs, and not considering productivity losses and other costs these workplace practices may impose?

Goh, Zenios, and I, as part of our research, also derived estimates for the incremental costs of people's exposure to harmful workplace circumstances. Fortunately, the US government surveys people to ascertain their self-reported physical and mental health and whether or not they have been diagnosed with any one of a number of major disease categories. The survey, the Medical Expenditure Panel Survey—Household Component, conducted by the Agency for Healthcare

Research and Quality, also asks about the total of all direct payments for medical care during the year, including out-of-pocket expenses and costs paid by insurance, Medicaid, Medicare, and any other sources. These data permit us to estimate costs by an individual's health status.

Combining the information on the effects of workplace conditions on various measures of health status, the information on what medical conditions and self-reported poor health cost, on average, and the prevalence of the various workplace circumstances that contribute to poor health, permits us to estimate the total costs of workplace exposures, as well as the extra health-care costs attributable to each specific workplace exposure.

My coauthors and I estimated that the incremental health-care costs from stress-inducing work conditions is about $190 billion annually, or approximately between 5 and 8 percent of the total US health-care budget. The inescapable conclusion: workplace conditions are a significant contributor to health-care costs in the United States.

Table 2 presents our estimates of incremental workplace costs by specific workplace condition.

TABLE 2. Incremental Health-Care Costs by Workplace Exposure

WORKPLACE CONDITION	ANNUAL EXCESS HEALTH-CARE COSTS
Unemployment	$15 billion
No insurance	$40 billion
Shift work	$12 billion
Long work hours	$13 billion
Low fairness	$16 billion
Job insecurity	$16 billion
Work-family conflict	$24 billion
High job demands	$46 billion
Low job control	$11 billion
Low social support	$9 billion

The biggest contributors to excess health-care expenditures are not having insurance, work-family conflict, and high job demands. Note that there isn't complete correspondence between the factors that make health-care costs higher and those that result in excess deaths. That's partly because the chronic illnesses caused by stress-related factors such as work-family conflict and high job demands create health conditions that result in people using the health-care system more intensively but not necessarily dying. When someone dies, health-care costs stop, which is why chronic diseases that persist over a long period of time often cost more than, for instance, sudden death from a heart attack, an outcome that research shows follows from layoffs and job loss.

Even more than was true for mortality, psychosocial elements of the work environment such as fairness, work-family conflict, high job demands, and low control over a person's work environment contribute to excess health-care costs. Our cost estimates are almost certainly low, for the following reasons. First, as already noted, the analysis considers only direct medical costs that come from one of the four measures of health—self-reported physical and mental health, a physician-diagnosed health condition, or mortality. Our analyses do not consider any other costs, such as loss of working time or diminished productivity from suffering from a health problem. Indirect costs from things such as disengagement, being physically present but not feeling well enough to do one's best, and being distracted by stress are typically estimated to be about *five times* as large as the direct medical costs, an issue I return to toward the end of this chapter.

Second, our analyses estimate the health-care costs, just as they do the increased mortality, experienced solely by the individual who directly faces the various workplace exposures, without considering any possible spillover effects to family and friends. In the cases of absence of health insurance, work-family conflict, and economic insecurity, for example, the likelihood of spillover effects to other family members seems high. Access to health insurance occurs or does not occur for everyone in the immediate family. Work-family conflict affects family members besides the focal employee. And the stress arising from the economic insecurity that comes from the threat of layoffs or highly variable wages and work hours likely impacts everyone in a household.

The conclusion about costs is the same as the conclusion about mortality: workplace practices have an important effect on the health-care costs companies and society confront. This means that workplace arrangements are one reasonable place to intervene in an effort to reduce such costs.

IS THE HEALTH TOLL PREVENTABLE?

When my colleagues and I put our research paper through the peer-review process, one anonymous reviewer made an important point: the odds ratios from epidemiological studies and our analyses necessarily compared the health effects and costs of workplaces with varying management practices to a counterfactual world in which there was no workplace-induced stress at all. But such a world does not—and possibly cannot—exist. After all, companies face competitive pressures, and they pass at least some of that pressure on to their workforce, be it in the form of long hours, work-family conflict, or the economic insecurity that arises naturally in dynamic economies where firms rise and fall and employment fluctuates. So, we sought to come up with at least some reasonable ballpark estimate of the extent to which the health toll in the United States was realistically preventable.

One way to address that question is to contrast the United States to comparable, advanced industrialized capitalist economies that also operate in the global marketplace but with different regulatory regimes and different national norms about workplace conditions and practices. In conducting this comparison, we came up with a crucial insight: as countries get richer, they spend more of their income on health and also achieve better health outcomes in terms of levels of population health. As part of spending more on health, the first thing societies tend to do is, for the most part, remedy environmental exposures that lead to disease, death, and excess health-care costs. For instance, as countries develop and get richer, they invest in clean water and sanitation to prevent waterborne illnesses; they clean up the air, and by reducing air pollution, prevent various lung and respiratory diseases. Countries also will engage in aggressive programs of vaccination to forestall infectious diseases such as polio, measles, mumps, and pneumonia.

To the extent this line of argument—as countries get richer they eliminate preventable environmental causes of death and illness—holds true, we should expect to observe a negative relationship between a country's per capita income and per capita deaths (or health-care costs) attributable to specific environmental causes. We gathered data on the relationship between per capita income and the per capita death rate from air pollution and an infectious disease, tuberculosis, for a set of countries in Western Europe and the United States. We looked only at these two environmental causes of ill-health in part because other possible environmental causes of illness and death such as waterborne disease or polio occur so infrequently in advanced economies that data on their mortality consequences are unavailable.

As expected, there was a negative correlation between per capita income and per capita mortality from air pollution, with the correlation being –.44. In a similar fashion, there was a strong negative correlation between per capita income and per capita mortality from tuberculosis, with the correlation being –.57.

Having demonstrated the plausibility of the relationship between income and death from environmental causes, we extended the same logic to examine the relationship between mortality and health costs arising from the workplace with per capita income, under the assumption that at least some workplace harms would be preventable and prevented in advanced industrialized economies. Again we found the expected negative relationship, leaving out the United States. For health-care costs associated with workplace conditions, the correlation with per capita income was –.60, and for workplace-associated deaths, the correlation was –.65. Figures 2 and 3 show the graphs for mortality and health costs compared to per capita income. What is clear in those graphs is that the United States is an outlier. The United States is statistically significantly off the regression line in a direction that suggests that health costs and mortality are higher than would be expected given the country's wealth—its high level of per capita income.

We next estimated equations relating both mortality and health costs to per capita income, with the United States omitted from the

FIGURE 2. Deaths Per 100,000 Persons Attributable to Workplace Exposures

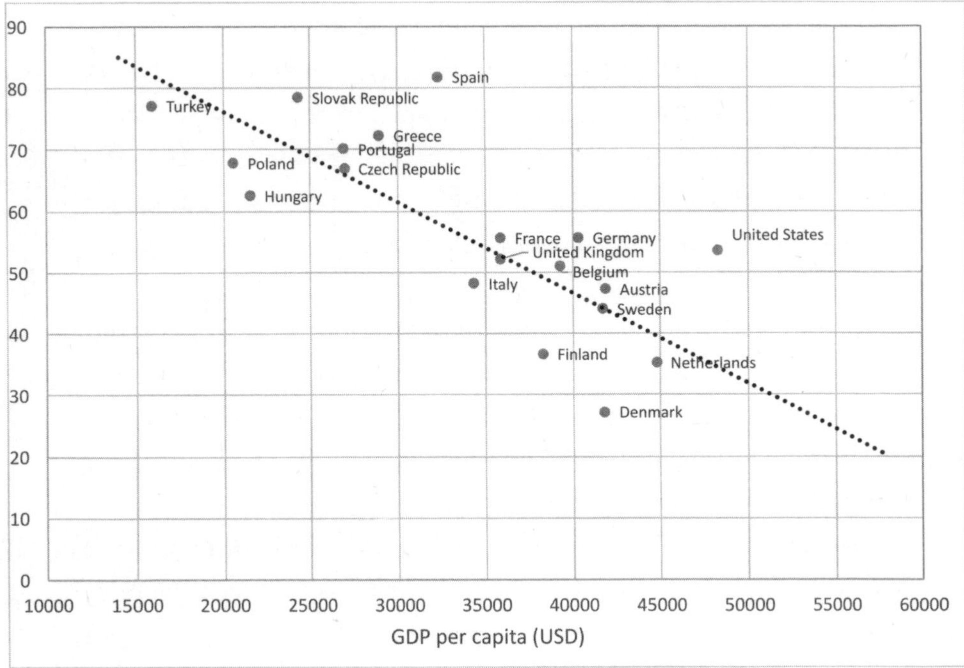

Source: OECD statistics database, Fifth European Working Conditions Survey (EWCS), authors' analysis

Notes: Regression line excludes the United States

sample used to calculate the regression equation. Once that equation was computed, we simply inserted US per capita income and then could see what the predicted level of mortality and health costs would be for the United States if it exhibited the same relationship between income and the health consequences of workplace practices as the rest of the OECD countries we had studied. When we compare the predicted values to the actual, observed values, we have a reasonable estimate of the extent to which the United States could prevent both costs and deaths—just by being similar to this set of Western European economies.

Doing this calculation showed that the United States experiences about fifty-nine thousand excess deaths and about $63 billion in incremental costs annually compared to what would be predicted given

FIGURE 3. Health-Care Cost (USD) Per Person Attributable to Workplace Exposures

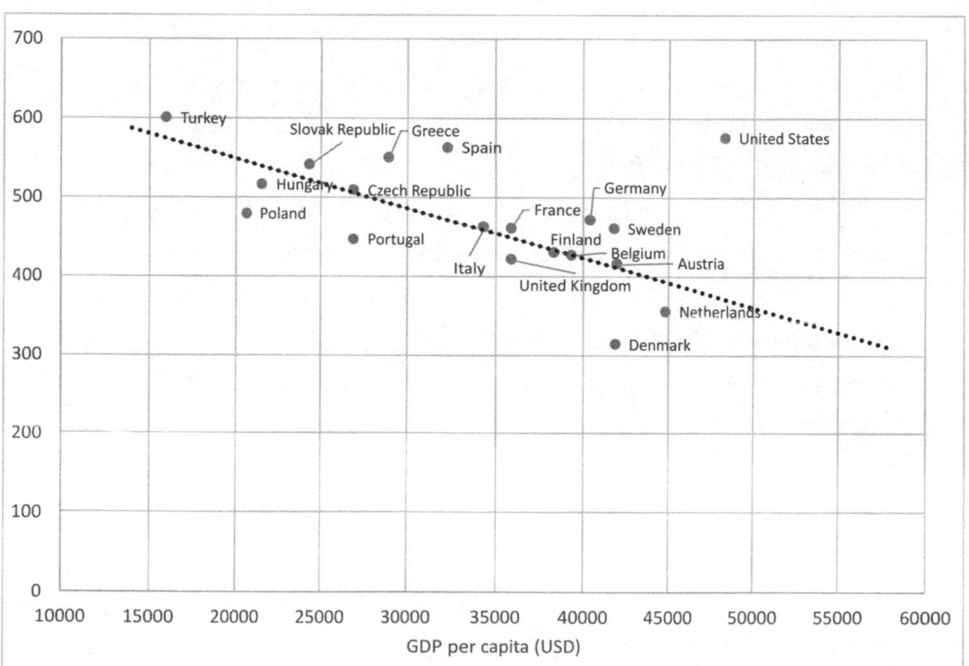

Source: OECD statistics database, Fifth EWCS, authors' analysis

its per capita income level. Considering the total toll we previously estimated (of about 120,000 excess deaths and $180 billion in costs), our analyses indicate that about half of the deaths and about a third of the incremental costs from workplace conditions appear to be potentially preventable if the United States were more similar to other advanced industrialized economies.

DIFFERENTIAL EXPOSURE TO WORKPLACE CONDITIONS HELPS EXPLAIN INEQUALITY IN LIFE SPANS

Inequality is a hot topic, what with growing income inequality not just in the United States but in many other countries as well. Inequality in health has also drawn increasing research and policy attention. Inequality in health, much like income inequality, has increased over the past decades in the United States and Britain as well as in other countries.[39] One study reported that "in 2008 US adult men and women with fewer than twelve years of education had life expectancies not much better than those of all adults in the 1950s and 1960s," and that the differences in life expectancies by race and education had widened substantially over time.[40] In the United States, there is "a 20-year gap in life expectancy between the most and least advantaged populations."[41] British epidemiologist Michael Marmot noted that, in Washington, DC, average life expectancy changed by one year for people living near adjacent subway stops.[42]

For many reasons, including the moral component attached to life and, therefore, life spans, inequality in health outcomes seems less tolerable than inequality in other things such as income. As Sudhir Anand, an Oxford University–based development microeconomist, commented at a conference on equity and health, "We should be more averse to . . . inequalities in health than inequalities in income. The reasons involve the status of health as a special good which has both intrinsic and instrumental value. . . . Health is regarded to be critical because it directly affects a person's well-being."[43] More than a decade ago, the World Health Organization decided to measure health inequality "as a distinct dimension of the performance of health systems." That is because "average achievement is no longer considered a sufficient indicator of a country's performance on health; rather, the distribution of health in the population is also key."[44]

It is well known that socioeconomic status is related to health status and that there is a social gradient for health. While there are many reasons for expecting people with different backgrounds to have different health outcomes, recently more attention has been focused on the effects of working conditions on health inequalities.[45] As one review noted, "It has long been recognized that adults with better jobs enjoy better health than those with less prestigious, less remunerating employment."[46]

What previous research has not yet done is to ascertain how much of the inequality in health outcomes comes from differential access to jobs with different amounts of exposure to harmful workplace environmental elements. However, the work Goh, Zenios, and I did to estimate overall mortality and health cost effects provided both a model and the data necessary to undertake the task of estimating the workplace-attributable component of inequalities in health. We reasoned that one factor accounting for the observed inequality in average life spans for different sociodemographic groups was the difference in the jobs held by persons of different races and particularly those who had more or less education. It seemed plausible that less-educated people would be more likely to hold jobs without health insurance, do shift work, face more economic insecurity, and be in positions with less job control and higher job demands. Because these conditions all affect mortality, differences in job environments might help account for the enormous (and increasing) disparities in life span.

And that is precisely what we found.[47] Different education/race groups do face very different job environments, and these differences account for between 10 and 38 percent of the differences in life expectancy across demographic subgroups. Although our estimates are at a single, contemporary point in time, research on the growing effect of educational attainment on income suggests that education has become increasingly important in sorting people into jobs. Consequently, it is likely that this effect and the resulting variation in exposure to harmful workplace conditions helps explain the growing inequality in life spans over time. If we believe that, to paraphrase the Gates Foundation, all individuals deserve an opportunity to live a normal life span because all lives have equal value, we should focus on reducing the disparities, or their effects, of differential exposure to workplace practices on human health.

THE COST TO EMPLOYERS

Employers also suffer from management practices that produce unhealthy work environments. In more than three decades of research, University of Michigan professor emeritus Dee Edington has consistently demonstrated two important findings. First, it is possible to identify people who are at risk from moving from good health to poor health. Because people with high health risks incur significantly higher medical claims costs,[48] a sensible strategy for employers is to try to prevent people from moving from the low-risk to the high-risk category. Edington has noted that "good health can be fostered or maintained only in a healthy environment and culture. This means employers . . . should . . . create work environments and cultures that encourage people to live healthy lifestyles."[49] Workplaces free from or low in the ten workplace exposures that create stress foster healthier employees and reduce medical claims and insurance costs.

Second, with relatively few exceptions, once people are in a high-risk health category and develop some chronic disease such as heart disease or diabetes, it is difficult and unlikely that they will move back into the low-risk category. Consequently, Edington argued that employers should be less focused than they tend to be on managing the costs of high-risk people and much more focused on *preventing* low-risk people from becoming high-risk in the first place. As in many other aspects of management, prevention is both less expensive and more effective than remediation.

Beyond medical claims and health insurance costs, employers face at least three other adverse consequences from operating work environments that make people sick. First, if people get sick enough, they quit. It is no accident that almost every person I interviewed about the health effects of work had left the place of employment where they were suffering. A study of university professors observed a statistically significant correlation between poor physical health and turnover intentions, with poor physical health resulting from work role and family role stress.[50] A study of the effects of job insecurity in Europe found that insecurity increased the frequency of mental health complaints and also the intentions of people to quit.[51] Because turnover is costly and ill-health contributes to turnover, workplace environments that create ill-health drive up turnover and its associated costs.

Second, sicker employees incur higher workers' compensation costs. A four-year study of 3,338 long-term employees of the Xerox Corporation reported that high-health-risk employees incurred higher workers' compensation costs. The study also showed that workers' compensation costs were highly skewed, with the top tenth percentile of employees incurring costs accounting for 54.4 percent of the total of all workers' compensation costs.[52]

Third, less healthy employees are less productive—a finding that should be completely unsurprising. When people are sick, they are distracted by their ailments and they have trouble concentrating. They may need to stop work more frequently, or talk to their coworkers about their health issues; they may be more tired, and in general be both physically and mentally less able to complete work. Numerous studies demonstrate the productivity effects of ill-health, with many of such studies showing that the productivity costs of employee ill-health are higher than the direct medical claims costs incurred by sick workers. For instance, a study of 564 telephone customer-service agents found that a Worker Productivity Index was correlated with employees' number of health risks.[53] Research using the Work Limitations Questionnaire reported that there were significant relationships between medical conditions and impaired work performance for some 16,651 employees of a large financial services firm.[54] A review of some 113 published studies concluded that there was good evidence for a relationship between health and productivity.[55]

The evidence presented in this chapter, both from our own analyses and from other sources, makes the case that the toll in both excess mortality and health-care costs from harmful workplace practices is high in the United States. Moreover, unhealthy employees cost employers in higher workers' compensation costs, medical insurance costs, and, perhaps most important, diminished productivity on the job. The workplace, as it is currently being managed by many if not most employers in the United States, exacts a toll for *both* employees and their employers—a situation that cries out for remediation.

Chapter 3

Layoffs and Economic Insecurity:

A LOSE-LOSE PROPOSITION

IN DECEMBER 2008, ARCELORMITTAL, which had taken over a steel plant in Lackawanna, New York, from the bankrupt Bethlehem Steel, announced it was finally closing the 260-person plant. What followed was all too predictable. George Kull, an employee at the plant, fifty-six years old, died of a heart attack three weeks later. Then a coworker, Bob Smith, forty-two, went to the doctor with chest pains. Smith survived his heart attack when doctors inserted stents into the blocked arteries. Next, Don Turner, fifty-five, who had worked at the mill for decades, also died from a heart attack. After Bethlehem Steel had closed coke ovens that were part of the same complex in 2001, two employees committed suicide.[1] White-collar workers, too, suffer health effects from layoffs and the resulting economic insecurity. In 2012, John Fugazzie oversaw dairy and frozen foods for the A&P supermarket chain. Then in October of that year, Fugazzie, fifty-seven years old, got laid off. Unable to find a new job, within ten months of being let go by A&P, Fugazzie had a heart attack.[2]

This chapter focuses primarily on the health consequences of layoffs, which are truly a lose-lose proposition, in that there are severe health effects for employees and the evidence suggests that layoffs provide little to no discernible benefits to employers. But layoffs are not the only cause of economic insecurity. Some other sources of economic stress are worth mentioning.

First, there are the consequences of contingent and part-time work and contract labor arrangements. Workers in the so-called gig economy and, for that matter, even skilled freelancers and contract workers confront uncertainty as to when and from where their next work will come and, consequently, face greater fluctuations in income, even as their financial obligations such as food and housing remain stable. Therefore, people in the on-demand economy need to constantly be "in the market" to ensure ongoing work and to maintain their reputations and visibility. One study of relatively highly paid contractors in Silicon Valley found that free agents didn't really feel free because of the need to be always searching for their next gig and therefore frequently took less leisure time than regular employees.[3]

Moreover, freelancers, part-timers, and contract workers typically do not receive health or retirement benefits. Consequently, they face the insecurity and stress of providing these safety nets for themselves. It is important to recognize how much this part of the labor market has grown. A survey by economists Lawrence Katz and Alan Krueger found that the proportion of people working in alternative work arrangements had increased some 50 percent in the ten years from 2005 to 2015. Moreover, "94 percent of the net employment growth in the US economy from 2005 to 2015 appears to have occurred in alternative work arrangements."[4]

Second, even for people in more regular, long-term jobs, typically working for one or maybe two employers, there is a growing sense of precariousness that arises from two causes. The first source of insecurity is the increasing use of just-in-time scheduling. Widely used in retail, many workers in settings ranging from hospitals to offices find that their schedules and hours fluctuate widely as employers call them in only as needed. One survey found that nearly 40 percent of retail workers don't get a minimum number of hours per week and 25 percent work on-call shifts, sometimes finding out they will work just two hours before their shift starts. "Other data has found that nearly half of part-time workers across the workforce and just under 40 percent of full-time workers don't find out their schedules until a week out or less."[5]

Varying, uncertain work schedules and work hours—and wages—wreak havoc on people's lives. For instance, as a person in a part-time service job at an international airline commented, "The company would distribute shift schedules in advance, but then it would adjust them at will, often with only a couple of days' notice and without bothering to consult the affected workers . . . the disruption to our lives soon became unbearable. The unpredictable hours were problematic, but even more demoralizing was the sense of being treated like a machine part."[6]

Companies recognize the issue raised by scheduling. Gary Loveman, former CEO of casino operator Caesars, noted:

> Scheduling unpredictability was the single biggest source of stress in people's lives. We have a lot of people who are single with children or with an ill parent. They have to have coverage. We would like to match demand for services in the hotels with the number of people we have working there. . . . This has only gotten worse in recent years, as companies have tried to skinny down their use of labor.

The toll from scheduling variability has prompted some states and cities to propose laws and regulations to ensure reasonable notice of when people will work. And because of the costs—in turnover and employee dissatisfaction—from scheduling issues, some companies have proactively implemented more employee-centric practices. Whole Foods, for instance, posts schedules two weeks in advance and prevents managers from altering them at the last minute, while Walmart has introduced a system that "allows workers to pick their own hours."[7] Loveman, whose strategy at Caesars was to improve customer service, "disallowed a lot of the manipulations of schedules that would happen almost real time. We told managers, 'You just can't do this stuff.' We caused managers to recognize that people have commitments." Retailers that are known as great places to work already understood this issue and offered employees stable, regular hours. As we see many times in the case of the workplace and health, what's good for workers is also good for their employers, who enjoy lower turnover, higher quality people, and a higher level of commitment and performance.

Another source of insecurity and stress even for full-time employees comes from feeling constantly under the gun. People feel that they are always being assessed and evaluated, and if they even temporarily don't perform as well as expected, they will be dismissed. There is less forgiveness in work cultures and not much patience with, or tolerance for, the invariable natural fluctuations in job performance. One recent research review noted that while job performance was traditionally considered to be a static, trait-like construct—e.g., there were "high performers" and "low performers"—"recently researchers acknowledged that short-term . . . within-person fluctuations in job performance are substantial and meaningful . . . studies estimated that roughly half the variance in job performance is within individuals."[8] A tough, judgmental evaluating culture confronted with natural individual variation in performance is likely to punish people for uncontrollable swings in performance levels.

A very experienced, busy executive coach doing work primarily with people in high technology and venture capital industries told me that many if not most of her clients—all of whom were incredibly successful and mostly very well paid—nonetheless felt "under the gun" and under a lot of job performance pressure. This was particularly true in places like Oracle, Salesforce, and Amazon, whose high-pressure work cultures are well-known. One consequence of these performance pressures was the long work hours (and consequent health effects) we will explore in Chapter 5. Another consequence was the reluctance of the clients to ever really disengage and turn off the connections to these companies, behavior that increased work-family conflict and stress. A third consequence was a sense of insecurity and instability in the employment relationship.

The research I conducted with Stefanos Zenios and Joel Goh that I summarized in Chapter 2 estimated approximately twenty-nine thousand excess deaths annually in the United States resulting from economic insecurity and thirty-five thousand additional deaths from unemployment and its effects. These empirical estimates imply that more than sixty-four thousand people a year die in the United States from not having a job or from confronting economic stress and job insecurity.[9]

MORE EMPLOYMENT IS CONTINGENT AND PRECARIOUS

Layoffs and other forms of economic insecurity such as contingent, part-time, and contract work have become increasingly commonplace in contemporary labor-market arrangements. Sociologist Arne Kalleberg's comprehensive study of job market conditions in the United States noted that "employment relations have become more precarious and insecure."[10] Among numerous indicators supporting this assertion are the following: although perceptions of economic insecurity are, not surprisingly, tied to the unemployment rate and general labor market conditions, even after controlling statistically for the unemployment rate, the "odds of perceiving greater risk of job loss" grew by 1.5 percent annually between 1977 and 2006.[11] Even prior to the recession of 2008, *New York Times* economics writer Louis Uchitelle had documented the increasing frequency and overuse of layoffs with their devastating consequences.[12] As one review of the literature on employee downsizing noted, more than 6.5 million jobs were lost during the recession that began in December 2007, and layoffs were common in countries throughout the world.[13] Even Japan and other societies that in the past have embraced more employment security increasingly have layoffs and other forms of economic insecurity as labor markets become more "flexible"—a phrase that actually means becoming riskier for employees.

Fewer companies that appear on the Great Place to Work Institute's lists of best places to work explicitly (or even implicitly) promise long-term employment and espouse no-layoff aspirations than in the past. As Wharton professor Peter Cappelli noted some time ago, average organizational tenure, particularly for male employees, has been falling, and to use his apt phrase, there is now a "new deal at work"—a deal that is, in most places and for most employees, considerably more transactional, unstable, and less relationship-based than in the past.[14]

The World Employment Confederation (WEC), which describes itself as the "voice of the employment industry at global level, representing labour market enablers in 50 countries and 7 of the largest international workforce solutions companies,"[15] released a white paper in September 2016 nicely describing the new world of work.[16] Some of the highlights:

- Between 1987 and 2015, the global working population doubled as India and China joined the world's market economy;
- New technologies facilitate more flexible work arrangements with people working outside of standard core hours and working beyond physical premises to doing work wherever someone is;
- Wage and salaried work constitutes only about half of global employment and represents only about 20 percent of workers in places such as South Asia and sub-Saharan Africa.

While the WEC sees these trends as positive—helping to grow the businesses and reach of labor market intermediary companies—contingent, contract, and alternative employment arrangements, many of which offer fewer protections and benefits, are clearly on the rise.

Economic Insecurity Produces Poorer Health

Economic insecurity is stressful, and stress adversely affects physical and mental health. It should scarcely be surprising that research consistently finds evidence that working in less secure, more contingent employment arrangements is adversely related to physical and mental health—*and not just for the people directly facing economic insecurity.* In part because of social contagion effects—people working with those facing economic insecurity themselves feel less secure—"the effect of job insecurity on health was the same in the exposed and unexposed groups,"[17] suggesting that job insecurity can lead to adverse health effects for both temporary *and* permanent employees. These effects occur even in countries with generous social welfare and income maintenance policies.

For instance, a longitudinal study of some nine hundred employees in Sweden found that people who worked in temporary help arrangements evidenced higher risk of both poorer self-rated health and psychological distress.[18] A study in South Korea found that people facing employment instability suffered health effects as large as the effects of smoking.[19] A meta-analysis concluded that job insecurity affected both physical and mental health with, not surprisingly, larger effects on mental health outcomes.[20] One review of the empirical research on the effects of job insecurity on health concluded that "reductions in job insecurity should be a point of intervention for government policies aimed at improving population health and reducing health inequalities."[21] Of course, precisely the opposite trend is occurring, with growing levels of insecurity and precarious employment.

Economic insecurity leads to people feeling a lack of control over their lives. Using both experiments and field data, a recent study found that economic insecurity was associated with increased consumption of painkillers and produced actual physical pain and reduced pain tolerance, with the absence of control providing one mechanism explaining these results.[22]

While the data on layoffs, reviewed below, show large health and mortality effects, any form of economic insecurity seems to adversely affect health.

HEALTH EFFECTS OF LAYOFFS: THE EVIDENCE

Layoffs aren't good for people's physical or mental health. Layoffs induce feelings of economic insecurity, which is stressful. Layoffs, in the United States where health insurance coverage was, prior to the Affordable Care Act, often determined by employment status, result in diminished access to health care, with the negative health effects that result from reduced access to medical care that I describe in the next chapter. Layoffs affect people's feelings of self-worth because they implicate people's capacity to provide for their own and their families' economic needs and harm their social status because of an absence of a job.

Not only do layoffs create physical and mental health problems for the people who are laid off, as already noted, but economic insecurity and job loss also have consequences for others not laid off. Even employees who survive layoffs face at least two adverse outcomes. First, people in plants that have experienced more layoffs report feeling greater economic insecurity as they wonder if they will be the next to go and if and when the layoffs will stop.[23] Second, as studies of health-care employees demonstrate, typically layoffs cut more people than they reduce the work that must be done. Therefore, those who survive layoffs wind up with greater workloads, something that also increases stress.[24]

Some people muster a countervailing argument about the effects of layoffs on health, noting that job loss might have some positive health effects. Because much of the stress encountered in everyday life comes from working, "a reduction in time at work, therefore, may reduce the prevalence of stress-induced illness."[25] Moreover, when people no longer have a job, they presumably have more time to engage in healthful activities such as pursuing hobbies and undertaking exercise. Notwithstanding the possibility of these positive consequences of job loss, as one review of the literature on the effects of economic decline concluded, "Much research shows that undesirable job and financial experiences increase the risk of psychological and behavioral disorder," including increased drug and alcohol use and the incidence of suicide.[26]

The costs of the ill-health created by layoffs are mostly borne by those laid off and the larger society, not by the companies doing the layoffs. That is because once people are laid off, they are no longer on an employer's books, covered by employer-provided health insurance or any other employee assistance programs. And not only do layoffs impose costs, including substantial costs in terms of death and ill-health, but it is far from evident that they are beneficial to company performance. As we will see, not all companies lay people off at the first sign of economic problems. Those companies that seek to retain their people often not only enjoy better performance but also spare their workforce and the country the loss of life and the psychological and physical effects that come from this socially destructive practice.

Studying the health consequences of being laid off is not as straightforward as it might first appear. That's because even if one observes a relationship between ill-health and being laid off, it is possible that losing one's job is a *consequence* of being in poor health rather than causing bad health. Although various laws presumably protect people from losing their jobs because of health problems, enforcement is spotty. Some of the studies I summarize overcome this problem of inferring causality by using panel designs that permit us to see what comes first—bad health or layoffs—under the reasonable assumption that for one thing to cause something else, the cause must precede the effect (so if layoffs precede bad health, it is illogical to argue that the health problems caused the layoffs). Other studies take advantage, if that's the right word, of plant closing events. When a plant closes, everyone in the facility loses his or her job, so it is implausible to argue that poor health caused individuals to be chosen for job loss.

As briefly summarized below, the evidence on the ill-health effects of layoffs is extensive. Moreover, the studies are not just from the United States but also from countries with more generous social safety nets and more employee protections such as Finland, Denmark, and New Zealand. All the studies show consistent results. The fact that results are similar across countries suggests that much of the effect of layoffs on health (and by extension, on health-care costs) occurs almost regardless of the level of social services and support provided by governments. The evidence shows that layoffs are harmful to health regardless of where, or for that matter, when, they occur, and some studies show that the adverse effects of layoffs persist even when people can find new jobs.

Layoffs Increase Mortality

Many studies demonstrate that being laid off increases a person's risk of dying compared to people not laid off. Some studies have even begun to explore a few of the pathways that produce this result. For instance, being laid off increases the risk of committing suicide. Being laid off increases the likelihood of being unemployed. Finding a new job is often difficult, and numerous studies "provided unequivocal evidence of the adverse effects on health and well-being as a result of being unemployed."[27] The studies cover a number of different countries and also a variety of research designs.

Researchers in New Zealand followed a cohort for eight years that was comprised of 1,945 people made redundant by a meat plant's closure, and compared them to 1,767 people from a neighboring meat plant that remained open. Even after adjusting for age, gender, and ethnicity, those laid off had a 2.5 times higher risk of inflicting serious self-harm and a 17 percent higher likelihood of being admitted to a hospital with a mental health diagnosis.[28]

A study in Sweden followed the employees of every establishment with more than ten employees that closed in 1987 and 1988. The overall mortality risk for men increased by 44 percent in the four years following job loss. And for both men and women, there was an approximate doubling of the increase in suicide and alcohol-related mortality.[29]

Another study followed almost 9,800 Danish men born in 1953 and explored what happened as a consequence of important events that occurred to these individuals between the ages of forty and fifty-one. The Danish men who had experienced one job loss were 44 percent more likely to have died than those who had not lost their jobs. The study also examined the effects of broken partnerships, defined as either a long-term relationship or marriage. Broken partnerships also increased mortality risk, but interestingly there was no relationship between broken partnerships and job loss. The empirical results suggest that the increased mortality risk for job loss was not because of the effect of losing one's job on also losing one's relationship.[30]

A study in the United States that combined administrative data on date of death and individual earnings and employment information from the state of Pennsylvania examined employment histories for male workers from 1974 to 1991 and mortality from 1974 to 2002. Like most studies of the causes of mortality, it included statistical controls for factors such as age and earnings. In the first years following job loss, mortality increased by 28 percent and then settled into a range of 15 to 20 percent higher risk of mortality for the following twenty years. The effect of job loss on increased mortality occurred mostly through the effect of job loss on income—displaced workers experienced a permanent decrement in subsequent earnings. This finding is completely consistent with recent job market experience during the recession where people who lost their jobs not only had difficulty in finding new employment but, even when they did, were quite likely to wind up working for lower hourly rates of pay and fewer hours than before. The study's authors noted that their estimated rate of increased mortality from layoffs implied a decrement of life expectancy of one and a half years for someone who loses his job at age forty.[31]

It is important to note the consistency of the size of the estimates of the effects of layoffs and job loss on suicides and overall mortality.

The large literature on the effects of unemployment on health, the inverse relationship between income level and mortality and ill-health, and the studies of layoffs on the increased risk of death paint a very consistent picture supported by a great deal of evidence: layoffs kill people.

Layoffs Lead to Poor Health

Kate Strully, a sociologist at the State University of New York at Albany, used data from the Panel Study of Income Dynamics in the United States to examine the effects of job loss on health. She distinguished job loss from plant or establishment closure—sort of "no fault" job loss—from being fired as well as from voluntary quitting. Her analysis controlled for health status at the start of the study, age, race, gender, family income, and education, all factors that might be expected to affect health. In addition to looking at self-reported health status, the study also asked respondents if a doctor had told them they suffered from a health condition, when they received the diagnosis, and what the condition was. Strully found that "job loss because of an establishment closure increases the odds of reporting fair or poor health by approximately 54%. . . . Conditioning on respondents being healthy at baseline, losing a job because of an establishment closure increases the odds of a new likely health condition by 83%."[32] Even people who found new jobs experienced adverse health consequences, at least by some measures. Strully wrote: "Respondents who had found new jobs at the time of the survey face a 97% increase in the risk of developing a new likely health condition."[33]

A study of acute myocardial infarction (heart attacks) followed more than thirteen thousand adults from 1992 to 2010. The study found that almost 70 percent of the sample had experienced one or more job losses during this time. The risk of suffering a heart attack increased monotonically the greater the number of job losses—people who suffered one job loss were 22 percent more likely to suffer a heart attack, while those with four or more job losses were 63 percent more likely than people with no job losses to experience a heart attack. These results held even when individual factors such as smoking, alcohol consumption, and obesity were statistically controlled.[34]

Layoffs also adversely affect employees who work in units experiencing layoffs but who manage to keep their jobs. Those who survive layoffs nonetheless face heightened economic insecurity and psychological stress—they don't know if they will be the next to go. And as extensively documented, most companies take out more workers than work. Consequently, those employees who still have their jobs find that they must do much more work to compensate for the reduced number of people now expected to get about the same tasks accomplished. Burnout and job stress typically increase following layoffs, resulting in adverse health consequences for those remaining employees.

One of the more analytically rigorous studies of this effect was conducted in the municipality of Raisio, Finland, in the early 1990s. Finland experienced a severe recession in the early 1990s with the number of Finish municipal employees declining 12 percent between 1990 and 1993, even as the overall unemployment soared from 3 percent in 1990 to 16 percent in 1993. A prospective cohort study of employees begun in 1990 demonstrated the effects of downsizing and explored the differences for employees in units that had downsized quite a bit compared to those in units that downsized less severely. Absence because of sickness was more than *twice* as high among employees in units that had experienced major as compared to minor downsizing, and downsizing increased the prevalence of smoking. As expected, downsizing caused increased work demands and heightened economic insecurity, which helped explain the effects of layoffs on absence and smoking behaviors.[35]

Most of the studies of the effects of layoffs on mortality and health have, naturally enough, focused on the people who get laid off or, in fewer instances, their coworkers who face increased economic insecurity and higher workloads. However, the act of laying people off can be stressful in and of itself, and that stress can contribute to poor health for the managers charged with getting rid of people. That is precisely what one study of 410 managers—some of whom had and some of whom had not implemented layoffs between 2000 and 2003—found. Managers who had given notice of potential layoffs reported more health problems, more use of medical care to deal with those health problems, more difficulty sleeping, and a higher intent to quit their jobs compared to otherwise similar managers. The research further found that it was emotional exhaustion that accounted for the effect of issuing layoff warnings on managers' health.[36]

Layoffs Increase Workplace Violence

Layoffs not only increase the mortality risk of those laid off. Through their effects on workplace violence, terminations also increase the mortality risk for those doing the terminating and innocent bystanders. To take just one of many examples, on November 14, 2008, Jing Wu, who had been fired from his job at a semiconductor start-up in Mountain View, California, returned to the company's headquarters and requested a meeting with three executives. In the conference room, Mr. Wu pulled out a gun and killed the CEO, the vice president of operations, and another executive.[37]

Workplace violence is not some rare occurrence that affects just a few people. In 1992, the Centers for Disease Control declared that workplace homicide was a serious public health problem, with more than eight hundred workplace killings annually.[38] Suicides in the workplace increased 28 percent just between 2007 and 2008 as the recession was beginning, while in organizations with more than one thousand employees, more than 50 percent of those responding to a survey reported at least one incident of workplace violence in the preceding twelve months.[39]

Ralph Catalano, a professor at the University of California, Berkeley,

School of Public Health, has done extensive research on the effects of economic insecurity on numerous outcomes, including workplace violence. One study found that "among respondents with no history of violent behavior at first interview, those laid off before the second interview were 6 times more likely to report such behavior than were similar persons who remained employed. The effect survived controlling for age, gender, socioeconomic status, ethnicity, marital status, and having a diagnosable psychiatric disorder."[40] Another study found a relationship between layoffs and the incidence of civil psychiatric commitments, with men being two times more likely to be committed when community layoff rates were higher.[41]

The Internet is filled not just with examples of violent responses to job loss but also with recommendations about how to administer layoffs to reduce the threat of violence. Such recommendations include not doing layoffs on Friday, having security officers both present and visible, and escorting those laid off out of the building and ensuring they do not have keys or other means to gain access. Layoffs provoke strong emotional reactions. Sometimes those reactions entail taking one's own life, and in some instances, the reactions involve lashing out and taking the lives of others, particularly those seen as responsible for the layoff.

Job Loss Induces Unhealthy Individual Behaviors

Studies of depression and anxiety consistently find an increase of between 15 and 30 percent in reported symptoms among people who have lost their jobs compared to those who remained stably employed.[42] Depression and anxiety, along with the stress of job loss, would be expected to increase the incidence of unhealthy and harmful individual behaviors, and that is precisely what the research finds. Carefully conducted studies demonstrate that being unemployed increases the use of alcohol,[43] cannabis,[44] and other drugs.[45] For instance, one study reported that being unemployed for more than twenty weeks doubled alcohol intake overall, with an increase of heavy drinking of 400 percent among Swedish males.[46] Some research shows that, not surprisingly, the risk of substance abuse following job loss is particularly pronounced among people who had previous histories of alcohol or drug use—the stress of unemployment coupled with their prior exposure and behavioral history makes such individuals particularly susceptible to reverting to previous unhealthy choices.[47]

This research suggests that individual behaviors, including harmful behaviors such as alcohol and drug abuse and overeating, are affected by situations. Situational effects on behavior is a fundamental principle of social psychology. Job loss, then, has both a direct effect on ill-health through stress and also affects health because it contributes to individuals coping by consuming drugs and alcohol, which further compromises health.

DO LAYOFFS ENHANCE ECONOMIC PERFORMANCE?

If layoffs improved corporate performance, then the costs of the layoffs in physical and psychological ill-health and increased health-care spending would need to be balanced against the economic benefits arising from the layoffs. Note, however, that even in this case there would be some concern about making socially optimal decisions. That's because the benefits from reduced payroll costs go mostly to the companies doing the layoffs while the costs are incurred mostly by the broader society and the individuals affected. Consequently, there is a misalignment of costs and benefits. Companies, which do not face the full costs of their layoff activities, are, just as they would be with any underpriced activity or resource, likely to use layoffs too much. And the employees who are affected, because they do not capture any of the benefits of the layoffs that accrue to the companies that are their former employers, will invariably prefer policies that restrict layoffs and the resulting labor market flexibility too much.

In this instance, however, the problem is even worse. That's because the evidence on the effects of layoffs on corporate performance is extensive and tells a largely, although not completely consistent, story—there is little evidence that layoffs provide benefits and much evidence that layoffs can harm the companies doing them.

In the first place, layoffs impose numerous costs on companies. University of Colorado professor Wayne Cascio outlined many: severance pay, paying out accrued vacation and sick pay, outplacement costs, higher unemployment insurance taxes, costs of rehiring employees when business improves, low morale and survivors who are risk averse, potential lawsuits, sabotage, or even workplace violence from aggrieved employees or former employees, the loss of institutional memory and knowledge, diminished trust in management, and reduced labor productivity.[48] Layoffs, which often seem to violate the psychological norm of reciprocity and implicit psychological contracts that say employee performance and loyalty should be rewarded, provoke diminished discretionary effort and employee engagement.

Layoffs often do not provide business benefits, because layoffs by themselves seldom if ever solve any underlying business problem, for instance, of quality, productivity, or market acceptance. In most instances, the problem struggling companies face is *not* excessive costs but instead insufficient revenues. Frequently cost-cutting efforts only drive customers away by reducing the value proposition being offered to the market, making the revenue problem even worse. There is a vicious cycle in which businesses offer less, customers defect, and then the businesses must chase the declining revenues by making even more cuts, and so on.

The US airline industry provides a wonderful illustration of this dynamic. Between 2000 and 2007, the number of premium trips, defined as full-fare coach, business, or first-class one-way journeys, flown by US airlines declined by 47 percent. Meanwhile, the number of trips flown by private aircraft increased so that private air travel that represented just 15 percent of the premium trips flown in 2000 grew to be 40 percent of such trips by 2007. Maybe some of this change reflects the increased security and hassle that followed the tragedy of September 11, 2001. But the airline industry is consistently panned in surveys reported in the American Customer Satisfaction Index out of the University of Michigan, often ranking just above cell phone companies in terms of customer satisfaction. The industry has added fees and cut services. And no industry can lose almost 50 percent of its best, highest-paying customers and expect to prosper.

Other data also support this view that the airlines' problem is revenue caused by driving customers away rather than costs. A survey done by industry association IATA reported in 2008 that because flying had become so unpleasant, people were flying less, costing the industry almost $10 billion in revenue that year, according to survey estimates. In what is essentially a fixed cost industry—the marginal cost of carrying extra passengers on a flight is very, very low—that incremental revenue would have made the difference in creating a profitable industry even in the 2008 recessionary economic climate.

If downsizing does not positively affect economic performance, it is logical to suppose that economic performance in turn does not strongly predict the implementation of downsizing programs. Instead, downsizing and layoffs are caused by other factors. That is precisely what Art Budros found when he examined the adoption of downsizing programs at *Fortune* 100 companies over the period of 1979 to 1994.[49] Budros concluded that downsizing was affected by the proportion of firms that had already initiated a downsizing program—an adoption or imitation effect—and also by deregulation and industry culture. Budros's subsequent writings consistently reported no significant relationships between economic conditions and downsizing.[50] Other scholars have reported similar results, with the evidence showing that downsizing among referent firms—similar, comparable workplaces—increased the likelihood that a given company would also do layoffs.[51] In other words, the institutional context and simple imitation of the behavior of other companies affected the adoption of downsizing programs more than did economic performance or the efficiency imperatives that emanate from poor performance.

Layoffs and Stock Price

Most studies of the effects of layoffs on stock price use an "event study" methodology that assesses whether companies that downsize earn abnormal stock market returns compared to others in the period immediately following the announcement of the layoffs. The evidence strongly suggests that layoff announcements have at best a neutral but most frequently a negative effect on stock price and shareholder returns. One study of 141 layoff announcements that occurred between 1979 and 1997 reported a negative return for companies that announced layoffs, with larger (as a proportion of the workforce) and permanent (as contrasted with temporary) layoffs producing stronger negative stock price reactions.[52] Another examination of 1,445 downsizing announcements between 1990 and 1998 reported that downsizing had a negative effect on stock market returns, with larger negative effects created by larger downsizings.[53]

A study comparing layoff announcements in the United States and Japan observed negative abnormal shareholder returns in both places following downsizing announcements.[54] A study of 214 layoff announcements by major Canadian companies listed on the Toronto Stock Exchange in the 1980s found that over the three-day time period when layoffs were first announced, the stock market value of companies announcing layoffs fell about one-half of a percentage point in response to the downsizing information.[55]

A recent review of twelve studies examining the effect of layoffs on stock market returns concluded that "on average, downsizing announcements have a negative effect on stock price," with nine of the twelve empirical examinations uncovering a negative effect on share values.[56]

At some level, the idea that stock prices should decline following a layoff announcement is not surprising, as layoffs often mean that the organization is not doing well. One study of the effects of layoffs on stock price examined whether there were differences depending on the announced reason for the layoffs. Companies citing declining demand as an explanation for the downsizing experienced negative stock returns while those who accounted for the layoffs with efficiency explanations did not have their stock prices affected.[57]

Layoffs and Profitability

Wayne Cascio studied the profitability of companies in the Standard and Poor's 500 over the period 1982 to 2000. He found that companies that downsized remained less profitable than those that did not get rid of staff. Another study examined 122 companies and statistically controlled for their prior profitability. Nevertheless, downsizing reduced subsequent profitability, and the negative consequences of downsizing were particularly evident in industries that had a lot of research and development.[58] An American Management Association survey that assessed company perceptions of the effects of downsizing—likely to be biased in favor of layoffs, as companies and their executives do not like to admit that they have made mistakes—nonetheless found that only about half of the companies reported that downsizing increased their operating profits.[59]

Layoffs and Productivity

The same American Management Association survey just mentioned also found that only one-third of the companies reported a positive effect of downsizing on employee productivity.[60] A study assessing productivity changes between 1977 and 1987 using data from more than 140,000 US establishments covered by Census of Manufacturing data reported that companies that enjoyed the greatest increases in productivity were as likely to have added as to have cut employees.

The study concluded that the growth in productivity observed during the 1980s could not be attributed to companies becoming lean and mean.[61] Wharton professor Peter Cappelli observed that labor costs per employee—a measure of labor productivity—improved following downsizing, but sales per employee, a different indicator of employee productivity and firm profitability, decreased.[62]

One of the reasons why eliminating employees does not invariably enhance productivity is that often the best, most capable people head for the door when layoffs are announced, leaving the less talented people behind. Another issue is that sometimes companies need more people than they have retained to do the work that remains following a downsizing, so the firms wind up hiring back laid-off employees as contractors. This is not very cost-efficient. Having paid severance, firms then hire back people they have just laid off and are not only paying them but also paying the labor contracting firm's profit margin. An American Management Association survey found that fully one-third of the companies that had done layoffs wound up rehiring some of those laid off as contractors because their skills were still needed.[63]

Layoffs and Innovation

Layoffs can have several negative effects on companies' ability to innovate. First, the fear that accompanies downsizing reduces people's willingness to take the risks that accompany innovative activity. Second, when people leave, existing networks of relationships within the organization get broken. Accomplishing innovation entails searching for knowledge, coordinating activities across multiple units such as product design, manufacturing, sales, and marketing, transferring expertise within the company, and making projects happen. Disrupting existing networks of social relations makes these processes more difficult to quickly and effectively accomplish.

It is little wonder then that studies find that layoffs retard innovation. A study of more than two hundred employers in Portugal reported that downsizing reduced innovative behavior.[64] An examination of the work environment for creativity at a large high-technology company before, during, and after a major downsizing observed that creativity and most creativity-facilitating aspects of the work environment declined while the layoffs were going on, although they recovered somewhat afterward.[65]

Why Layoffs Seldom Help Employers

Layoffs, like virtually all decisions, have feedback effects, and the evidence indicates that these effects, including increased employee fear and disengagement and reduced effort, frequently swamp any positive direct effects that come from cutting costs by reducing the payroll. One summary of numerous research studies concluded that "there is general agreement that downsizing results in lower job involvement and reduced organizational commitment among survivors" and that "downsizing results in reduced creativity," has a "negative impact on different aspects of quality improvement," and "results in a significant decline in other dimensions of work performance."[66] As management writer Gary Hamel has often noted, it is difficult for companies to cut their way to success. Cutting people only makes the company smaller, not better, and certainly not necessarily better able to serve customer needs or, as we have seen, more productive, efficient, or innovative.

When companies begin cutting staff, employees head for the door if they have options, or to the watercooler to gossip and get social support from their colleagues if they can't easily move to a better workplace. Even as companies need effort and talent to improve their business results, layoffs drive talent away and cause the people who remain to be worried rather than motivated. That's why some years ago, Hap Wagner, CEO of Air Products at the time, told me, "It took us two months to decide to do layoffs, two weeks to do them, and two years to recover." David Cote, CEO of Honeywell, made this comment about seeking to avoid layoffs during the recession that commenced in 2008: "Most managers underestimate how much disruption layoffs create; they consume everyone in the organization for at least a year. Managers typically overestimate the savings they will achieve."[67]

If layoffs don't help companies, besides the fact that they are socially accepted and trendy, one might wonder why companies do them. Perhaps part of the answer comes from a study that examined the relationship between layoffs and top executive pay. Companies that announced layoffs in the previous year paid their CEOs more and gave those CEOs larger percentage raises than companies that did not have at least one downsizing announcement during the previous year.[68]

The evidence suggests that layoffs often do not help companies get better results. And the evidence shows that plant closures and layoffs harm human beings, creating psychological distress, physical maladies, and death.

COMPANIES DON'T HAVE TO RESORT TO LAYOFFS

On Wednesday, September 12, 2001, no planes were flying in the United States. On the day after two planes flew into the World Trade Center and one crashed in Pennsylvania, it was not clear when air travel would be permitted to resume nor was there any certainty as to what the operational and logistical conditions would be when flights resumed—what new security arrangements would be required and how they would work. As the United States was already beginning to experience the effects of a recession, it was certainly unclear as to what the level of ongoing demand for air travel would be. In the days following September 11, US airlines such as American, Delta, and United did what they had done so many times before—laid off employees, about eighty thousand in total. All the big airlines announced layoffs almost immediately after September 11. That is, all except one.

Southwest Airlines sent an e-mail to its employees and in that message noted that in its entire history it had never had a layoff or furlough. Although it could not promise that it would never have to lay people off, the airline made clear that it was committed to its people. Get back to work and provide great service to the customers when that became possible again, and the company would do its best to ensure the well-being of both its people and its patrons. Southwest, even as it offered its customers no-questions-asked refunds if they wanted them, maintained its flight schedule and made a scheduled $179 million contribution to its employee profit-sharing plan in the aftermath of September 11.[69] By the end of 2001, Southwest had not only made money for the year, it had been profitable even in the fourth quarter and had gained market share on its domestic US airline competitors. Going into 2002, the company had a market capitalization greater than the entire rest of the US airline industry combined.

The idea that all companies, particularly those operating in cyclical industries, must resort to layoffs as a routine part of how they do business is simply not true. For a long time Xilinx, a semiconductor manufacturer, avoided the cycles of layoffs and rehiring so common to that industry. In the tech recession of 2001 and 2002, when Intel and Advanced Micro Devices cut nine thousand jobs, Xilinx laid off none of its 2,600 people.[70] Toyota assiduously tries to avoid layoffs, even during times when the motor vehicle market is not doing well. Toyota has sought to retain employees on the payroll not just in Japan but in the company's US factories as well.

Arc welding manufacturer Lincoln Electric, headquartered in Cleveland, Ohio, has survived two world wars and numerous economic cycles without sacrificing its employees or their jobs. The company is famous for its profit-sharing incentive plan that produces variable compensation costs and helps Lincoln avoid layoffs. Because pay declines when profits go down during recessions, Lincoln Electric can eschew layoffs as its wage costs decrease. One of Lincoln's former CEOs described downsizing as "dumbsizing." And a more recent CEO, a longtime veteran of the company, noted, "I think my philosophy and that of my predecessors is that we can perform in an economically challenging environment, and we can spread that pain in a way that long-term will better represent our shareholders' interests without crucifying our employee base."[71]

SAS Institute, the largest privately owned software company in the world with 2016 sales of more than $3.2 billion, used the technology downturn in the early 2000s to hire hundreds of people and thereby gain both talent and market position. When the next economic recession hit in 2007 to 2008, Jim Goodnight, the CEO, noted that employees were frequently asking him if there were going to be layoffs. He sent out an e-mail encouraging people to watch expenses but assuring them that there would be no economy-related layoffs. As he told me, although sales did not grow as fast during the recession as they had in the past—no surprise there—profitability was reasonably good. With people assured of their jobs and their security, they could focus on their work and be more productive, and, because they were grateful to be working for a compassionate employer, they reciprocated with diligence and creativity—and with enhanced attention to keeping expenses in check.

Layoffs reflect company values. Large grocery chain Whole Foods Market went through the economic crisis of the late 2000s laying off fewer than one hundred people. Chip Conley, the founder and leader of Joie de Vivre Hospitality, one of the largest boutique hotel chains in the Unites States, tried to minimize layoffs even as the company's revenues fell more than 30 percent in the recession of the late 2000s. And having gone through that wrenching experience, when the economy recovered, Conley sold his stake in the hotel chain in part, he commented, so he would not have to go through the experience of laying off so many people again.

Some industrialized countries have adopted public policies that encourage employers to retain their workers. In many European countries, companies that lay off permanent staff are required to make large severance payments, thereby causing companies to have to balance the presumed savings from letting people go against these severance costs. Other policies require advance notice of layoffs and, in some instances, consultation with unions or workers' counsels. Although such policies are presumed to create inflexible labor markets that result in persistently higher unemployment and less growth in employment, the evidence on such effects is mixed.[72] Moreover, virtually no studies of labor market effects balance the costs of higher economic security against the benefits in health and well-being.

Germany, recognizing that when people lose their jobs they collect unemployment benefits and other social-support payments, has experimented with offering companies some fraction of these anticipated payments to induce them to retain workers, even on a part-time basis. The German policies have often been credited with reducing the extent of economic dislocation that would otherwise occur during recessions. The point is that public policy is an important factor affecting company decisions about layoffs. Moreover, the cost of layoffs needs to be considered in deciding about the benefits and costs of policies that seek to reduce economic insecurity and layoffs.

THE EXTERNALIZATION OF SOCIAL COSTS

There is no question that fewer companies today attempt to maintain a no-layoff policy than was the case in the past. This change reflects how much downsizing has become part of the accepted management tool kit and how social values have changed such that employees no longer expect to build their careers within a single company. Companies are, for the most part, no longer communities but instead a nexus of often temporary labor market contracts. The increased frequency of layoffs also reflects social values that apparently prize economic efficiency and returns to capital over human well-being.

But labor-market flexibility exacts a price on employees, in both their physical and mental health. For the most part, the companies doing the layoffs do not face the costs those layoffs impose. Once employees are no longer employed, employers are not responsible for their health-care costs nor do the now-former employers suffer from reduced productivity arising from psychological distress and harmful behaviors. Costs imposed by employer decisions that the employers don't see, let alone have to pay for, lead to the overuse of layoffs, which seem less costly than they are.

Unless and until organizations doing the downsizing confront the full costs of their decisions, society and individual employees will continue to pick up the burden for organizational decisions that will necessarily be suboptimal because of the mispricing of the consequences of layoffs.

Chapter 4

No Health Insurance, No Health

DAN IS A BRICKLAYER in upstate New York. Bricklaying is tough work—much bending, lifting, and carrying a lot of weight. At forty-five, Dan tells me he has pains in his back, shoulders, legs, and arms, but, fortunately, no serious health problems. One other fact to be aware of: upstate New York has severe winters, so for about four months of the year, unless Dan is very lucky to find some inside bricklaying work, he will not be earning any income.

About two years ago, Dan decided to go out on his own, and he now has one contract employee. It is a tough but in some ways better life than when Dan worked for others. He is learning how to bid on jobs and to balance workloads so he has just the right amount of work, not so much so that he can't do a good job and keep projects on schedule, but not so little so that he won't earn enough money to support himself. As a laborer, Dan always faced some degree of economic insecurity. Now he faces even more variation in how much he works and how much money he earns. But as his own boss he has more control over his work—with the positive effects that such control provides.

I ask Dan if he has health insurance. "No," he replies. What about Obamacare? He replies with a chuckle that "the Affordable Care Act is not that affordable." The inexpensive policies offered on the insurance exchange don't cover very much. With seasonal and uncertain income, Dan expresses reluctance to sign up for yet another monthly fixed obligation. I forgo asking him if he knows about the subsidies that help buy health insurance if someone's income is too low. Figuring out eligibility and applying for subsidies would be one more task in Dan's already long days—he tells me that sometimes he comes home after a twelve-hour day of demanding physical labor too tired to eat dinner. Navigating the health insurance marketplace would require him to interact with a government website that does not operate perfectly, with complex, multidimensional choices that change frequently, and to deal with numerous forms and organizations.

Dan tells me he is hoping for the best—to keep in good health so he does not need to access the health-care system. He says this even as he also tells me that he knows very few bricklayers who are able to work into their sixties, let alone until the age when they can become eligible for Medicare. Bricklayers often confront back, shoulder, neck, and leg problems—all of which require access to health care to address. Dan's plan is to build his business so he can hire other, younger bricklayers to do more of the demanding work as he becomes the supervisor and business development person. My conversation with Dan reveals a kind, sincere, helpful human being doing the best he can in an economy that has been hard on the middle class. I tell him I sure hope he doesn't get ill without health insurance.

Dan's story is not unusual. The United States was and remains fundamentally different in providing access to health care than any other advanced industrialized country. And America is also different, and not in a good way, in health outcomes. Compared to sixteen other rich nations, the United States has the fourth-highest mortality rate from infectious disease, the highest rate of maternal and infant mortality, and the second-highest mortality from noncommunicable diseases such as diabetes and heart disease. A comparison of twenty-one countries in 2000 revealed that the United States had the highest degree of inequity in physician use.[1]

There are three important facts to know about health insurance. First, not having health insurance, and not having adequate insurance with sufficient benefits, adversely affects health, mortality, and financial well-being. As described in more detail later in this chapter, about fifty thousand people die annually in the United States because they didn't have health insurance and therefore did not have access to preventive screenings or health care of excellent quality. People without health insurance also face the financial and other stress that comes from having impaired access to the health-care system and health-care bills that they cannot afford to pay. As noted in Chapter 2, the absence of health insurance has been the single largest contributor to the total of 120,000 excess deaths from work conditions annually in the United States.

Second, not having health insurance is *not* just a problem for a marginal segment of the population; for instance, for undocumented immigrants, the unemployed, those not in the workforce, or those younger than sixty-five (the age at which Medicare eligibility begins). The lack of health insurance and therefore the inability to access medical care has become an increasingly pervasive problem affecting many people, even those who work full time, in the United States.

Third, for people who receive health insurance from their employer, the good news is that they have health coverage. The not-so-good news: apart from the relatively small proportion of the private sector workforce that works under collective bargaining agreements, everything about a person's coverage is determined unilaterally by their employer. That means that the cost of someone's health insurance, the rules that determine which doctors and hospitals that individual can use, how much that person will pay for medications and treatment, and what specific treatments for what conditions the insurance will and won't cover, are all at the discretion of employers who can, and do, change coverage conditions all the time. Employees can easily find themselves struggling to understand benefits and fighting with their employer-provided health insurer over medical claims.

Even well-intentioned employers may not fully appreciate how their health plans operate, because health insurance is administered by insurance companies, not human resource departments. Therefore, employers have limited visibility into the situations their workers face. The result: a surprisingly large fraction of the US workforce, even people with health insurance, report delaying or not receiving medical care and not obtaining needed medicines or dental care because of costs. For instance, in 2015, Gallup reported that almost one in three Americans delayed medical treatment in the prior year because of the cost, a fraction unchanged even after the passage of the Affordable Care Act. Moreover, people who put off obtaining medical care because of costs were more likely to say they did this for a *serious* condition than for a nonserious one.[2] Even when people get care, they may face stress and have to expend time and energy dealing with their health insurers to get costs reimbursed, efforts that divert people from their primary job responsibilities.

THE FALSE CHOICE

Companies seem to believe there is some inevitable trade-off between offering health insurance benefits that benefit their people and saving money and keeping costs low to increase their profits. But like many of the presumed trade-offs between aspects of employee well-being and dimensions of organizational performance, the choice is a false one. Keeping employees healthy—and satisfied with their health care—is completely consistent with economic performance, particularly if you consider the costs of people wasting time fighting with insurers, turnover, and employee disengagement and dissatisfaction.

According to Dean Carter, the head of human resources for outdoor clothing manufacturer and retailer Patagonia, his company offers health care on the first day of employment for all their full- and part-time employees—anyone not seasonal or temporary. Moreover, the premiums are zero for employee-only coverage. Even though Patagonia operates in a competitive business, it believes providing employees with health-care coverage is both consistent with its values and good business. As Carter noted:

> We believe that everyone should have health care. There was some concern in the beginning that people would choose not to have health care, even part-time people. And these jars would appear around the company, because "Bill" just had a hospital stay, and can you help raise money to help him out? We believe that's something people shouldn't have to do. Everyone just gets health care, and we have really low maximum out-of-pocket expenses and we try to keep the co-pays low.

Such a system not only helps retain people but also reduces their stress and permits them to concentrate on their work rather than worrying about health-care access and cost.

Administrative Nightmares and Their Costs

Collective Health is a venture-backed provider of customer-focused, service-oriented health insurance solutions to employers designed to benefit their employees. The story of the company begins with Ali Diab, who had sold a company to Google and had stayed on at Google. In 2013, Diab experienced sharp pain in his abdomen that an emergency scan revealed was caused by his intestines twisting in on themselves, cutting off circulation to about ten feet of his small intestine. He needed emergency surgery.

After successfully confronting a painful, dangerous, life-threatening condition that took time for recovery, Diab faced insurers claiming that some of his treatments were experimental and therefore not covered, and that other treatments and medicines were unnecessary; still other claims were denied because he'd failed to obtain required preapprovals. To make a long story short, the insurers proposed leaving Diab with a six-figure medical bill. Diab was a senior executive at Google. He knew Larry Page, Google's cofounder. Page called the insurance provider, which fixed things, and he also offered Google's resources if necessary to help with the expenses. As Ali Diab emotionally recounted to me, it was bad enough to face a severe health crisis that terrified him and his family without having to go to war with an insurer—a war that he won mostly because of his great connections and senior position.

Ali Diab decided to cofound Collective Health to make the health insurance experience easier on employees. By providing patient advocates to employees and by using the most innovative information and information technology, Collective Health promised that employees would spend less time dealing with health claims. And because employees would experience more of the benefits rather than the burdens associated with coverage, they would develop more loyalty and deeper connections with their employer. Third, as an organization with focused expertise on health care, the health insurance market, and employee health, Collective Health would be able to relieve some of the burden confronted by in-house human resource and benefits people, another gain for employers.

Simply put, employers pay a lot of money for health insurance coverage, but that coverage is often administered in a way that irritates employees and imposes burdens of stress and time on both employees and human resource executives in their companies. It is as if neither side of the deal profits. Companies pay money for arrangements that all too frequently upset their employees and absorb wasted time learning about and fighting over benefits.

The almost absolute discretion employers in the United States have to determine conditions of access to health insurance—and consequently health care—is different from what people in any other advanced industrialized country confront. All other industrialized countries provide health coverage to all their citizens regardless of age or employment status.[3] Employer-centric health coverage is not just a mixed blessing for employees. It also poses demands on employers.

Providing coverage requires a lot of effort on the part of employers to purchase coverage that affords reasonable benefits without costing too much. Employers often view the multitude of decisions to be made in health-plan design as a burden. Overseeing the many choices of insurance companies and other vendors, and hiring the benefits consultants who help employers make those decisions, costs money.

Even more important, when employers make health insurance decisions that upset their workforce, something that is quite easy to inadvertently do, the employers risk responses ranging from people besieging a beleaguered human resources department to increased employee turnover to possible unionization efforts. Thus, it is far from clear that employers benefit from the current employer-centric health insurance arrangements—a situation that has provided a business opportunity as well as a cause to companies like Collective Health.

LESS IS NOT MORE

A few years ago, I was preparing to make a presentation to the Human Capital Leadership Council of what was then Hewitt (now Aon Hewitt, post-merger) about how organizational decisions affect human health. The council consisted of the heads of human resources from some of Hewitt's best customers—some of the largest and best-known US corporations that at the time included Hewlett-Packard, American Express, Marriott, Cargill, and Google. As I was previewing my talk, which would include a discussion of the health effects of not having health insurance, my inside "partner" at the firm told me to drop this part of the presentation, because, he said, "These are all large employers. All of them offer health insurance. So this is not a relevant issue for them." Not quite, for reasons I will soon explain.

As I was preparing this book, a friend, reviewing the outline, said, "Why do you have a chapter on health insurance? Isn't access to insurance and care a nonissue now that the Affordable Care Act has passed?" Holding aside that attempts to repeal Obamacare continue as this is written, even the ACA has failed, by a lot, to provide universal health coverage, as bricklayer Dan's experience makes clear.

Or consider the dilemma faced by casino workers in Atlantic City. Atlantic City has lost about half of its casino jobs in the past seven or so years. With the jobs went health coverage. Many of the remaining casinos, owned by private equity firms or by companies facing financial stress, have eliminated or reduced health insurance benefits. Many hotel workers in Atlantic City are organized by a labor union that surveyed its Atlantic City members and shared the results with Stanford colleague and health policy expert Arnold Milstein. Milstein shared some of the survey data with me.

Seventy-two percent of the people responding to the survey said that the cost of health insurance had affected their ability to pay their monthly bills. Seventy-two percent said that they were unable to address current health problems. Sixty-three percent believed that their health was deteriorating because they did not have health insurance, 75 percent could not afford new health insurance options, and more than half of the respondents reported symptoms of depression. The idea that access to health insurance and health care is a problem that has disappeared is simply wrong. If anything, the issue is getting worse.

Health insurance costs are often economically significant, not just to individuals, but to companies, too. For instance, General Motors, at one time at least, spent more on health insurance than it did on steel.[4] Employers typically spend some $12,000 per employee on an employee-plus-spouse health insurance plan per year. For an employer with one thousand employees, the cost of $12 million per year is large enough to get management's attention. For even larger employers, health-care costs are very salient. Employers that choose to offer insurance can face cost disadvantages compared to competitors that choose not to.

The public policy goal of taking health insurance out of competition among companies, so there is not a race to the bottom in what they offer, is one reason that many other countries do not leave the decisions and costs about health insurance with employers. Instead, the governments and populace of most other advanced economies believe that in relatively wealthy societies, access to health care is a fundamental human right that should not be subject to employer cost concerns. Because health insurance is at once costly and discretionary, the two recessions of the early and late 2000s that encouraged employers of all types and in all sectors of the US economy to re-emphasize cost control adversely affected employee access to health insurance coverage and increased the already large number of people in the United States who did not have health insurance.

As noted by the Kaiser Family Foundation, by 2010, just before the Affordable Care Act began being implemented, there were more than forty-nine million nonelderly uninsured people in the United States.[5] The growing number of uninsured arose because employer-provided health insurance coverage among the nonelderly had fallen from 69.3 percent to 58.8 percent between 2000 and 2010.[6] By 2011, some 40 percent of all employers did *not* offer health insurance to *any* of their employees. Moreover, even of the 60 percent of employers who did offer insurance, on average more than one in five of their employees (21 percent) were ineligible for coverage, either because they worked part-time, had insufficient total work hours, or had worked for the employer for too short a period to meet eligibility standards.[7] Moreover, "low-wage workers who are offered coverage often cannot afford their share of premiums, especially for family coverage."[8]

As health insurance has become increasingly unavailable to workers, it has also become increasingly expensive to keep for those employees who do have access to coverage. In just the ten years between 2001 and 2011, the average employee contribution for individual coverage increased from $355 to $921 per year (a 159 percent increase) and the average contribution for family coverage went from $1,787 to $4,129 (a 131 percent increase) annually. By 2015, the cost of individual coverage had further increased to $1,071 and family coverage to

$4,955.[9] Both family and individual coverage expenses paid by employees increased at a faster rate than total health insurance premium costs because not only were employers shedding coverage and raising eligibility requirements, they were also shifting costs to employees.

Employers have not only reduced access to health insurance and increased employee cost burdens, but, in an additional move to cut costs, the health insurance plans provided often do not cover all medical needs or do so with such high co-payments and deductibles that people forgo treatment.

Data from a federal government survey are revealing. In 2014, after the implementation of the ACA, the proportion of people reporting forgoing either medical treatment or prescription drugs because of costs was actually *higher* than it had been in 1997, before passage of national health insurance legislation, although both were lower than in 2010, just after the recession and prior to the ACA taking effect. Moreover, although the percentage of people reporting forgoing medical care or medicine because of cost was obviously much higher for the uninsured than for insured individuals, even among the insured, almost 6 percent of people reported forgoing or delaying medical treatment because of cost.[10] An analysis of the employer-centered American health-care system in the *New England Journal of Medicine* argued that "the increasing prevalence of underinsurance may well be the most serious trend," even worse than the absence of insurance in its implications for health. The report provided data showing substantial cost shifting to individuals and rising rates of underinsurance that limited access to treatments.[11]

Because of employer decisions, "having a job does not guarantee a person will have access to employer-sponsored coverage; in fact, about 38 million of the uninsured [77 percent] are in families that have at least one worker."[12] Moreover, 61 percent of the uninsured were in families that had one or more individuals working *full time*. Survey data shows that the uninsured are more likely to be minorities, to have no education beyond high school, to be in low- or moderate-income families, and to be young. And more than four-fifths of the uninsured are either native or naturalized US citizens, which means that the problem of not having health insurance is not one affecting mostly undocumented workers.

These facts mean that the profound racial and income disparities in health outcomes, an increasing focus of both research and public policy attention, can be at least partly attributed to the racial and family income differences in who has employer-sponsored health insurance. For example, one analysis reported that while people of color comprised 34 percent of the US population, they accounted for 52 percent of the people without health insurance.[13]

Employer decisions to provide health insurance are, as already noted, a typical collective action problem. If everyone provides insurance, no single company is at a cost disadvantage from doing so. Moreover, the (higher) costs of treating the uninsured don't get shifted from those who do not provide insurance to those who do. Such cost shifting occurs because doctors and particularly hospitals and clinics raise their rates for those who have insurance to recoup the uncompensated costs of caring for the uninsured. For instance, one study using very detailed state-level data reported that in 2002, uncompensated care just in the state of Maryland totaled $529 million.[14] But as in all collective action situations, there are strong incentives for individual employers to defect. By not providing insurance, they can cut their costs below the competition and offload employee health care to others.

As the proportion of employers who don't provide insurance at all or who make it unduly expensive so that fewer people avail themselves of it increases, other employers who do provide affordable insurance are at a growing competitive cost disadvantage. The cost-shifting implications of providing insurance grow larger, because those who provide insurance pay twice—once directly through their insurance contributions and once indirectly through the taxes they pay to fund public health programs that provide health services for those without insurance. Thus, insurance experts in compensation consulting firms have told me that there will come a tipping point at which more and more employers will abandon the provision of private health insurance altogether because of competitive necessity and also because providing health-care coverage will no longer be seen as normative, as something that good employers routinely do. This will happen even under the ACA, because the "fine" for large firms that fail to offer health insurance to their employees is substantially less than the actual cost of providing that insurance coverage.

When norms change, behaviors change, too. Of course, no one is sure at precisely what level such a tipping point will be reached. But I have been in meetings with senior human resource executives from some prominent, large, and economically successful companies where the discussion has turned to the possibility of employers getting out of the business of providing health insurance to their employees, regardless of what has occurred or might happen in the future at the national policy level—something that all around the table agreed would never have even been considered in the past.

The Affordable Care Act, as of 2016, has extended health insurance coverage to perhaps thirteen million of the forty-one million previously not covered. It is up to the states to decide whether to expand Medicaid programs to provide coverage to children and the poor. Some states have taken advantage of federal funds available to encourage such expansion, but many have not. The data showing that the uninsured are, for the most part, working adults—people just like Dan the bricklayer—means that the effects of health insurance on people's well-being remain relevant.

THE HEALTH AND ECONOMIC EFFECTS OF BEING UNINSURED

What are the effects of employer decisions to offer health insurance coverage? The most important are, first, health and mortality and, second, bankruptcy and financial stress.

Health Insurance and Health

Decisions about health insurance are important for the simple reason that health insurance or its absence profoundly affects individual health and mortality. An Institute of Medicine (IOM) study using data from 1971 to 1987 on people between twenty-five and seventy-four years old and Census data from 1982 to 1986 on individuals between twenty-five and sixty-four estimated that being uninsured increased mortality risk by 25 percent in working-age adults. This result held even after various other factors that might affect mortality were statistically controlled.[15] Based on this estimate of increased mortality and the number of people uninsured at the time, the IOM report estimated there were eighteen thousand excess deaths per year in the United States. As the number of uninsured grew over time, the Urban Institute, using the IOM's original methodology, estimated that there were 137,000 excess deaths because of being uninsured just between 2000 and 2006, with 22,000 excess deaths occurring in 2006 alone.[16]

The IOM methodology assumed that increased mortality from not being insured was identical for all age cohorts. But this is almost certainly not the case. The risk of being ill from any cause increases with age, and the risk of having cancer or heart disease, for instance, is also age-related. Not having insurance if you aren't sick clearly would have many fewer health and mortality consequences than being uninsured when confronted with a serious disease. And there is another complication in this initial analysis. Being uninsured is itself related to health status. Prior to the passage of health reform under President Obama, it was frequently the case that when people got sick, they would lose their health insurance coverage, and exclusions for preexisting conditions were routine parts of insurance contracts. Taking these factors into account, one study noted that after adjusting for the effect of people's health on the likelihood of having health insurance, the mortality difference between having and not having health insurance coverage reached 42 percent, almost double the increased mortality risk estimated in the Institute of Medicine study.[17] Another analysis that used data on adults aged fifty-five to sixty-four estimated that just among this ten-year cohort of near-elderly individuals, more than thirteen thousand people died annually because they did not have health insurance.

A recent review of the scientific literature generally supports the original conclusion of the Institute of Medicine study: that "health insurance reduces mortality" and that "uninsurance shortens survival."[18] In part, this is because having insurance increases the use of recommended care. This review of the evidence noted that one reason the United States has worse life expectancy than many other industrialized countries is that "worse access to good-quality health care contributes to our nation's higher mortality from medically preventable causes."[19]

Other studies show an even higher death toll from an absence of insurance. A longitudinal panel study of about nine thousand people aged seventeen to sixty-four between 1988 and 2000 uncovered a 40 percent higher likelihood of death for those uninsured even after statistically controlling for age, gender, body mass index, smoking, regular alcohol use, leisure exercise, and physician-rated health status. This analysis estimated that there were almost forty-five thousand excess deaths annually because of lack of health insurance. As a comparison, an absence of insurance caused more deaths than kidney disease.[20]

In addition to these studies of excess deaths from all causes, studies of the mortality outcomes from specific diseases also consistently reveal higher death rates for those who do not have health insurance compared to similar others that have such insurance. One study of 189 patients born with cystic fibrosis who had at least one hospitalization at a university medical center found that the median survival for patients without health insurance was 6.1 years compared to 20.5 years—more than three times longer—for those individuals with private insurance.[21] Another study of mortality from cystic fibrosis compared Canadians to Americans. That study found that "Canadians with cystic fibrosis survive, on average, more than 10 years longer than Americans with the same disease, largely because of differences in the two countries' health insurance systems." Although there was no difference in death rates across the two countries for people in the United States who had private health insurance, the "Canadian death rate was 44 percent lower than that of Americans on Medicaid or Medicare and 77 percent lower than Americans without insurance."[22]

A study of women with breast cancer found that, even after controlling for the extent of the disease when the patient presented for treatment, the adjusted risk of death was 49 percent higher for uninsured patients compared to those with private health insurance.[23] An analysis of women with cervical cancer, a disease where prognosis is highly related to the stage of the cancer at time of discovery, reported that uninsured women were about 1.4 times more likely to present with more advanced stage cancer than women with private health insurance.[24] And an analysis of stroke patients reported that, depending on the type of stroke, being uninsured increased the risk of death between 24 and 56 percent.[25]

Researchers have also discovered at least some of the causal pathways and processes that connect health insurance to health outcomes. One causal relationship relating insurance to mortality is the connection between having health insurance and obtaining preventive screening for various health conditions. Research demonstrates "the efficacy of preventive health service use (e.g., cholesterol screenings, mammograms . . . Pap tests) in reducing morbidity and mortality," and the data consistently show that "uninsured adults are less likely than those with insurance to use preventive services."[26] Many people alternate between being insured and uninsured, for instance, as they change employers or move from being unemployed to finding a job. Panel evidence with comprehensive statistical controls for socioeconomic status shows that even intermittent periods of being uninsured substantially reduced people's use of preventive screenings and that the effects of not having insurance on reducing people's obtaining useful screenings persisted for some time even after they got insurance.[27]

Access to health insurance also affects people's compliance with treatment regimens, including getting their prescriptions filled. The Kaiser Family Foundation reported that "more than a quarter of uninsured adults say they did not fill a drug prescription in the past year because they could not afford it."[28] One study compared what happened to thousands of people with and without insurance following either experiencing an unintentional injury or the onset of one or more chronic medical conditions. After an adverse change in their medical condition, people without insurance were less likely to obtain any medical care, had fewer doctor office visits, and filled fewer prescriptions. Moreover, people without health insurance were about twice as likely to not have received any follow-up medical care. Not surprisingly, then, even seven months after a "health shock," those without insurance were almost 50 percent more likely than those with health insurance to report worse health status.[29]

Having insurance also seems to be related to receiving better care once diagnosed with some disease or health condition. That is because being insured provides access to a wider—and better—set of doctors and hospitals that are not as financially constrained and therefore can offer a broader set of treatments and more comprehensive care, including follow-up treatment. One innovative study used turning sixty-five, the age at which people become eligible for Medicare insurance, to examine the effects of insurance on treatment and health outcomes. The analysis considered unplanned admissions to the emergency department for severe asthma, heart attacks, and strokes, and explored differences between those admitted just before and those admitted just after their sixty-fifth birthday. The study showed that people over sixty-five received more services and therefore experienced a

20 percent reduction in deaths, even for a patient group that was severely ill, with the difference in mortality persisting for at least nine months after being hospitalized.[30] Another analysis, comparing states that expanded their Medicaid coverage with otherwise similar states that did not, estimated that expanding access to health care through the Medicaid expansions reduced all-cause mortality by about 6 percent, with some of the effect coming from reducing the incidence of receiving delayed care because of costs.[31] These studies are consistent with others that show that insured individuals receive more and better care and also more timely care than those without insurance.

Health Insurance and Financial Problems

Numerous studies have found a relationship between having health insurance and bankruptcy and other forms of financial distress. One report noted that "almost 40% of uninsured adults have outstanding medical bills." And another study in Oregon reported that "the uninsured were more likely to experience financial strain from medical bills and out-of-pocket expenses." As a Kaiser Family Foundation report on the uninsured noted, "The uninsured live with the knowledge that they may not be able to afford to pay for their family's medical care, which can cause anxiety and potentially lead them to delay or forgo care."[32] Financial stress, just like other forms of stress, is negatively related to both physical and emotional health as well as to mortality.[33] Stress has direct effects on health and also induces unhealthy behaviors such as smoking and alcohol and drug abuse that further compromise health and increase the risk of premature death.[34]

There is little doubt that medical bills, even for the insured but particularly for the uninsured, contribute to bankruptcy and other symptoms of financial problems, although the magnitude of these effects remains in some dispute. One examination of 1,771 personal bankruptcy filers in five (of the seventy-seven) federal district courts estimated that about half cited medical causes for the financial distress. "A lapse in health coverage during the two years before filing was a strong predictor of a medical cause of bankruptcy."[35] Nonetheless, about three-quarters of those filing for bankruptcy had insurance at the time of the onset of their medical costs. Another study compared changes in household assets, excluding the value of an owned residence, for near-elderly individuals who were newly ill with insurance to those in the same age range who were newly ill without insurance. Assets in households with a newly ill, noninsured person declined between 30 and 50 percent more compared with matched individuals who were covered by health insurance.[36] Although medical debt is quite common, "medical debt is greater for people without health insurance."

Medical debt and bankruptcy obviously are traumatic and stress-inducing. "One national survey found that 44 percent of those with medical debt used all or most of their savings to pay outstanding medical bills . . . one in five medical debtors took on large credit card debt or a loan against their home to pay medical bills. . . . People with medical debt are often subject to legal judgments, wage garnishments, attachment of assets including bank accounts, or liens on their homes, which can lead to foreclosure."[37]

As this partial review of the extensive existing evidence shows, an absence of health insurance is truly hazardous to an individual's financial and physical health and adversely affects mortality. Therefore, employers who offer health insurance at reasonable cost positively affect their employees' well-being, while those who do not put their workers at serious physical and psychological risk.

HEALTH INSURANCE AND THE OPERATION OF LABOR MARKETS

When some employers provide health insurance and others don't, numerous problems arise. Such problems are particularly severe when and if insurers can deny coverage for preexisting conditions, something that was quite common prior to the passage of health reform under President Obama. These problems affect not only employee well-being but company performance as well.

The first problem comes from restricted labor mobility, frequently referred to as "job-lock." Most theoretical perspectives on human capital, which view labor as subject to market forces, acknowledge the positive function of labor sorting and matching. Simply put, employers have needs for certain technical skills and other attributes, and these requirements change over time as competitive conditions change. To take one example, manufacturing jobs that once required limited mathematical and reasoning skills now require more of such skills as numerically controlled machine tools and more complex manufacturing processes have grown in prominence. On the other side of the equation, employees have both a set of skills and tastes that also change over time as individuals acquire training and learn through job experience what employment conditions they like and don't like.

Labor markets work best when employers can freely select workers and workers can freely move to employers who offer not just the best financial deal but also the best setting for their talents and abilities. Many scholars and policy experts acknowledge that when employee-employer job matching is restricted, "the economy-wide results will be lower labor market efficiency and productivity."[38] That's because "labor market mobility enables workers to obtain employment where they are most productive," so "immobility due to disparities in the availability of scope of health insurance across employers can eliminate potential gains in productivity and income, adversely affect worker satisfaction, and alter the volume and quality of goods and services produced."[39]

Non-portable pension benefits are one source of job-lock, and indeed one of the purposes of deferred compensation schemes such as pensions is to tie employees more tightly to their employers, thereby reducing turnover costs. However, having health insurance tied to employers and making coverage difficult to obtain for those who already have some disease restricts labor mobility in ways that disrupt optimal labor matching. Employees stay at employers where they no longer are interested or maybe even competent at their jobs because they are afraid to risk losing their health insurance benefits if they enter the labor market and either don't find a job right away or don't find an employer that provides adequate coverage.

Estimating the magnitude of job-lock effects from decisions reflecting health insurance concerns is invariably difficult using available panel data on job mobility. Nonetheless, the empirical evidence, which employs sophisticated methodologies and a variety of controls for other factors that might affect mobility, provides reasonably consistent estimates that show substantial mobility reductions. One study using data from the 1980s estimated a 25 to 31 percent reduction in mobility because of health insurance concerns, an effect that was even larger for employed women than for men,[40] while another study focusing on dual-earner men found mobility reductions of about 36 to 51 percent.[41] Another analysis reported that chronic illness reduced job mobility by about 40 percent compared to otherwise similar workers.[42] There is also evidence that public policies that make obtaining health insurance after leaving an employer easier to obtain, such as "continuation of coverage" mandates, reduce the magnitude of health-insurance job-lock effects on mobility.[43] Reductions in labor mobility between 25 and 50 percent are substantively significant and suggest that the theoretical problem of mismatched employees and employers has important productivity and efficiency consequences.

A second problem arises from the current set of health insurance arrangements in the United States: a form of adverse selection. Most group health insurance plans do not have exclusions for preexisting conditions and are open to all employees who meet the relevant eligibility requirements, such as hours worked or length of employment. Not all employers, however, offer health insurance. Moreover, the health insurance offerings on the private, individual market largely do (or did, prior to the passage of health reform legislation) limit coverage to new medical problems and exclude preexisting illnesses. Therefore, employees with medical problems will be drawn to seeking employment at those employers who offer health insurance. Employers who offer such health insurance will, as a consequence, tend to attract a higher percentage of sick people who have higher medical costs. Thus, there are increasing incentives over time for those employers who do offer health insurance to reduce or restrict coverage to cope with the cost disadvantages they face because of this adverse selection effect. Moreover, choosing employment based on the health insurance coverage offered clearly interferes with sorting processes premised more on skills and interests, resulting in additional productivity and efficiency losses.

The labor market distortions created by job-lock and adverse selection make it increasingly costly for employers to offer health insurance. These facts help explain why privately provided coverage has declined over time as we have already seen. But unavailability of private coverage does not "solve" the problem of health costs. Instead, health costs are merely transferred to other payers, most often either the public or medical providers who furnish uncompensated care, even as such costs get increased because treatment gets delivered to patients who are sicker and have more advanced disease because they have delayed seeking care because of uncovered costs.

PROVIDING HEALTH CARE ON-SITE

Good employers take care of their employees by providing health insurance. Healthy employees are more productive. Offering health insurance helps attract and retain people.[44] Employers who offer health insurance—and other benefits—signal that they care about their people. Offering health benefits, particularly when competitors are cutting benefits, activates the norm of reciprocity and causes employees to reciprocate with greater levels of loyalty and engagement.

But employers who are concerned about employee health confront some dilemmas. First, as already discussed, as health-care costs escalate, companies that want to do the right thing are caught in a competitive bind—confronted with issues of adverse selection as sicker workers flock to workplaces that offer health coverage and with the problem of competing with companies that have lower costs because they have externalized—offloaded—their employee health costs to the larger society, to care providers, or both. Second, employers confront a health-care system in the United States beset with administrative costs—the costs of marketing health-care plans to employers and their employees, reviewing and paying claims, adjudicating appeals of claims denials, providing pre-authorization for tests and procedures—many of which have a tangential relationship to providing health care. Gail Adcock, the chief health officer who oversees health benefits and is in charge of on-site health care at the large software company SAS Institute in North Carolina, told me that "managed care was mostly about managing costs, not care," something that not only drove up the administrative overhead but also created distrust among employees. Some Harvard researchers have estimated that administrative overhead consumes almost one-third of US health-care spending, and this large administrative burden is one reason why the United States spends so much on health care without achieving better outcomes.[45]

One growing employer response to these issues has been to offer health care on-site. This is a solution that not only reduces the enormous overhead burden created by insurance companies, but also permits employers to get closer to their employees' health issues so they can intervene earlier in the disease process, thereby saving money and also keeping their workforce in better shape. It is well known that a relatively small proportion of employees with serious medical conditions account for a disproportionate share of health costs, and that the risks of people moving into the high-utilization/high-cost population can be predicted, affording the possibility of early intervention and prevention that can reduce health costs.[46]

Decades ago some companies had company doctors on-site or nearby—particularly companies located in remote locations or those that faced a high risk of injury or disease. Over time, such arrangements disappeared as organizations chose to focus on their core activities and as the employment relationship became more transactional, with less of a sense that employers needed to take care of their workers. But there are many cost advantages for employers offering health care on-site. First, seeing a doctor at the workplace saves travel time. At Sprint's Overland Park, Kansas, facility, employees "could sign out, drive to their own doctors somewhere in the region, and typically come back the next day. Or they could walk across the campus . . . see a physician in one of the clinic's three exam rooms, and make it back to their desk . . . in about a half hour."[47]

A second advantage is the cost savings. Overhead of doctor's offices and hospitals is eliminated, as are insurance middlemen with their costs, for all visits by employees and their families to on-site health facilities. Health-care providers are typically salaried rather than paid on a fee-for-service basis, which also cuts costs. Another major advantage cited by numerous employers is reduced absenteeism and better employee health and productivity. People are more likely to visit an on-site clinic that is not only more convenient but often offers a lower co-pay for the visit—in many cases there is none. With more frequent contact with employees, the medical staff can intervene earlier to prevent disease problems from getting worse and encourage healthier behaviors—and have better ability to follow up with people to ensure those behaviors take hold. Yet another advantage cited in employer surveys is the greater use of evidence-based guidelines for treatment and electronic health records that facilitate care coordination. "Studies point to a relatively substantial return for on-site health centers of $2 in savings for every $1 invested, and some studies indicate levels of $3 to $6 for every $1 invested."[48]

These advantages have led to widespread adoption of the on-site model. "According to . . . the National Business Group on Health, 23 percent of surveyed employers with more than 1,000 employees reported offering on-site medical services in 2007" with that number expected to grow.[49] And on-site medical care has even diffused to smaller employers. So, for instance, Wilson Tool International in White Bear Lake, Minnesota, and Turck, Inc., in Plymouth each have an on-site medical facility even though both have only about four hundred employees.[50] A number of companies are now in the business of operating on-site medical facilities for companies, and the service is growing in popularity.

Of course, on-site clinics are suitable primarily for relatively minor illnesses and routine care such as immunizations. But nonetheless, the time used to access even such routine care is enormous. And the ability to cut costs while providing a physical manifestation of companies' commitment to their employees' well-being provides some compelling advantages for the on-site model.

EVERYONE'S LOSS

The data are clear: the absence of health insurance leads to higher levels of mortality, worse health, financial strain including bankruptcy, and increased anxiety and stress. The United States continues to have a large population of individuals who lack health insurance and a surprisingly high proportion of people who must forgo medicines and treatment because of cost issues even if they have insurance. Those without health insurance are for the most part working, many of them full time, and are overwhelmingly either US citizens or legal residents. Even for people with employer-provided health insurance, costs have been shifted from employers to employees, resulting in insurance premiums and co-payments that have increased at rates even faster than the growth in health-care costs and have adversely affected access to care. And people with health insurance—and their employers—often confront administrative difficulties in obtaining reimbursement for health-care expenses, diverting employees' attention from their work and increasing their level of stress.

Health insurance concerns produce job-lock and restricted labor mobility that negatively affects productivity. Worries over accessing health care impact people's job performance, and their ability to obtain care affects their absence behavior. Administering health-care plans consumes enormous amounts of resources, and much of those costs fall on employers who pay for benefits consultants, human resources staff to administer medical plans, and for the overhead of the health-care providers that they use. These overhead and administrative costs are one reason that some large employers have moved to a model of offering on-site care for relatively minor and routine medical problems.

It is hard to see who, other than health insurance companies and insurance brokers and benefits consulting firms, gain anything from the current arrangements. Moreover, health care and who pays for it has become an increasingly politicized issue. It is not just politically fraught on the national and state government levels, although disputes are frequent in government at all levels. Health-care costs are also politicized inside organizations, where chief financial officers fixated on cost reductions sometimes lock horns with human resource leaders interested in employee well-being. As with any such political struggle, forecasting how things will evolve is almost impossible.

What's missing in much of the discussion—in government and inside workplaces, in the discussion of health insurance, health-care costs, and employee health—is the human toll these contradictions and paradoxes cause. People face unforeseen medical bills as prescriptions go on or, more frequently, off formularies. As one individual told me, it seems particularly inhumane that individuals confronting serious, sometimes life-threatening illnesses, should also have to cope with insurance companies, insurance plans, and their benefits office, and be at the mercy of these entities about what are often life-and-death decisions.

In this as in so many other aspects of work environments covered in this book, considerations of human sustainability are largely missing from the financially driven discussions and decisions. And it is far from clear that employers benefit from having financially stressed employees navigating a health insurance thicket of forms, policies such as where care can be accessed and what prior approvals are required, and ever-changing cost and benefits offerings.

Chapter 5

Health Effects of Long Work Hours and Work-Family Conflict

KENJI HAMADA WAS FORTY-TWO years old when he died of a heart attack at his desk in a Tokyo office. His widow said that Hamada was working seventy-five hours a week and spent almost four hours a day commuting back and forth to work. He had worked forty straight days prior to his death. "He was so stressed out, working day and night," she maintained.[1] In late 2016, a twenty-four-year-old employee of the large advertising firm Dentsu jumped to her death after telling friends about enduring harassment and long hours on the job. The employee was working Saturdays and Sundays and put in more than one hundred hours of overtime a month.[2]

The Japanese even have a word for death from overwork—*karoshi*. The first reported case of karoshi occurred in 1969 when a twenty-nine-year-old, married male worker in the shipping department of Japan's largest newspaper died from a stroke. After that, karoshi became much discussed and worried about in Japan, where death from overwork has been formally recognized as a cause of death by the Workers Compensation Bureau in the Ministry of Labor. "In 2012, the Japanese government compensated 812 families who were able to show a link between overwork, illness, and death, including 93 suicides."[3] By 2015, claims had risen to 2,310, "but the true figure may be as high as 10,000—roughly the same number of people killed each year by traffic."[4]

One Japanese study noted: "Nowadays, there are almost no workers who do not know the word. . . . Many Japanese workers and their families are anxious about *karoshi*." Notwithstanding the public discussion and scrutiny, the problem persists. A survey conducted in October 2016 found that nearly one-quarter of the companies surveyed said that some employees were working more than eighty hours of overtime a month.[5] Starting in 1987, Japan's Ministry of Labor began to publish statistics on karoshi, although these statistics are not considered completely reliable because it is difficult in individual cases to unambiguously attribute sudden or premature death to overwork as contrasted with other causes.[6]

Long work hours and the adverse health consequences they cause are a problem in many countries besides Japan. A forty-eight-year-old Chinese banking regulator, Li Jianhua, died of a heart attack after twenty-six years of hard work as he rushed to finish a report. Gabriel Li, who worked in the Beijing office of advertising firm Ogilvy, died in May 2013, on his first day back from medical leave. Other deaths attributed to overwork in China include "a 24-year-old employee at Ogilvy Public Relations Worldwide" and "a 25-year-old auditor at PricewaterhouseCoopers."[7] Chinese factories, particularly those assembling electronics products for many iconic companies such as Apple, HP, Cisco, and others, are notorious not only for their low wages and stressful, inhumane working conditions but also for their extremely long and sometimes unpredictable working hours. Indeed, customer-facing companies such as Apple can keep their supply chains lean while introducing new products and new models so quickly after their designs are finalized explicitly because their subcontractors are willing to do whatever it takes—literally waking workers in the middle of the night—to ramp up production.

Not surprisingly, China also has a word for death from overwork—*guolaosi*. Overwork apparently is an enormous problem in China: "About 600,000 people a year die from toiling too hard, according to the *China Youth Daily*. State-controlled China Radio International puts the toll at 1,600 a day." A survey of Chinese employees working in Beijing, conducted by the dean of the School of Labor Economics at the Capital University of Economics and Business, reported that 60 percent of the respondents said they were working more than the legal limit of two hours a day of overtime.[8]

Sometimes people believe that long work hours only bedevil emerging economies. That is because advanced industrialized countries often regulate work hours. Such regulations include restricting the hours that younger, school-age people can work, mandating overtime pay for certain employees working more than some prescribed number of hours per day and/or per week, and requiring a number of weeks of paid vacation or paid time off to delimit the hours people work on an annual basis.

But not all jobs are effectively covered by such regulations. Vulnerable groups such as immigrants worried about deportation or low-wage workers concerned about losing their jobs may be reluctant to assert their rights. Some positions, such as managerial and supervisory jobs as well as professional work are often exempted from overtime pay provisions. As one person told me, at Airbus, the French-headquartered airplane manufacturer with substantial operations in a country with a supposed thirty-five-hour workweek, mid-level managers typically work sixty hours per week and often stay until 8 p.m. Professional and managerial work hours have increased as Airbus has grown and become more successful. However, unlike in some countries such as the United States, at Airbus managers seldom work on the weekend and they do take their five weeks of vacation.

Some industries and occupations are particularly prone to excessive work hours. For instance, investment banking, regardless of where it is located, is notorious for long hours and associated adverse health effects. As previously described, in 2013, Moritz Erhardt, a twenty-one-year-old intern at Bank of America's Merrill Lynch unit in London, died after working until 6 a.m. for three nights in a row. He apparently had worked all night eight times in two weeks. A report about his death noted that "Mr. Erhardt appears to have been one of the many interns caught on the so-called magic roundabout—a process whereby a taxi takes an intern home, waits outside while they shower and change, and then drives them back to the office to begin another long day." Another intern commented, "They get you working crazy hours and maybe it was just too much for him in the end."[9]

Long work hours characterize law practice, too, with its billable-hours culture so that the more people work (and bill), the more money the firm makes. Writing about her ex-husband who died from complications associated with drug use, Eilene Zimmerman noted that "he had been working more than 60 hours a week for 20 years, ever since he started law school and worked his way into a partnership in the intellectual property practice of Wilson Sonsini Goodrich & Rosati."[10]

High technology, with its Red Bull–fueled all-nighters, is another place where overwork reigns. The Palo Alto Medical Foundation operates a mobile medical facility in the Silicon Valley with two examination rooms and a laboratory. The van serves more than two dozen of the area's largest employers. Why a mobile van? As the head of PAMF's employer health services explained, "People are so freaking busy they can't even imagine going out to the doctor."[11] Forty percent of the people the van sees don't have a primary-care physician, even though they earn high incomes and work for companies that offer health insurance. The employees are simply too busy to take care of themselves. "Some patients don't even get off their mobile devices while being examined."[12] The result: "30-year-old engineers with 50-year-old bodies, complete with potbellies, curved spines, dulled skin tones, joint issues, reduced vitality, and elevated risks of diabetes and heart disease."[13]

Thus, the problem of excessive work hours and the resulting deleterious health effects can be seen at least to some extent in most if not all countries and in many different jobs and industries. "Working long hours is common and has increased in many developed countries in recent years."[14] Working hours in the United States are particularly long and irregular, a situation that has gotten worse over time. As David Waldman, vice president of human resources at the Robert Wood Johnson Foundation, noted, "Overwork is not new in this country. . . . But in some ways, it seems like it's hitting critical mass."[15] In the United States, "the average number of hours worked annually . . . has increased steadily over the past several decades and currently surpasses that of Japan and most of Western Europe," so that while in 1979, the United States did not have the longest work hours, by the 2000s the country stood out for its long working time. A study using time-diary data found that almost 30 percent of US employees reported working on the weekend, a proportion higher than that seen in France, Germany, the Netherlands, and the United Kingdom, and more than twice as high as Spain. That study also examined the proportion of US employees who reported working at night, between 10 p.m. and 6 a.m. In the United States, more than one-quarter of all people reported working at night, a proportion substantially higher than that in any other country included in the study.[16]

Long hours have become the norm for successful employees interested in advancing their careers. As one executive coach told me, almost all of her clients work a ten- to twelve-hour day, like from 8 a.m. until 6 p.m., take some time off for dinner, and then go back to work from, for instance, 8 p.m. until midnight or even later. And most will also work at least one day on the weekend. These hours are so much a regular part of people's work patterns that the coach no longer even offers sympathy when people complain about the strains such working arrangements put on their health and their relationships. It is just expected as part of the "price" for career success—and in many instances, exceptional levels of income and responsibility.

Moreover, even when people are presumably not "at work," the separation between work and nonwork time has decreased because of the omnipresence of electronic devices that leave employees always on call and potentially working even when they are not physically in the workplace. One survey reported that 81 percent of respondents said they checked e-mail on the weekends, 55 percent said they logged in after 11 p.m., and 59 percent said they looked at e-mail while on vacation.[17] People check e-mail at funerals and at the birth of their children. Describing the scene at her lawyer ex-husband's funeral, Eilene Zimmerman poignantly wrote:

> Quite a few of the lawyers attending the service were bent over their phones, reading and tapping out e-mails. Their friend and colleague was dead, and yet they couldn't stop working long enough to listen to what was being said about him.[18]

Employees are frequently expected to be potentially available for work-related calls and e-mails while at home or even while on vacation. At Uber, the ride-sharing company notorious for its hard-charging, demanding culture, an employee told *BuzzFeed*:

> "I got texts on the weekend. E-mails at 11 at night. And if you didn't respond within 30 minutes, there'd be a chain of like 20 people. . . . There was a three- to four-month period when I was getting woken up every Friday, Saturday, and Sunday at 3 or 4 in the morning to fix something," said an engineer. . . . "Months of that, on top of working 10-plus hours a day."[19]

It's not just high technology, I-banking, or law. This always-on, always available expectation is increasingly pervasive. Dean Carter, the head of human resources for Patagonia, told me about something that happened while he was working for the department store chain Sears years ago:

> I remember when I was at Sears I got an e-mail on Christmas Eve at 7. I responded Christmas day, the next morning, at 8 a.m. The response from one of the executives to whom the e-mail

was sent was, "Dean, I don't understand why you took so long to respond. We're in a transformation, and you need to be a lot more responsive."

Recognizing that work intrudes on nonwork time, in 2016, France passed a law that embodies a "right to disconnect." Although the law does not ban after-hours work-related e-mails, it does "require that companies with more than 50 employees negotiate a new protocol to ensure that work does not spill into days off or after-work hours." In justifying the need for the law, France's minister of labor noted how "employees were more and more connected to work outside of the office."[20]

While people may joke about France and its working-time regulations, a study of 365 working adults reported that "off-hour" e-mailing negatively affected employees, leading to burnout and diminished work-family balance. The study noted that the expectation to be constantly available on e-mail was a job stressor.[21]

There are many manifestations of long, excessive, or irregular work hours, all of which have health effects. One manifestation would be working very long hours in a day or week, thereby depriving the body of sleep and weakening the immune system. A Gallup study of more than seven thousand US adults found a positive relationship between more hours of sleep and self-reported well-being, with some 40 percent of the sample getting less than seven hours of sleep a night, the minimum number recommended for good health.[22]

A second example would be working excessive hours over the course of a year, by not taking paid time off, if such time is even available, to go on vacations and take holidays to get away. One study reported that about a third of American employees do not use all the vacation days to which they are entitled,[23] while a more recent survey found that more than half of US workers eligible for paid vacation did not use all the time allotted, leaving a median of seven vacation days unused.[24] About a quarter of Americans do not get any paid vacation at all.[25]

A third symptom would be not taking time off when a person is ill, under the belief that taking care of oneself while sick could put one's job or income at risk or in some way demonstrates that the worker is insufficiently concerned about the company's well-being. The BBC reported on a 2014 survey that found that more than 25 percent of US employees said "they always go to work when they are ill," while "nearly a quarter of US adults have been fired or threatened with the sack for taking time off to recover from illness or to care for a sick loved one."[26] A representative survey of one thousand American adults reported that 62 percent said they had gone to work sick.[27] Working while ill is not just bad for the individual's productivity and for possibly making coworkers sick. Mexican fast-food chain Chipotle "partly blamed a 2015 outbreak of the norovirus vomiting bug on employees who had come to work sick."[28]

A fourth case of work-hour problems would be shift work, working hours at variance with normal bodily rhythms such as working at night. As one fifteen-year longitudinal study of paper mill workers found, the incidence of heart disease increased by more than two times for people who worked shifts for more than ten years.[29]

Companies Have a Choice

It is important to understand that long work hours and not taking sick or vacation days are not some inevitable result of contemporary economic realities such as global competition and technological change. We know that because firms vary dramatically in their work-hour policies, even companies operating in the same country and in the identical industry. Work time is the result of managerial decisions and discretion. "There is a long-hours culture in some workplaces; long hours are used even when they are not strictly needed for business reasons."[30] One study using survey data from Britain reported that about one-third of the variation in weekly hours of work came from firm-level differences, with such differences being particularly important in the private-services sector.

In Dublin, Ireland, a few years ago Google tried an experiment called "Dublin Goes Dark." In the experiment, staff were invited to leave anything that beeped at the front desk when they left for the day. "Phones, iPads, and computers stayed at HQ and so, it seems, did the stress. 'Googlers reported blissful, stressless evenings,' wrote Laszlo Bock, the head of Google's People Operations" at the time.[31]

Clothing company Patagonia has standard work hours and offers on-site childcare. Their head of HR commented, "When childcare closes at 5:30, basically the parking lot empties. Everyone leaves. I rarely see cars in the parking lot after six." The company moved to a nine-hour workday so that every other Friday, people can have an extra day off—twenty-six three-day weekends a year. And people do not get calls or e-mails during their three-day weekends. As one person said, "It just doesn't happen."

Zillow Group, which operates a real estate website, is yet another example of a company seeking to encourage people to limit their hours so they have a healthy work-life balance. As one person noted, "It's not until you're a part of the company, and not until you realize that a lot of people don't take their laptops home, or they are able to drop their child off at day care and come in at 9:45, that it hits home that this culture really, actually does value work-life balance."

Landmark Health, a start-up providing in-home care to people who are often dealing with five or more medical conditions, trains its employees as part of their onboarding process to be sensitive when they send e-mails. Unless the communication concerns patient care, people are told not to send e-mails at night or on weekends or holidays. Obviously, numerous other companies have adopted progressive practices that try to manage work hours, limit times when employees are on call, and provide flexible work schedules.

If work hours and the ability to separate oneself from work vary according to company decisions and culture, not just because of business necessity, then work hours—and their consequences—are a policy variable controllable to some extent by employers and potentially modifiable by changes in social norms and labor market regulations. Therefore, employers and governments have discretion over work hours and also the health effects of those work hours on people.

SOME CAUSES OF LONG WORK HOURS

Both employers and employees conspire to make work preeminent among competing life priorities and, as one consequence, encourage and venerate long working hours. Many people, both employees and their bosses, see putting in long hours as demonstrating commitment and loyalty to the employer and the job. Furthermore, employees often see their work as important. People who work hard and make sacrifices for their work would tend to see that work as important because of pressures for cognitive consistency, as a way of justifying and making sense of their effort. But if that work is important, indeed essential, then it should take priority. That is possibly one reason that some research has found that people who work in nonprofits work longer hours, because they see their work as being driven by a higher purpose.[32] But, of course, nonprofit employees suffer burnout and the other consequences of long work hours, too.

Employees see long work hours as signaling their toughness and strength. An accountant told me, "You see this a lot, particularly in the Silicon Valley culture. People say, 'I can last longer than you. I can work harder than you.'" So, in the contest for promotions, work hours become one way of competing. The accountant, while working for a health-care organization, commented:

> When I started there, I would come in and say, "I got four hours of sleep last night." My boss, the VP of finance, would

> tell me, "I got three." It was never like, "You should take a day off." And of course then this is how I would treat my staff. I would say, "This is not acceptable. Why didn't this get done? I don't care how late it is."

Employees see putting in "face time" as necessary in an increasingly competitive labor market with ever more people competing for fewer promotion opportunities, a result of companies having reduced middle management layers and jobs. Even high-earning professionals—or maybe particularly high-earning professionals—work ever longer hours and pay the price for doing so. Sylvia Ann Hewlett's 2004 survey found that 62 percent of high-earning respondents worked more than fifty hours a week and 10 percent worked more than eighty hours weekly. Almost half said they were working more than fifteen hours a week more than as recently as five years ago. These folks forgo vacations regularly. And although seemingly successful, at least in financial terms, some 69 percent believed they would be healthier if they worked less, 58 percent stated that work interfered with relationships with their children, and 46 percent thought that their work hours affected their relationship with their spouse.[33]

Decades ago, leisure time was a marker of social class. A tan meant that you could afford to take a nice vacation, and beach attire was a status marker. Today, higher-class, higher-earning individuals actually work more than their lower-income counterparts. In a perverse twist, longer work hours have become a status symbol—a marker of how important, indeed indispensable, someone is. Summarizing this phenomenon for Arianna Huffington's new venture Thrive, Drake Baer wrote:

> Busy is now cool. It's even become an aspirational bit of American culture. . . . The higher up you go, the busier your calendar gets. . . . References to "crazy schedules" in holiday cards have . . . shot up since the 1960s. . . . When Americans hear

"busy," they think status. . . . Displays of busyness show that society values you, that everybody wants a piece.[34]

As such, people *want* to put in long hours to signal how valuable they are.

Why Companies Like Long Hours

Notwithstanding the nil to negative relationship between work hours and performance reviewed below, many companies have cultures that seemingly venerate long hours and forgone vacation. After all, who could be against "hard work"? Most employers seek loyalty and commitment from their employees. They want employees who are willing to devote the extra effort required to triumph against the competition. It is, of course, difficult to directly observe someone's loyalty and commitment. It is much easier to assess indirect indicators of employee dedication, and the hours someone puts in on the job is one such indicator, and so is whether employees use all their allotted vacation and paid time off or give their lives to the workplace. Employers often use work hours, something readily observed, as an indicator of an important employee attribute more difficult to observe, dedication.

Because employers see long work hours as a signal of employee effort and loyalty, employers reward those who put in long hours, in part because employers favor those who are willing to make sacrifices for the organization. What could show more organizational commitment than being literally willing to work yourself to death for the company? Studies consistently demonstrate an effect of work hours on salaries and changes in wages over time, even for people who are ostensibly not paid by the hour (in the case of hourly pay, obviously, income varies directly as hours increase).

Employers also prefer longer rather than shorter hours because of the implicit belief that work output is related to the number of hours worked—the more hours, the higher the output. This relationship certainly holds for some sorts of jobs and particularly in the past when there was less technology, creativity, and mental concentration involved in production. But for creative work, for work that requires thought, for innovation, it is scarcely obvious that, beyond some point, more hours will result in more productivity. Indeed, for many jobs, there comes a point at which output suffers from just putting more time in. That's because after a while, long work hours produce fatigue and boredom, which lead to making more mistakes and also to being less thoughtful and insightful.

If employers like long hours and those who work endlessly, then employees learn that long work will be rewarded and respond accordingly. Before the key cards we use to open doors and access equipment such as printers became ubiquitous and low-tech sign-in sheets were more common, stories abounded in the Silicon Valley of employees who would sign in to their workplace on the weekend and then leave, nap, or do other, nonwork things while supposedly in the office. Even today, employees will reset their computer clocks to show they are sending e-mails in the middle of the night, leave office lights on and coats or sweaters on the backs of their chairs to indicate they are at work, and engage in numerous other such ploys to make their boss think they are always working. The purpose of the deceptions—to show employers and, more specifically, the employees' direct supervisors, how hard they were working. Of course, face time does not equal work time, and time spent at a workplace is not highly correlated with the work that someone does. But the signaling, symbolic outcomes from apparently putting in long hours remain important for people's careers.

Because women generally tend to have more family responsibilities than men, women are sometimes able to put in fewer hours at work. The reduced hours result in diminished career success. One study by business school professors Olivia O'Neill and Charles O'Reilly found that statistically controlling for hours worked eliminated the oft-observed male-female earning differential.[35] They argued that this effect would become even more important over the course of a career. Initially, people are hired on the basis of promise and there is variation in knowledge and competence. But careers are for the most part organized as tournaments—at each level, people compete for promotions, and those who lose fall out of contention for even higher-level promotions. Over time, the less competent or those who have less time to put into their work get weeded out. Consequently, at higher organizational levels, differentiation is based mostly on motivation and effort—hours—as there are few remaining differences in capability. In other words, hours matter even more as careers unfold. Although not every study of this issue reported that controlling for work hours eliminated the effect of gender on salaries, numerous studies do find that controlling for hours worked reduces the male-female earnings differential.

Employees, then, become complicit in the long-work-hours culture. Seeking to stand out and demonstrate commitment, each individual puts in more time. Even when employers provide paid vacation and ostensible flexibility, few employees may avail themselves of these benefits. For instance, at IBM peer pressure abounds so that many employees never take their full vacation and check e-mail and voice mail while away on vacation.[36] But dedication and commitment are relative concepts—demonstrated mostly in comparison to others. The dynamic of a rat race is created, in which, to show how valuable and dedicated someone is, that individual puts in more time than his or her peers, and as they ratchet up their work hours correspondingly, so does the individual trying to stand out. Until finally people are pulling all-nighters until they get sick or die.

Much as in the case of layoffs, there is good epidemiological evidence of the harmful effects to human health of long work hours and also shift work, but little evidence that long work hours actually benefit employers. As such, long working hours impose often unrecognized and unaccounted for costs on human beings without apparent offsetting benefits for their employers. Here is yet another management practice that could be changed to positively affect employee physical and mental health without jeopardizing organizational performance. Indeed, a different approach could even improve company results.

LONG AND IRREGULAR WORK HOURS HARM HEALTH

"Paul" (not the individual's real name) worked for a major television network producing news shows for about fifteen years. As Paul explained, "Working in the news business, in order to get a promotion, you have to work the worst shifts. I worked weekends, I worked prime time, I worked in the field. I did breaking news." For instance, Paul covered the Tucson shootings when Congresswoman Gabrielle Giffords was severely wounded and six people were killed. On such assignments, Paul sometimes wound up sleeping in the greenroom for three hours and then going back to work. Because of the irregular sleeping patterns, Paul said that he lost the ability to sleep for any longer than three to four hours at a time, even when he wasn't on call or wasn't working. He continued:

> As a result of the sleep deprivation, I faced what I called a three-punch: hypothyroidism, no exercise, and bad food. You had no time to prepare your own food. At 6:30, you'd be sitting there going, "I'm really stressed out. Man, I really need some Doritos," and you'd hit the vending machine. I went through eight different presidents of the network.
>
> Between when I became a senior producer in 2008 and I finally quit because I couldn't take it anymore in 2012, I gained sixty pounds. My metabolism was bad and all the things that would keep me healthy—my bodily functions—were just breaking down.

Whether long work hours are voluntarily embraced as a way of advancing one's career or forced on people by their employers, or whether the long hours arise from the fact that people earn so little on an hourly basis that they must work multiple jobs and excessive hours to get by, the evidence is clear—long work hours adversely affect physical and mental health and increase mortality. Moreover, research has begun to identify some of the specific pathways through which long work hours adversely affect health.

First, as the case of Paul illustrates, long work hours often result in sleep deprivation and disrupted sleep patterns, and a lack of sleep is unhealthy. One study in the province of Quebec, Canada, reported that short sleep duration had a bigger effect on obesity than did high lipid intake or lack of exercise.[37] Another article noted the many metabolic effects of sleep deprivation, including elevated levels of the stress hormone cortisol and impaired carbohydrate tolerance, increasing the risk of diabetes.[38]

Second, long work hours have been related to drug abuse, particularly of stimulants or hard drugs such as cocaine, which can act as a stimulant.[39] Between 2005 and 2011, "emergency room visits related to nonmedical use of prescription stimulants among adults aged 18 to 34 tripled," while between 2010 and 2012, people who entered substance rehabilitation centers citing simulants as the primary drug they abused increased by more than 15 percent compared to the prior three-year period. One start-up founder, ironically working on a health technology application, had on average just three hours and twenty-five minutes of sleep per night over a nine-month period, before entering an addiction center to address her health problems. Medical experts note that stimulants can cause anxiety, addiction, and hallucinations, and worry "about added pressure in the workplace—where the use by some pressures more to join the trend."[40]

Third, long work hours are stressful, as excessive work hours exacerbate work-family conflict, which has its own negative health effects, as we will see later in this chapter. Long hours are often a response to excessive job demands in the workplace, reflecting the stress of work pressures. Fourth, long work hours leave people without time to relax and refresh.

And fifth, the longer the time spent at work, the greater the possible exposure to possible stress-inducing workplace exposures such as workplace bullying and nasty bosses. It is little wonder, then, that in occupations where fatigue can have potentially fatal consequences if people fall asleep or are not alert, such as airplane pilots, truck drivers, and medical personnel, regulations mandate rest periods and limit work hours and work schedules. And yet even in these occupations, employers often push back seeking to relax or eliminate work-hour restrictions.

The evidence of the effects of work hours on health is reasonably extensive and has been around for many decades. Nonetheless, insufficient attention has been paid to incorporating this research into policies and practices that would limit the costs and harm that long work hours cause.

The Evidence

More than a half century ago, a study found a higher incidence of coronary heart disease among men who worked more than forty-eight hours per week.[41] A study of almost 7,100 British civil servants aged thirty-nine to sixty-two without heart disease found that over a ten-year period, people who worked ten hours per day were about 45 percent more likely to have suffered a heart attack, and those who worked eleven hours per day were 67 percent more likely to have had a heart attack than those who worked eight hours per day. Working hours predicted future heart attacks even when typical risk factors such as age, gender, blood pressure, and cholesterol levels were statistically controlled. Because of the longitudinal design of the study, it is easier to establish causality—work hours cause heart attacks, not the other way around.

Using 2001 California data from more than twenty-four thousand working-age individuals, analyses showed a positive correlation between hours worked per week and self-reported hypertension, itself a risk factor for heart attack and stroke. Compared to people working between eleven and thirty-nine hours per week, individuals who reported working between forty-one and fifty hours per week were 18 percent more likely to report having high blood pressure, and those who worked more than fifty-one hours per week were 29 percent more likely to have elevated blood pressure.[42] A study of almost one thousand employees at a Japanese construction manufacturing company explored the effects of workaholism on health. *Workaholism* is defined as voluntarily choosing to work and having trouble disengaging from work activities. The study reported that workaholism was negatively related to both job performance and life satisfaction and was positively associated with ill-health.[43]

A meta-analysis of twenty-one study samples reported small but statistically significant correlations between hours of work and overall symptoms of ill-health as well as physiological and psychological ill-health.[44] And a National Institute of Occupational Safety and Health review of fifty-two research reports investigating the association between long working hours and illnesses as well as job performance concluded:

> In 16 of 22 studies addressing general health effects, overtime was associated with poorer perceived general health, increased injury rates, more illnesses, or increased mortality. One meta-analysis of long work hours suggested a possible weak association with preterm birth. Overtime was associated with unhealthy weight gain in two studies, increased alcohol use in two of three studies, increased smoking in one of two studies, and poorer neuropsychological test performance in one study.[45]

Long work hours also adversely affect mental health, as long working hours increase stress and fatigue and preclude adequate time to recover. For instance, a study of 473 nursing assistants working in nursing homes reported that there was a 400 percent increase in the odds of experiencing depression for people working more than fifty hours per week, more than two weekends per month, and more than two double shifts per month.[46] Another study compared 1,350 employees who worked overtime with 9,092 employees who did not work overtime. Both men and women who worked overtime had significantly higher anxiety and depressive disorders. Moreover, the extent of the psychological problems was linearly related to the amount of overtime in a dose-response fashion, with more overtime causing more severe anxiety and depression.[47]

When Boeing fell years behind schedule on the 787 plane, there was enormous pressure on engineering employees and work hours went up significantly as the company struggled to complete work on this important new product. An individual close to the engineering community told me that burnout went up as employees struggled with the long work hours and physicians in the area reported much higher levels of illness among employees associated with the 787 program.

None of this should be surprising. After all, when people get sick and go to the doctor with ailments ranging from flu to more serious medical issues, I don't know any doctor who would prescribe more work (as contrasted, for instance, with bed rest) as a remedy. Stress weakens the immune system, and overwork is an important form of stress.

THE PERFORMANCE EFFECTS OF LONG WORK HOURS

As the evidence makes clear, we don't have to trade off longer working hours against better economic results. All too many companies seem to love employees who put in long hours, but the evidence makes crystal clear that organizations would be better off with employees who don't overwork themselves. Employees would be healthier, the health-care costs borne by both employees and employers would be lower, and employee productivity and innovation would not falter. Indeed, the latter is likely to improve.

When people work exhausted, they make mistakes. As one Uber engineer noted about a mistake with a master database in 2015 that took the service down, "If you've been woken up at 3 a.m. for the last five days, and you're only sleeping three to four hours a day, and you make a mistake, how much at fault are you, really?"[48]

Researchers at the OECD prepared a chart for the hours worked per person in OECD countries between 1990 and 2012 and the GDP created per hour worked. That chart "reveals that productivity is highest when people spend fewer hours working."[49]

During World War I, the British Health of Munition Workers Committee undertook a study to see how to increase the productivity of munitions plant employees. When Stanford economist John Pencavel analyzed those data, he found that the optimum number of work hours was about forty-eight per week. Below that number, output declined proportionately with the decline in hours worked. But "once workers clocked . . . more than 48 hours, output started to fall."[50]

In 2012, the International Labour Organization (ILO) published an extensive review of the research literature examining the effects of working time on productivity and firm performance.[51] That report highlights extensive research demonstrating that longer hours often *decreases* performance. For instance:

- A study using panel data for eighteen industries in the United States found that the use of overtime hours lowers average output per hour worked for almost all the industries in the sample. A 10 percent increase in overtime resulted in a 2.4 percent decrease in productivity.[52]
- An analysis of eighteen OECD countries, studying productivity at the national level since 1950, reported that an increase in working time was always accompanied by a decrease in per-hour

productivity. Once annual working time exceeds 1,925 hours, a 1 percent increase in working time leads to a .9 percent decrease in productivity.[53]

- An earlier ILO report noted that productivity improvements followed reductions in work hours.[54]
- A study of professional employees found that reduced hours improved employees' self-reported job performance.[55]
- A study of six workplaces providing dental health care ran an experiment on work hours. Employees in these workplaces were randomly assigned to one of three experimental treatments: a 2.5-hour reduction in weekly working time accompanied by increased physical exercise, a 2.5-hour reduction in weekly work hours without increased physical activity, and a control condition. The research examined both self-rated productivity and an objective measure, the number of patients examined. Both reduced working-hours conditions showed increases in the number of treated patients, and reduced work hours accompanied by increased physical exercise produced increases in self-rated productivity and also decreased absence from illness.[56]

Thus, the simplistic idea that more work hours produce more output is incorrect. After a while, exhausted workers produce more errors. Extensive empirical evidence is consistent with the idea that above a certain threshold, *reducing* work hours would increase *both* employee health and productivity and job performance. There is *no* economic trade-off required to improve people's well-being by having them work less.

WORK-FAMILY CONFLICT AND ITS EFFECTS

Paul, the news producer, worked in a unit where most of the employees were women, and most of the women were single. "We call them news nuns. I don't think any of them would like that term, but it's a long-held name." Of the forty-two people in the department when Paul arrived, within about five years there were only twelve left. Paul was the only person married with kids. For good reason. After Paul left the network, one day he talked to his daughter, who had been quite proud of his job as a news producer.

> I said, "Are you sorry that I'm not working there anymore?" And she said, "No, I'm glad. Because now you're here to listen to me and now you're here to tell me stories." Then she caught herself. She said, "Of course you did those things before, except you had Mr. Scrolly with you when you did it." Mr. Scrolly was my BlackBerry.

When people are in a situation in which they have more to do than they have time to do it, that is called role overload. When people have demands for behavior emanating from one role, such as that of employee, that are incompatible with the demands of another role, such as family member, that is called role conflict. Long-standing research literature on role conflict and overload consistently finds that people who confront conflicting expectations for behavior or more demands than they can handle are more stressed.[57] Thus, not surprisingly, role conflict and role overload are associated with poor outcomes ranging from increased turnover to lower job performance.

Work-family conflict takes two forms: family demands can interfere with job performance, as when an employee is distracted or loses time on the job attending to family-relevant issues such as caring or arranging for the care of an ill family member; this is often called family-to-work interference. The second form of work-family conflict, called work-to-family interference, is when job demands interfere with an individual's ability to fulfill family obligations such as meeting with teachers, coaching their children's sports teams, or having time to spend with spouses and other family members.

As would be expected, empirical research consistently shows negative physical and mental health effects of both work-to-family and family-to-work conflict. For instance, one study of almost two thousand adults in Erie County, New York, found that, even after statistically controlling for gender, race, education, family income, marital status, and number of children, higher levels of work-family conflict were associated with higher levels of depression, poorer physical health, and higher levels of alcohol consumption. A second study of about seven hundred households in Buffalo, New York, replicated these results. And both studies found that men and women were affected similarly by work-family conflict.[58]

A study of some 2,700 employed adults noted that people who reported experiencing work-family conflict were between two and thirty times more likely to experience a clinically significant mental health problem compared to people who reported no work-family conflict, with the magnitude of the effect depending on the specific mood or substance abuse disorder examined.[59] Of course, one possibility is that the health and psychological problems cause the work-family conflict rather than the reverse. To explore this possibility and better establish causality, a four-year longitudinal study reported that family-to-work conflict was related to poorer physical health and more depression while work-to-family conflict was related to elevated alcohol consumption.[60]

The role overload characteristic of work-family conflict affects marital interactions[61] and marital satisfaction.[62] Role conflict more generally has been found to relate to lying in organizational settings—a finding that makes sense because one way of balancing conflicting, incompatible demands is to lie.[63]

Physical and mental health problems, lying, diminished marital satisfaction, and similar outcomes are instances of what IESE professor Nuria Chinchilla has referred to as social pollution. To what end? Work-family conflict drives up sickness absence, something that harms employers.[64]

Providing more flexible work arrangements, giving more generous family leave, and working people less are all in the interests of both employers and the general public, each of whom face increased costs from the social toll of excessive work hours and work-family discord.

WHY SOME COMPANIES AND COUNTRIES ARE DIFFERENT

Not every employer and not every country encourages long hours and work-family conflict, of course, and evidence suggests they may be onto something. Patagonia's head of human resources, Dean Carter, described the very generous, family-oriented benefits the company provides:

> Family is really important here. We have integrated on-site childcare. Any parent, at any time, is encouraged to go hang out with their kid. You can eat lunch with them, eat breakfast with them. If you want to just sit on the ground with them for a play break, you can do that. We have really generous [paid] maternity and paternity leaves, twelve weeks for dads and sixteen weeks for new moms. You can have up to twelve weeks of paid leave to take care of an elderly parent.
>
> If I could pick one thing about the culture at Patagonia that has a bigger impact than anything else, I would pick that our childcare and family policies are really extraordinary. For example, if you're a mom and you're nursing and you need to travel for work, we will pay for the child to travel with you as well as a nanny to care for the child while you're working.

Countries and companies compete for talent with other locales and employers. Those that make it possible to reconcile the demands of work with the rest of life do better in that competition. At Patagonia, "We know that about 99 percent of our moms return to work, which is about 20 percent above the national average, because we make it super easy."

The "war for talent" is an already long-established phrase. Countries invest, through education and training mandates, in building the quality of their human capital. Companies, too, invest not just in training but also in identifying high-potential employees and instituting policies and programs to ensure their retention. Interestingly, work hours, scheduling flexibility, and policies that foster work-family conciliation are important means for accomplishing these goals.

At the company level, firms on *Fortune*'s Best Places to Work list regularly outperform their peers on shareholder returns. And these companies are more likely to offer job-sharing programs, compressed workweeks, telecommuting opportunities, and more generous family benefits to create environments more supportive of employees seeking work-family conciliation rather than conflict. Numerous organizations including Deloitte Consulting, Google, and some management consulting, accounting, and other professional service firms have sought to address issues of work hours and flexibility in order to attract and retain employees who increasingly do not want to trade off their life for a career. Family-friendly work environments offer companies an edge in recruiting and, possibly more important, in retaining employees.

Google, frequently rated as the best place to work in America, has a vision "of making its staff the healthiest and happiest on the planet." As described in a 2011 article:

> Google launched its "optimize your life" programme in 2010, as an extension of a new healthcare plan. . . . Google's emotional wellbeing benefits include an employee assistance programme . . . life coaching, deep-sleep sessions, brain training, support groups, and recharging spaces . . . within the office for 20- or 30-minute breaks.[65]

Of course, that's Google—they can afford it. But it is not just software companies that have chosen to take care of their people by providing reasonable working hours. At Whole Foods Market, in the hideously competitive grocery business and ranked fifty-eighth on the 2017 Best Companies to Work For list, 85 percent of surveyed employees said that they were able to take time off from work when they thought it was necessary.[66]

Companies vary with respect to work-hour issues and for that matter on other dimensions affecting employee health mostly because of the values—and behavior—of their leaders. The CEO of Landmark Health believes that his employees must take care of themselves if they are going to take care of others. Patagonia's founder wrote a book entitled *Let My People Go Surfing* and strongly believes that work should not be all-consuming.

But leaving decisions about work practices that will affect employee health to the discretion of a founder or a CEO puts employees' health and psychological well-being at risk to the vagaries of executive succession and founder whim. We don't leave food safety, for instance, to the discretion of the CEO, nor do we leave it up to the CEO to determine whether or not to pollute the environment. If employee health is as fundamentally important as these other things, it, too, should not be subject to a particular CEO's values, as it currently is. This is a subject to which I return in Chapter 8, the concluding chapter.

Both individual companies and countries vary in how they approach work-family conflict. The United States, as is well known, is different, and not in a good way—being the only advanced economy not to require employers to provide paid time off for either vacations or illness and also having fewer mandates that make balancing work and family easier. A report from the Center for WorkLife Law at the University of California's Hastings College of the Law noted:

> Of 20 high-income countries examined in comparison with the United States, 17 have statutes to help parents adjust working

> hours; 6 help with family care-giving responsibilities for adults; 12 allow change in hours to facilitate lifelong learning; 11 support gradual retirement; and 5 countries have statutory arrangements open to all employees, irrespective of the reason for seeking different work arrangements.[67]

Although causality is difficult to prove, it is interesting to note the possible effects of these policies, or their absence, on female labor force participation. "US labor force participation for prime working age women (age 25 to 54) has stalled and is now lower than it is in 14 of the 20 high-income countries. . . . Labor force participation for college educated women in the United States is lower than in any of the other 20 countries."[68]

Systematic evidence and numerous anecdotes suggest that working hour and work-family policies and practices affect companies' and countries' ability to attract, develop, retain, and utilize all of their human capital—something that is increasingly important in a world in which more and more work requires more and more creativity and skill.

WHAT WORKERS SHOULD DO

It is possible that public policy will address the social costs of excessive work hours and work-family conflict, but with a move toward decreasing labor market regulation worldwide, I would not hold my breath. Maybe employers will voluntarily take steps to remedy these problems, as some have already done. But once again, I wouldn't bet on it.

Simply put, workers—be they freelancers or employees—need to take care of themselves. And this means *not just economically*, although that is obviously crucial. In my research for this book, I often heard comments of the following form: "I know that my working unsustainable hours and neglecting spending time with my family can lead to bad outcomes, including physical and mental health problems. But I'm [only going to do it for a while longer, really don't have a choice, am not going to suffer the consequences for various reasons such as being young, having good genetics, and so forth]." Lots of people engage in various forms of magical or wishful thinking about how they will mystically avoid the health consequences of toiling in toxic work environments. Unfortunately, things seldom work out well, rationalizations and wishes notwithstanding.

My advice: Stop telling yourself stories about how bad consequences from poor choices won't happen to you, and stop making excuses for why you can't do what you know you should do to take care of yourself at work. Instead, limit your work hours to what is sustainable, understanding that people have different levels of stamina and that endurance levels can be modified. Take vacations and time off and spend sufficient time with family and friends to obtain the social support that so much research has shown is important to well-being. Don't schedule your baby's delivery for your employer's convenience by having a medically unnecessary caesarean section—holding aside physical considerations, the high rate of surgical deliveries is one factor (among many) driving up health-care costs.

And most important, as you think about possible jobs, employers, and other aspects of working life, recognize the profound mental and physical health consequences of your choices and actions. In other words, while plenty of people are suffering—and even dying—for a paycheck, you don't have to be one of them.

Chapter 6

Two Critical Elements of a Healthy Workplace

COMPANIES UNDERSTAND THE COSTS of turnover and employee absence due to sickness. Companies also know the importance of discretionary effort, and many do surveys to measure employee engagement. But employer efforts to build more enticing workplaces often focus on the wrong things—"trinkets" and perks that can be quickly implemented, rather than important dimensions of the workplace itself that are more challenging, but more important, to change. For example, the profusion of perks offered by Silicon Valley and other high-technology workplaces seems to be a source of endless fascination for business journalists and others. As one source noted, "Lavish perks are as much a part of Silicon Valley lore as are unicorns and behoodied billionaires." A search for "crazy employee perks" uncovered stories of companies offering employees "free helicopter rides, endless supplies of booze, on-site barbers, fitness classes, bike repair, and nap pods, ball pits, indoor basketball courts, arcade-size game rooms, and designated candy kitchens."[1]

The companies that attract, retain, and motivate a great workforce, and the workplaces that keep their employees physically and mentally healthy, do so not by offering people cute amenities. People are not that easily seduced by mere trinkets; sleep pods, free food, and letting people bring their dogs to work cannot make up for stressful work environments.

What matters—for employee engagement and productivity and, more important, for employee physical and mental health—is the work environment and the work itself. Not having a boss who heaps scorn and abuse, because the health hazards of workplace bullying and incivility have been well documented.[2] Having a private office or at least a workplace with comfortable temperature, good lighting, and acoustical privacy, so that the physical work environment does not impose stress.[3] And, most important and the focus of this chapter, two crucial elements of a healthy workplace that any company, in any industry, can provide without breaking the bank—and therefore ought to offer to enhance employee well-being: job control and autonomy and social support. What follows is evidence on the importance of these two dimensions of work environments and some examples of how to create healthy workplaces that provide people autonomy and control and that promote the social connections and support that foster physical and mental health.

JOB CONTROL, AUTONOMY, AND HEALTH

In the 1970s, British epidemiologist Michael Marmot and his colleagues noticed an interesting fact: the higher someone's rank in the British Civil Service, the lower the incidence of and mortality from cardiovascular disease (CVD, or sometimes CHD, as in coronary heart disease).[4] Why might higher rank be positively correlated with better health? Marmot launched a series of longitudinal studies, called the Whitehall Studies—because the British Civil Service is administered out of a building named Whitehall—to understand the causes of this relationship between hierarchical rank and health. These were prospective cohort studies in which people were recruited to participate, assessed initially and then again over time, and their health status monitored. Of course, as is typical and inevitable in field research, this was scarcely a random sample of the British population and, moreover, for ethical and practical reasons, people could not be randomly assigned to job conditions that varied in the amount of job control provided. Nonetheless, the studies could and did control for people's initial body mass index, blood pressure, cholesterol levels, blood glucose levels, age, gender, and many other factors that might affect health such as individual behaviors like smoking. Even with all those controls, social status, in this case measured by hierarchical rank, mattered for health. Why?

Research revealed that it was differences in job control, differences that are correlated with job rank, that explained the effect of civil service grade on CVD. Higher ranked British employees, like higher ranked employees in most organizations, enjoyed more control over their jobs and had more discretion over what they did, how they did it, and when, even though they often faced higher job demands. This finding makes intuitive sense, as the higher one is in an organizational hierarchy, the more discretion and decision-making power that individual typically has. In the second set of Whitehall Studies, Whitehall II, Marmot and his colleagues followed more than 7,300 people beginning in 1985 and ending in the period 1991 to 1993. They examined self-reported angina and also doctor-diagnosed narrowing of the coronary arteries. Marmot and his fellow researchers summarized their findings:

> Compared with men in the highest grade (administrators), men in the lowest grade (clerical and office-support staff) had an age-adjusted odds ratio of developing any new CHD of 1.50. The largest difference was for doctor-diagnosed ischaemia (odds ratio for the lowest compared with the highest grade 2.27). For women, the odds ratio in the lowest grade was 1.47 for any CHD. Of factors examined, the largest contribution to the socioeconomic gradient in CHD frequency was from low control at work. Height [which is often taken to reflect the effects of early-life health and well-being] and standard coronary risk factors made smaller contributions.[5]

These results mean that, after adjusting for age (because health problems and mortality generally increase as people age), men and women in the lower ranks had about a 50 percent higher probability of reporting chest pain and angina and men had more than twice the likelihood of having physician-diagnosed narrowing of the arteries than those in higher ranks. Moreover, job control was the single most important predictor of developing heart disease—more important even than smoking, for instance, in accounting for developing CHD.

Of course, coronary heart disease is only one health indicator, albeit an important one. The Whitehall Studies also assessed how differences in absence from work because of sickness varied across hierarchical ranks. Marmot and his colleagues found that men in the lowest civil service grades had *six times* the rate of absence because of sickness than did men in the highest grade. For women, the differences were smaller but still important, with those in the lowest ranks being absent between two and five times as much as those in the highest.[6] And the Whitehall data related work stress, measured as the co-occurrence of high job demands and low job control, to the presence of metabolic syndrome, a cluster of risk factors that predict getting heart disease and type 2 diabetes. Employees who faced chronic stress at work were more than twice as likely to have metabolic syndrome compared to those without work stress.[7]

Nor are the health effects of job control on health limited to British civil servants. The Wisconsin Longitudinal Study followed a random sample of more than ten thousand men and women who graduated from Wisconsin high schools in 1957. The long-term survey asked questions about health, job characteristics, and other important control variables such as education, childhood health, and individual health-related behaviors such as smoking and drinking. Of course, this is not a completely random sample, as in 1957 there were relatively few minorities among Wisconsin high school students and a substantial fraction of people did not finish high school. Nonetheless, the data permit reasonable assertions about causality because people provided information over time. One analysis followed people to study their changes in health between ages fifty-four (the 1993 survey) and sixty-five (the 2004 survey). During this eleven-year period, 7.4 percent of the women and 11.2 percent of the men died. The study assessed self-reported physical health as one outcome, but did not relate job characteristics or other variables to death. Nonetheless, the study found that job control in 1993 was statistically significantly related to self-reported physical health for women, though not for men, eleven years later.[8]

Other research has also found a relationship between measures of job control and health. A cross-sectional study of hospital employees in Europe reported that in Western Europe, there was a positive relationship between job autonomy and health.[9] A study of 8,500 white-collar workers in Sweden found that people who had gone through reorganizations where the individuals had influence in the reorganization process and achieved greater task control exhibited higher levels of well-being compared to those with less influence and discretion. The higher-control group had lower levels of illness symptoms for eleven out of twelve health indicators, were absent less frequently, and experienced less depression.[10] An Indiana University longitudinal study of 2,363 Wisconsin residents over a seven-year period found that individuals who were in jobs with high demands but low job control experienced a 15.4 percent higher mortality rate.[11]

Not surprisingly, job control affects mental health as well as physical health outcomes. After all, not being in control of your work environment is stressful and also sends a message of powerlessness, regardless of the jobholder's salary or formal status. A study of almost seven hundred people from seventy-two diverse organizations in the northeastern United States reported statistically significant negative relationships between job control and self-reported anxiety and depression.[12] The more job control people had, the lower their levels of anxiety and depression.

Why Lack of Job Control Is So Harmful

If you want to drive any organism—a rat, a dog, or a human being—crazy and create a whimpering, downcast, and helpless being, one of the surest ways is to administer random punishments, not linked to any specific behavior, or to in other ways impose capricious demands that remove people's sense of control over their environment. I suspect most people who have worked for any length of time have suffered the effects of arbitrarily changing deadlines and work assignments, or criticism that seemed unwarranted by job performance and did not come with enough information to permit the individual to do better. During my research, some people told me how business trips got "rearranged" even while they were on the road, with no rationale provided. Others related stories of ever-evolving performance evaluation criteria that made it tough to know how to succeed at work. Still others talked about having workplace scouts sense the boss's mood on arrival at the office, so employees could anticipate if they were going to be in for a good or bad day.

And someone told me the following story, which is all too typical: A leader inherited a team, and each of them had a P&L to manage. The one who was doing the best on her numbers, and was also seen by the organization (and her own team) as the best people manager, was fired. Under pressure by the appalled organization to say why, the leader told his second in command that he owed nobody an explanation.

When leaders act capriciously, people do not know what to expect or what to do. The results are both psychologically and physically devastating. The learned helplessness literature makes the case that although there are many events that we cannot control, "such uncontrollable events can significantly debilitate organisms; they produce passivity in the face of trauma, inability to learn that responding is effective, and emotional stress."[13] Little wonder that job control predicts morbidity and mortality, with higher levels of job control creating better health and longer life spans.

According to the learned helplessness literature, uncontrollable events adversely affect people's motivation, their cognitions and learning, and their emotional state.[14] And the reasons are logical. An absence of control reduces motivation. If through their actions people cannot predictably and significantly affect what happens to them, they are going to stop trying. Why expend effort when the results of that effort are uncontrollable, rendering the effort fruitless? That's why research shows that severing the connection between actions and their consequences, leaving people with little or no control over what happens to them at work, decreases motivation and effort.

A person working for a company organizing digital health conferences told me that after presenting a preliminary agenda for an upcoming conference to their boss, the response was, "I don't see a point of view. I need you to take this away and come back with something better." The person described their reaction: "Along with just being overworked, that makes me not feel valued. Why bother when I'm not getting any help or feedback so I can do a better job?" Seemingly random criticism, as in this case, causes people to give up: "Why should I even continue?"

Or consider the case of learning. People are adaptive in that they learn, albeit imperfectly, from watching what happens to others and from their own personal experience—don't put your hand on a hot stove or you will be burned, what various foods taste like, how to succeed in various environments. People's ability to learn by observing the connection between actions and their consequences permitted them to attain some degree of mastery over their environment and provided evolutionary advantage. But the most fundamental principle of learning is that various actions produce reasonably predictable consequences, so people can comprehend what they need to do to achieve the desired results. Think about the difficulty of driving a car if randomly from one moment to the next the brake became the accelerator and then the transmission. Research shows that not only is learning difficult when outcomes are uncontrollable, but even worse, "experience with uncontrollability may produce a difficulty in learning that is actually successful. Uncontrollability may retard the perception of control"[15] even if people have achieved some degree of mastery.

And an absence of job control leaves people feeling depressed. Part of feeling good about oneself comes from a sense of mastery and success that results from competently performing self-relevant tasks. But in a condition of low job control, people have less responsibility and discretion, resulting in not feeling as competent or successful. As a consequence, people are more likely to experience stress and depression. Particularly for previously successful people, experiencing failure on the job and not knowing what to do to fix the situation invariably leads to withdrawal, either by leaving the company or by expending less effort, or both. Moreover, not having control over what you do and what happens to you is stressful, and stress produces other negative emotional states such as depression and anxiety. Job control affects people's ability to learn, their motivation, and their emotional states—and consequently, their physical and mental health.

WHAT IS JOB CONTROL AND WHY IS IT SO RARE?

When you're a child, people—parents, teachers—tell you what to do. As you get older, you get more responsibility—a driver's license, the ability to set your own hours for when you eat and sleep—and you begin to make choices that affect your life, such as what to study, where to live, with whom to associate, and how to spend your time each day. And then, one day, you get a job, and depending on your boss, your employer, and the design of your work, your choices about what to do and how to do it, at least while at work, can disappear, leaving you in an infantilized state. That's too bad. People, at least most people, want to make decisions and use their experience and skills at work. When people cannot make decisions and do not have sufficient control over their work, they are stressed and suffer ill-health, as extensive evidence makes clear.

A Berkeley-trained lawyer working in the toy industry told me that many people in corporations are promoted based on abilities other than their skill at managing people, such as the capacity to manage a budget or being effective at meeting project deadlines, among other things. Because many managers can't manage, in the sense of coaching and facilitating others to do their jobs better, one of the worst "sins" that this person and many other people encounter at work is micromanaging. When managers micromanage their subordinates, those individuals lose their autonomy and sense of control to the bosses who won't delegate. The lawyer commented:

> My current employer is very face time oriented. You're expected to be here in your chair and if you're not, that's treated with suspicion. And telecommuting and flex time and all sorts of things are really looked down upon. And that's demoralizing and disengaging. I need autonomy. I need to feel like I have some control, even if it's just illusory or over small things. But some autonomy, so I can feel like I am exercising my free will as a human being over what happens to me during the course of my day. Living with micromanagers is no fun.

Work doesn't have to be this way. At Patagonia, Dean Carter, the head of human resources, noted that the company's founder and co-owner, Yvon Chouinard, thought of the company as a place where "everyone kind of knows the role that they need to do, and does that work independent of extreme management. He leads using a principle he calls 'management by absence.'" Patagonia helps to ensure there won't be micromanagement by having "a really flat organizational structure. We try to have more people than a manager can micromanage. That's all by design." A Patagonia leader in their information technology unit noted that their founder had written a book, *Let My People Go Surfing*, and that one of the company's values is that "when the conditions are good for doing those outdoor sports [surfing in Ventura, skiing in Reno], allowing people to go and take advantage of them."

One of the four leadership principles at Zillow is "empowering your team." As a learning and development person from the company said, "the manager's role is to support the team and be there to help remove roadblocks, not to be the dictator." Heather Wasielewski, who runs human resources at Landmark Health after working for more than a decade at DaVita, noted: "If somebody feels like the work that they're doing is not valued, if they personally don't feel like they have a voice at the table, if they feel like they're dictated to or micromanaged, they're going to feel less fulfilled and more tired."

People often believe that providing job control is possible only for some jobs, and for some people. But that is not the case—every job and person can be given more decision-making discretion and latitude to control their work. Collective Health, a San Francisco–headquartered company focusing on health benefits administration, is also concerned about the health of its own workforce. Andrew Halpert, a physician hired into the company in the role of senior director of clinical and network solutions, told me how Collective Health had designed the jobs of "patient advocates," the people who answer the phones to resolve customer issues that aren't readily solved. Of course, the company, competing in a tight labor market for talent, has what he referred to as "table stakes" in the recruiting world—the nice work space, healthy food, and so forth. But the company also hires different types of people and gives them more autonomy and influence. Halpert noted:

> Unlike most of the health plans in which their call center is going to be in a midwestern state staffed by people who have

> been doing call center work for years, we're hiring kids out of top universities like Stanford but also Penn and UC Davis. The typical profile is someone who majored in human biology and maybe wants to pursue a medical career but meanwhile wants a job and to work for an interesting start-up. Then you say, "How are you going to keep smart people engaged and happy and not burnt out and dissatisfied?"
>
> First of all, we train them really well. And they have really good technical tools so they're able to do their job. But at the end of the day, a lot of what they're doing is talking on the phone to people. One thing we do is we move people physically around on the floor every few weeks, so it feels a little different. We also rotate them into different types of tasks. So one week they're doing coordination of benefits issues, and one week they're working on out-of-area problems. So they're seeing more of the big picture.
>
> The person who runs the group tells people that as soon as they identify an issue, to surface it and work with people in other groups such as engineering to resolve it. In other words, they're empowered to work with the team to resolve the issue they've discovered. If you have smart people, and they're actually thinking and they have the right tools, they will solve issues more efficiently. Otherwise, the issue comes back again and again and then there's an appeal. On the "how much did I pay" criterion it looks like it's more expensive, because the Collective Health call costs more because it's being handled by someone who is better qualified and better paid who is also spending more time resolving the issue. But we solve problems, unlike other systems where claims and problems just go on with a life of their own.

Empowered people working with their teammates to create a better experience for the customers has several positive outcomes.

First, the system provides a benefit, health insurance that the clients' employees see as a real benefit and not as a hassle, thereby increasing employee retention. Second, this way of organizing work and empowering people increases Collective Health's own employee retention by providing people with more interesting and impactful work. And third, this arrangement is more efficient at resolving problems that don't just go on and on and find their way to the desks of human resources people in the client organizations.

As the preceding example illustrates, job control affects employers, not just employees and their health. Research going back decades consistently shows that job autonomy—the amount of discretion you have to determine what you do and how you do it—is one of the most important predictors of job satisfaction and work motivation, frequently ranking as more important even than pay.[16] Job autonomy also positively affects job performance,[17] in part by increasing motivation and partly by permitting people to use all of their capacities and information to do the work in the best way possible.

As with many other situations discussed in this book, there is no real trade-off between designing jobs to improve people's health and designing jobs that increase motivation and performance for the benefit of employers. Jobs that provide individuals more autonomy and control serve to increase their motivation, job satisfaction, and performance—and also make individuals healthier and live longer.

Why Isn't There More Job Control and Autonomy?

If job control is good for people and providing people discretion as to how to do their jobs is also good for their employers, why aren't delegation and discretion more widespread in the workplace? Why do so few people have much control over what they do and when and how they do it? Research on workplaces shows that in many countries, job autonomy has been decreasing.[18] That decrease in autonomy, made possible in part by increased computer monitoring of work of many types ranging from how many calls someone handles in a call center to how many patients a doctor sees and how many tests a physician orders, is one reason that surveys by Gallup and other major human resource consulting firms consistently provide evidence of widespread employee disengagement from and dissatisfaction with their work.

The question of what limits job autonomy is precisely what social psychologist Robert Cialdini, two doctoral students, and I set out to study almost twenty years ago. Our intuition was that people like to feel good about themselves and their efficacy and competency—they are motivated to self-enhance—and therefore individuals engage in motivated cognition to develop beliefs and perceptions that ratify their sense of competence. Two psychological consequences arise from these self-enhancement motives. First, individuals frequently suffer from an illusion of control, believing that because they have touched something or intervened in a situation, the outcome is or will be better because of their intervention. The classic illusion of control studies demonstrated that people held inappropriately higher expectations of success in affecting random events.[19] Second, because people like to think well of themselves and believe in their ability to positively affect outcomes, individuals tend to evaluate work products more positively if they had a higher level of intervention—or perceived intervention—in the production of the work. Simply put, individuals hold a faith in the effectiveness of their supervision over the work of others.

To test these ideas, we ran an experiment with three conditions. Two people came to an experimental session and expected that one would be a supervisor (randomly determined) and the other person would be doing some work, in this case, producing a rough draft of an advertisement for the Swatch watch. Both participants were actually supervisors, but each assumed that there was a counterpart in another room working on the task. In the control condition, people saw only a final advertisement. In the surveillance condition, they saw an intermediate draft of the advertisement and could fill out a standardized feedback form and make comments but were told that because of communication difficulties, the person in the other room would not get their input. In the feedback condition, they saw the identical intermediate draft advertisement, filled out the feedback form, and believed that the person in the other room received their guidance. In all three conditions, people at the end of the study saw the identical advertisement and rated that ad, themselves as supervisors, and their subordinates.

People who believed that they had given feedback on the work to their "subordinate" rated the ad, themselves, and their subordinate about twice as highly compared to those who only saw the final advertisement, with the surveillance condition falling in the middle. This difference is not only statistically significant, it is substantively meaningful to rate things twice as good simply because the person doing the rating had the illusion that they were providing some minimal level of oversight. And it turns out just being in the study influenced people's judgments. People who did not participate in the study at all rated the advertisement even lower, suggesting that merely participating in the study caused people to evaluate the advertisement more positively. If people rate themselves, their subordinates, and the work product more highly just because they believe they have had some intervention in its creation, no wonder it is so difficult to delegate. When people cede control to others, they perceive those others and themselves as less effective and the work product as inferior compared to when they provide supervisory oversight.[20]

While psychological biases may make delegation difficult, research on both job performance and health effects suggests that job control is a crucial workplace dimension affecting both health and productivity. And as the case of frontline employees at Collective Health and decades of research on job autonomy illustrates, it is possible to design more autonomous work in all sorts of jobs.

SOCIAL SUPPORT AND HEALTH AND WELL-BEING

In a video describing the DaVita culture, one woman explains how, when confronted with breast cancer, work colleagues launched bake sales to raise money for her and brought her food, lots of food. A single mom describes, almost in tears, how the company and coworkers helped her after she was hit by a car in a crosswalk and broke her pelvis, leaving her scarcely able to care for her young child. In both instances, what is clear is that the individuals appreciated not just the specifics of the help they received but, as important, the sense that they were part of a community. Adhering to the company's Three Musketeers'–based motto, there would be "all [coming together] for one."

If job control is one important aspect of a healthy workplace, social support is another. Research going back to the 1970s consistently demonstrates a connection between social support and health.[21] Having friends protects "your health as much as quitting smoking and a great deal more than exercising," even though survey evidence suggests that the "number of Americans who say they have no close friends has roughly tripled in recent decades."[22]

The evidence shows that social support—having family and friends who people can count on, and having close relationships—has both a direct effect on health and also buffers the effects of various psychosocial stresses and strains on people's health, the so-called buffering hypothesis. For instance, one review noted that "people who were less socially integrated had higher mortality rates" and that "individuals with low levels of social support have higher mortality rates . . . especially from cardiovascular disease. . . . However, there is also preliminary evidence linking support to lower cancer . . . and infectious disease . . . [and] mortality."[23] A 2012 Gallup survey of people in 139 countries showed that even after controlling for age, education, gender, and marital status, people who reported having family and friends who they could count on in times of trouble were more satisfied with their personal health.[24]

Studies and meta-analyses—statistical aggregations of numerous independent empirical research reports—consistently find evidence for both the direct effects of social support on health and evidence that social support helps buffer the adverse effects of stress,[25] including workplace stress,[26] on disease.[27] Moreover, more recent research has uncovered some of the specific physiological pathways through which social support affects health. Utah health psychologist Bert Uchino described evidence linking social support to changes in "cardiovascular, neuroendocrine, and immune function," with social support correlated with more positive "biological profiles" for these "disease-relevant systems."[28]

None of these findings should be surprising. People's need for social contact, for affiliation, to be with other people has been repeatedly demonstrated. One review of this literature noted that "people form social attachments readily" and "resist the dissolution of existing bonds. Belongingness appears to have multiple and strong effects on emotional patterns and on cognitive processes."[29] Isolating individuals as in solitary confinement in prisons is a harsh punishment, considered by some to overstep legal boundaries. Separating prisoners of war as a way of breaking them and getting them to reveal secrets is a well-established practice because it is often effective. Social support and social relationships promote well-being. Which raises the question of precisely *how* companies can and do promote a culture of strong interpersonal relationships and social support.

First, Do No Harm

Workplaces often have practices that make things worse in terms of building relationships and providing support. Changing the environment to make things better is not that hard—stop doing the things that create toxic work environments.

Possibly the most important suggestion: get rid of forced ranking, the grading-on-the-curve performance review process made famous—

and still embraced by—former General Electric CEO Jack Welch. As *Financial Times* writer Andrew Hill noted, so-called stack ranking has been blamed for Microsoft's "lost decade," and Microsoft's employees often mention forced ranking as the most destructive process inside the company. One of the costs: infighting and reduced collaboration.[30] The effect of forced ranking to reduce collaboration and teamwork is one reason why consulting firm Deloitte argued that forced ranking is dead, unpopular with both evaluators and the people being evaluated and increasingly abandoned by companies.[31]

But beyond the effect on teamwork and collaboration, pitting people against each other weakens social ties among employees and reduces the social support that produces healthier workplaces. Although there is not yet systematic evidence of the effects of forced ranking on health nor data on how evaluating people against each other diminishes social support, clearly pitting people against each other increases internal competition. For instance, at ride-sharing company Uber, forced ranking created a competitive culture that employees described as unfair and like a black box, fostering uncertainty and increasing the stress that comes from being subject to a capricious and uncertain review process.[32]

And then there's GE. As one former senior GE manager recounted to me:

> Everybody was fighting for turf. Everybody was fighting to control things and own things. Immediately I had to kind of fight to hold on to my turf for the job that I had been hired to do. . . . You assumed that there were only going to be so many people who got promoted. You almost had a celebrity death match, like with Jim, who was my peer. It was this idea that probably Jim or I would get promoted, no matter how good we both were. That kind of cage-fighting mentality was in the culture. You climb up, you climb up, you climb up, and then you get

spit out. You get fired, and the next group of young punks are coming up trying to take your job.

The stress from the internal competition—and the fact that this internal competition created a rat race in which people worked crazy hours and traveled excessively—took a toll on this individual and many others that he knew.

Another common condition of contemporary workplaces also contributes to an absence of social support: organizational chaos and a lack of feedback and particularly positive reinforcement. Companies run very lean in terms of the number of managers, which makes providing any sort of positive feedback and social support difficult because people are too busy to take care of others. For instance, a graduate with a degree in advertising got a job at Ogilvy & Mather as her first job. In part because the part of the company where she was working was growing very rapidly and people didn't have time to mentor or provide much help for a new graduate, she felt "uncared for." She commented, "If someone had said something like, 'you did a great job on this,' the next time I'd do an even better job. I definitely needed the reinforcement that wasn't there."

With some modest investment in the process of management so people would have senior support and guidance, and with the elimination of practices like forced curve ranking that set people against each other in an environment of intense internal competition, companies would be well on their way to eliminating harm from work arrangements that diminish social support.

Provide Support for People Having Difficulties—and to Everyone

As we have already seen, economic insecurity is an enormous source of stress, and stress is related to ill-health. Many workplaces have embraced a transactional approach to their workforce—people are seen as factors of production and the emphasis is on trading money for work, with not much emotional connection between people and their workplaces.

However, companies that seek to build an environment of social support often implement programs and activities that do two things: first, demonstrate that the company itself is committed to providing support for its workforce, and second, letting people engage in activities that demonstrate mutual caring for each other. In addition to providing tangible support, these actions signal to employees that others are there to help in times of trouble—and that emotional support and sense of connection to bosses and colleagues can be as important as any other benefit.

SAS Institute, often found near the top of best places to work lists and a company whose business strategy is premised on long-term relationships with its customers—and its employees—signals in ways large and small that it cares about its employees' well-being. For instance, soon after a program manager joined the company, he learned his mother had terminal cancer. The company located nursing care and coworkers helped build a wheelchair ramp at her house. When a SAS employee died in a boating accident one weekend, the question was what would happen to his children, currently enrolled in company-subsidized day care? How long would they be permitted to stay? The answer: as long as they wanted to and were age-eligible, regardless of the fact that they no longer had a parent employed by the company.[33] And perhaps nothing signifies SAS's commitment to its employees' well-being more than its investment in a chief health officer whose job entails not just running the on-site health facility but ensuring that SAS employees can access medical care that can keep them healthy and care for them if they get sick.

Southwest Airlines has always had a culture of caring for each other as well as taking care of the customer.[34] The large health-care and dialysis company DaVita has the DaVita Village Network, which "gives teammates the opportunity to help each other during times of crisis, such as a natural disaster, an accident, or an illness through optional payroll contributions and DaVita provides funding to match up to $250,000 per year."[35] When southwest Florida was hit by a series of hurricanes in 2004, a dialysis administrator noted, "The DaVita Village Network provided our housing while our homes were uninhabitable and provided funding for food until we were able to get back on our feet."[36]

Google, particularly while Laszlo Bock was running human resources, offered support for its employees who went above and beyond what was required or even expected just because it was the right thing to do. As Bock wrote, "Not everything we do falls neatly into our framework of efficiency, community, and innovation. Some programs exist purely because they make life better for our people."[37] Such as Google's decision in 2011 to increase maternity leave in the United States to five months. But perhaps the company's death benefits program is the most extraordinary:

> In 2011 we decided that if the unthinkable happened, the surviving partner should immediately receive the value of all the Googler's unvested stock. We also decided to continue paying 50% of the Googler's salary to the survivor for the next ten years. And if there were children, the family would receive an additional $1,000 each month until they turned nineteen, or twenty-three if they were full-time students.[38]

The cost was trivial, according to Bock, "about one-tenth of one percent of payroll." But the psychological payoff is enormous. As Bock described, "In 2012 our benefits team received this anonymous e-mail from a Googler":

> I'm a cancer survivor and every six months I have a scan to check if the cancer is back. You never really know when the news is going to be bad . . . so while I'm laying on that scanner

> bed I write and rewrite the e-mail to Larry [Page] asking that my stock continue to vest for my family, even though I'm going to die.
>
> When I got your e-mail about the new life insurance benefits it brought tears to my eyes. Not a day passes that I'm not appreciative of this company that does so many thoughtful and impactful things to my life. This . . . is one of those things and it goes on the already long list of reasons I'm proud to work at Google.[39]

To be clear, Bock and Google were focused on doing things to build community. Bock believes that "a sense of community helps people do their best work."[40] These instantiations of social support foster employee physical and psychological health. They also signal to employees that they are valued, and thus help in the company's effort to attract and retain people to the organizations.

Create a Culture of Community

People are more likely to like and help others with whom they share some sort of unit relationship, to whom they feel similar, and with whom they are connected, including being connected through shared experiences. The evolutionary logic is that a survival advantage accrues to those who can quickly ascertain friend from foe, us from them, and those with whom they share genetic similarities. Thus, it makes sense that similarity is a fundamental basis of interpersonal attraction[41] and people almost automatically help others and comply with requests from those with whom they share even incidental and random characteristics such as birthdates or fingerprint patterns.[42] Companies can readily, if they so choose, create a culture that builds a sense of community and fosters shared connections.

First, fix the language, so that people are less separated by title, and use language that is consistent with the idea of community. DaVita sometimes refers to itself as a "village." The company's CEO often calls himself the "mayor" (as a leader of a village might be called). Employees are constantly referred to as "teammates," and certainly never as "workers," a term that denotes both a somewhat lower status and also people who are distinct from the "managers" or "leaders."

Second, encourage shared connections through social and other events. At DaVita academies, training and socialization events that bring together a few hundred people at a time from within a region, people were organized into teams to design and perform skits, often in costumes—sometimes quite silly costumes. As one employee commented in a video profiling the company, people develop a deeper connection when they sing a song together, do a skit together, or act silly together—engaging in actions that reduce interpersonal barriers.

Or if you don't want to go that far, have people eat together and share other social interactions. Many companies have cafeterias that not only save time by people eating without having to go off-site but also bring people into contact and create a sense of community by sharing meals. At Patagonia, people enjoy the same types of outdoor recreation. That plus the long tenure of many employees has built a sense of community, as an executive in their Reno facility explained:

> There is this sense of community at Patagonia. I think that . . . encouragement to get out and do the things that we're passionate about, combined with the fact that a lot of people here have worked for Patagonia for many years . . . means that the relationships and the mission of the organization are as or more important than the day-to-day work. That's a unique feeling to any organization I've been a part of.

Organizations sometimes offer their employees volunteer opportunities to help local nonprofits. The workplaces thereby derive the benefits that accrue from having people who may not otherwise work together doing something for a common goal. A 2013 UnitedHealth survey found that 76 percent of people who had volunteered in the last year felt that volunteering had made them feel healthier and that 78 percent said that volunteering reduced their stress level. And 81 percent of employees who volunteered through their workplace "agreed that volunteering together strengthens relationships among colleagues."[43]

Holiday and birthday parties, and events that celebrate shared successes such as product launches or other business milestones—almost anything that brings people into contact in a pleasant and meaningful context—helps build a sense of shared identity and strengthens social bonds. Southwest Airlines is famous for its Halloween parties where people dress up and have fun.[44] Former CEO Herb Kelleher was famous for dressing up—sometimes as Elvis Presley. Having fun together builds social bonds and a sense of community.

The message of this chapter is simple, although it is too infrequently implemented. Giving people more control over their work life and providing them with social support fosters higher levels of physical and mental health. And these management practices also enhance employee retention and engagement, providing a payoff both to the company and to its people.

Chapter 7

Why People Stay in Toxic Workplaces

People who work in harmful, even toxic, circumstances *know* they are suffering. They feel the stress, understand what they are doing to cope, and in many ways are quite cognizant of the psychological and physical toll.

Not only that. They often join companies with some sense that they are not finding nirvana or anything close. When a young Korean-American woman, let's call her Kim, with a degree in human-computer interaction, joined Amazon.com in their e-commerce department in Seattle, she knew what she was getting into with respect to the work environment and culture. As she told me, "I knew there was some negative stigma about the company, but it was all kind of hush-hush. You don't really talk about that kind of thing, because it's unprofessional." Kim accepted the job offer, notwithstanding the information about a possibly unpleasant workplace, because of the prestige of the company. "Everyone says, 'If you can work at Amazon, you can work anywhere,' so I chose Amazon because of the status and because it was such a new and booming company."

Soon Kim was suffering from workplace stress because of the long hours and the pressure coming from a chaotic organizational structure, political infighting, and a difficult boss whom she could never satisfy. She had headaches, stomachaches, and skin rashes. She felt bad about herself. To get through her depression, she told me she engaged in binge eating and binge drinking. Prior to joining Amazon, she had dreams of going to college, getting a good job, and contributing to society. "Once I was at Amazon, I was like, 'I don't care anymore.

I will take any drug that comes my way. I will take any opportunity to, I guess for lack of a better way of saying it, feel something better than what I am currently feeling.'" Kim told me that Asians often look younger than their age. In her case, she said she soon looked as old as her mother.

Kim's story is not unusual. One Amazon employee noted that while on vacation, she went to a Starbucks every day to use the wireless connection to get work done. "That's when the ulcer started."[1] And it's not just Amazon. Several people told me about breaking down at work, and the numerous stress-related symptoms such as headaches, skin rashes, and stomach distress they suffered. People working in toxic environments that compromise their physical and mental health know that they are not in places that permit them to thrive. Just like Kim, some people accept jobs even as they are well aware that the place won't be good for their well-being. But they join, and stay, nonetheless.

A former senior executive at General Electric described how he recognized the negative effects of his work environment on his weight, health, and family, and had thought numerous times about quitting. He was traveling 150,000 to 200,000 miles a year and sometimes was away from home and his wife and two children for three weeks at a time. "What kind of company keeps you away from your family that long?" he said. The health-care company financial executive I have previously described was cognizant of the toll her long hours were taking and how her efforts at "self-medication"—alcohol, stimulants, and narcotics—neither solved the problem nor improved her health. In fact, I encountered very few people in my research who were not aware of the toll toxic work environments exacted on them.

All of which raises a fundamental question: Why do people, who mostly recognize they are working in harmful environments, nonetheless choose to remain?

ECONOMICS

One answer as to why people stay on in harmful work environments is obviously sheer economic necessity. Unless people have inherited wealth, they need gainful employment to earn the wherewithal to pay their bills. One person, working in a place where "everything was due as soon as possible, people worked late almost every day, and we had these dreaded weekly meetings where the CEO criticized our work with no constructive feedback," nonetheless stayed because her husband was going through graduate school and she was the breadwinner. She stayed to keep the family economically viable.

Moreover, some organizations, rationally enough, decide where to locate their expansion sites in part based on where they can find available labor willing to work for possibly less money and not be too particular about working conditions. When plants and businesses close, employment choices diminish, and people have to work somewhere. Amazon tends to locate its warehouses in economically struggling areas so the company can tap into surplus labor that will be grateful for almost any sort of gainful employment. For instance, an article describing Amazon's decision to open distribution centers in Chattanooga, Tennessee, and in South Carolina noted:

> The Amazon announcement represents this year's biggest job addition by any new business to Tennessee . . . local recruiters and company officials note that the sites . . . were within a labor market that could supply the thousands of seasonal workers Amazon needs. . . . Around some Amazon facilities, "work campers" live in recreational vehicles while they perform seasonal jobs for the Internet giant.[2]

Amazon is scarcely the only company to make location decisions using this criterion. Surplus labor and the correspondingly low wage rates high unemployment can produce, as well as workers who are willing to put up with tough work environments, are features attractive to many companies. An Internet search for location criteria produces scores of checklists and articles, many of which, like one on siting call centers or data centers, list "labor costs and availability" either first or near the top.[3]

Putting call centers in places with lower wages and high unemployment and manufacturing plants in areas where other manufacturers have left also permits companies to take advantage of government incentives to open facilities. Such incentives include property and other tax breaks, low interest loans, and occasionally free land or even buildings offered by communities anxious to obtain employment opportunities. In Chattanooga, Amazon got the site for free and a deal that permitted it to pay just 27 percent of the normal property tax bill. Once the facilities open, the companies are able to recruit a labor force more likely to put up with difficult working conditions and nonetheless remain—because the workers have fewer options.

Thus, the stagnating wages and pervasive economic insecurity so much in the news makes people grateful to have any job, and all the better if that job comes with a good income and the status of being associated with a prestigious organization that will bolster your résumé. Other aspects of work, such as its effect on physical and mental health, can take a back seat to the need to earn a living.

COMPANY PRESTIGE AND INTERESTING WORK

A second, related reason to put up with difficult working conditions is to gain the credibility that comes from working for a prestigious place. As the general manager from GE put it, "I took the job because I had never run something that large before and I figured at the age of thirty-six, it was good to invest in my career. . . . And to be clear, I benefited from leading one of the divisions at GE. I come back to

Silicon Valley and when people find out I ran a division at GE, they look and think, 'this person must know what he's doing.'" Kim explicitly mentioned the prestige of Amazon in deciding to work there, and few people I talked to did not, in fact, mention the reputational benefits that accrued from being employed by a well-known, prestigious employer, notwithstanding possible other negative aspects of their jobs.

Moreover, even in places where people were stressed, they were, for the most part, doing interesting, challenging work in their chosen profession. An event planner told me about the exciting events she got to organize, albeit under pretty stressful working conditions. The person who left the electric utility with PTSD told me that, prior to burning out from the overwork, she enjoyed being able to interact with local officials as she helped the utility in its government relations work. The GE executive enjoyed the leadership challenges he confronted in running a substantial business. A widow writing in the *New York Times* about her lawyer ex-husband who died from complications associated with drug abuse while working for a very prestigious Silicon Valley law firm noted: "He loved the intellectual challenge of his work."[4]

People obtain prestige and do things they are trained to do and enjoy doing. So they stay. And they stay, in part, because they are not particularly attuned to the physical and psychological toll the work is taking on a daily basis, and also because they often believe—or convince themselves—that things probably would not be that different elsewhere.

Without in any way diminishing these explanations, people in all jobs and occupations often have at least some degree of choice. There are healthier and less healthy work environments in virtually all industries. And some of the healthier, more humane places to work—think Google or SAS Institute, for instance, often ranked near the top of best places to work and best employers for families lists—are quite prestigious and résumé-enhancing.

For example, the retail industry is well known for low wages, economic insecurity that comes from fluctuating hours, the scheduling software that makes people's work time unpredictable, and limited benefits. Nonetheless, the Container Store, a retailer of packaging products and materials, has frequently ranked high on the list of best places to work. At least when founder George Zimmer ran it, Men's Wearhouse, a retailer of tailored men's clothing, offered higher wages, used fewer part-timers, and had an employee-centric culture that placed it on the Best Places to Work list. Costco, under the leadership of cofounder and former CEO Jim Sinegal, offered higher wages and more benefits than its competitor, Sam's Club. It also created a humane work environment that caused people to stay for years in what is typically a high-turnover industry. Airlines vary in their use of layoffs and their demands for wage concessions. For instance, Southwest, unlike its US peers, has never laid anyone off nor asked for wage givebacks.

The point: some work environments are toxic; others, even in the same industry or geography and with equal levels of prestige, less so. Therefore, people have choices. People would be well-served to consider the health consequences of their workplaces as they decide where to work; this holds true regardless of their level of education, geographic location, or particular job.

TWO EXPLANATIONS THAT DON'T HOLD WATER

There are other economics-based explanations offered for why people remain at workplaces that jeopardize their health, although the evidence for these accounts is surprisingly scarce.

Economists and others who believe that people are rational argue that workplaces can't be as bad as I've described, or people just wouldn't stay. The concept of revealed preferences, originally developed for consumer behavior but subsequently extended to other choice situations, states that individuals, through their behavior in a marketplace (in this instance, the labor market), reveal their preferences.[5] As Nobel Prize–winning economist Amartya Sen noted, the idea of revealed preferences makes it "possible to define a person's interests in such a way that no matter what he does he can be seen to be furthering his own interests in every isolated act of choice."[6] Revealed preference, in other words, is tautological. So, no, people don't reveal themselves to be masochists by remaining in unhealthy workplaces. Nor do they necessarily "prefer" where they work or not recognize the downsides of their work environments.

Another idea adduced to help explain why people stay in unhealthy places is that of compensating differentials. That idea maintains that even if people work in harmful environments, their compensation will rise correspondingly to reward them for the extra hazards and burdens they encounter.[7] This account argues that people consciously and deliberately choose to earn more in return for taking more risks with their safety and health at work. There's only one problem. Notwithstanding the intuitive logic of this idea, the empirical evidence for compensating differentials—that people get paid for the risks they take at work—is surprisingly weak.[8]

People fully comprehend the conditions at work. People know if they get paid time off and how much of their vacation, if they get any, they have used. Vacation and sick days are often printed on pay statements. When a high-technology executive's husband complained to her about her travel schedule and work hours, this talented and intelligent individual obviously realized the family costs of her work choices.

I don't buy the arguments that people are unaware of their working conditions—although they may not fully recognize the magnitude of the health costs they are incurring. Nor do I think that many individuals have somehow consciously and thoughtfully "chosen" to put themselves in harm's way to earn a living or to receive (nonexistent) "hazard" pay for putting up with poor work environments. As growing research demonstrates, people are scarcely rational decision-makers—about jobs or much else.[9] Instead, people get trapped, in a variety of ways, into staying in harmful work environments.

PEOPLE DON'T HAVE THE ENERGY TO LEAVE

Inertia helps explain why people stay in bad working environments. Numerous people told me that it often was easier just to stay where they were, unpleasant though that workplace might be.

Looking for a new job is itself a job and takes energy. People sometimes get trapped in harmful workplaces because, with not enough sleep and lots of workplace-induced stress, they do not have the physical or mental energy to fulfill their current work obligations and look for a new job at the same time. In a sense, the very fact that they are stressed and overwhelmed makes it impossible for them to escape the situations that are making them sick. A Salesforce marketing employee put it this way:

> You're stuck between a rock and a hard place. I was not at my best. I was not on my A game. You have to understand, last fall you could have asked me out for dinner for Friday and I would have said, "Sure," and a minute later asked you, "When?" You really think I was in a place to interview for and get a job and then hit it out of the park in the first six months?

The executive continued:

> You have all this shame and embarrassment because you are stressed and think it's you. I felt like my brain literally did not work. I literally could not remember conversations ten seconds later. I thought I was going to get fired. The reason I wanted to take a medical leave is that I had a really good personal brand, but the last several months I hadn't been able to do a thing. And

> I was worried it was going to affect my brand at Salesforce. I felt I might be better off taking a leave of absence. I would walk into work with tears streaming down my face because I felt like, "I don't want to go to work. I can't do this. I don't know how I will get through the day."

In that condition, looking for, let alone finding, another job seems, and probably is, impossible. So one simple but important reason that people stay in harmful work environments is that they are too psychologically wounded and too physically stressed and overwhelmed to muster the energy to leave.

AREN'T YOU GOOD ENOUGH? PRIDE AND EGO

One GE general manager I talked to stayed at GE just three years because of the work culture. But his tenure might have been even less. On several occasions when he went in to quit, his bosses would ask him, "Aren't you good enough to be a GE leader?" Of course he was good enough, he told himself, so he stayed, at least for a while. As he told me, once he started working, "There was a sense of 'oh my goodness, they basically did not tell me what was really going on in this division because the place was a train wreck.' So I have a choice. I can suck it up or I can run out the door. I decided to suck it up—that's why they hired me."

If you quit, you are, by definition, a "quitter." Who wants to be known, even to oneself, as a quitter? His GE bosses told him, "If you were a leader, you'd be able to figure out how to get things done and navigate the environment." The implication: If you were any good, you'd be able to successfully cope with the job demands and achieve success. So what's wrong with you? And who wants to admit that they aren't any good?

Kim's first response to her growing sense of unease at Amazon: "What's wrong with me? I started blaming myself." Amazon makes it clear that the place isn't for everyone, only for the best. The implication: if you can handle the work environment, you are good; if not, you are a weakling, a failure. In an Amazon recruiting video, a young woman says, "You either fit here or you don't."[10] Amazon's top recruiter noted, "This is a company that strives to do really big, innovative, groundbreaking things, and those things aren't easy. . . . When you're shooting for the moon, the nature of the work is really challenging. For some people it doesn't work."[11] A news article about Amazon reprised the saying: "Amazon is where overachievers go to feel bad about themselves."[12] In a competitive, performance-driven, metric-obsessed workplace, you can either hack it and thrive, or you can leave—and thereby admit to yourself and your family and friends that you can't take the pressure and that you aren't good enough to compete with the best.

People prefer, indeed are strongly driven, to think of themselves as competent and efficacious. One of the more powerful human motives is self-enhancement motivation—the desire to think well of ourselves.[13] There are numerous manifestations of this quest for self-affirmation. If people are asked to respond anonymously rating themselves on almost any positive trait ranging from sense of humor to intelligence to physical attractiveness to writing ability, more than half of the people in the group will say they are above average, a phenomenon called the above-average effect.[14] If people are told they possess an unusually large amount of some personal attribute or quality, these individuals will overemphasize and overvalue the importance of that particular trait for success. Thus, people think they are above average on positive attributes, and also believe that the attributes they possess are more than of normal importance for success.

As other manifestations of people's desire to self-enhance and think well of themselves, individuals think anything they have personally touched is going to be better and more successful for their having been involved in its development and creation. As I described in Chapter 6, when people provide feedback on the development of an advertisement, they view the (identical) advertisement as better; they view themselves as better managers, and their subordinates as better, too. Furthermore, once people own something, they value the item, be it a coffee mug, a pen, or a chocolate bar, more highly, simply because it is theirs, a phenomenon called the endowment effect.[15] The ways in which we self-enhance, and the implications of self-enhancement for understanding human behavior, are numerous and pervasive.

Few people want to admit to themselves or others that they aren't good at something, particularly if that "something" implicates their self-esteem. And for many people, work is integral to their self-concept and self-image. Particularly for people doing relatively high-prestige work in high-prestige organizations, there is no price too high or circumstance too difficult to face—because the alternative is to admit some weakness or failure. So, toughing it out in impossible circumstances becomes something to be sought, to be able to demonstrate one's competence, energy, and dedication.

Consequently, the ability to survive tough work circumstances has become a badge of honor. A friend who at one point held a very senior marketing job at Hewlett-Packard described how he traveled 250,000 or more miles a year, mostly on American Airlines. He flew so much for so long that he had the personal number of a senior American executive to help him deal with the inevitable snafus of flying. At Amazon, Dina Vaccari bragged about not sleeping for four days straight to meet a deadline.[16] Engineers in the Silicon Valley boast of their prodigious work hours, their ability to pull all-nighters, their ability to get the work done under almost any circumstances.

And the companies do things to help people keep up the pace. They provide on-site services such as cleaning, cafeterias, and car maintenance (and sometimes even cots) so that people do not have to leave the premises. They provide alcohol and food to ensure that people have the fuel to keep working. As one shrewd observer of high-technology companies commented, many workplaces adjust their food offerings to make it easier for people to keep going at a time when they might otherwise go home exhausted. She noted that while lunch offerings might feature salads and protein, "if you go to Facebook, look at what they give their people more of at happy-hour time, which is when people are going to start their second shift of work. It is going to be heavy fats, heavy sugar, heavy food." It may not be healthy, but fat and sugar are useful for providing the temporary boost of energy to help people continue working into the evening. And of course, companies also provide reinforcement and encouragement for people to keep working—the promise of promotions, status, recognition, the occasional award, and so forth. And always the query, either directly asked or implied: "Aren't you good enough to make it here?"

YOU CHOSE TO BE HERE: RATIONALIZATION AND COMMITMENT EFFECTS

Once people have made a decision, particularly if the decision is public—such as choosing a job, which someone's friends and family know about—and voluntary, in that the individual wasn't forced to make the choice, that person is psychologically committed to the decision. That means the individual becomes psychologically identified with the choice and its implications and motivated to continue behaving in ways consistent with the committing decision.[17] Commitment is a powerful psychological process that can cause people to escalate their investment of resources in failing courses of action, to adopt attitudes consistent with their decisions, such as revaluing the desirability of groups and jobs, and to behave in ways consistent with their original choice. So, for instance, people who make a donation or take some small action, such as putting up a political poster favoring a candidate, will then take further, more significant actions in the same direction. That's because once they have done something favorable toward a cause or candidate, the individuals are now committed to the implications of that first act—they must behave in ways supportive of the target.

Commitment implicates several psychological processes. A decision someone makes is "their" decision, and if we like our coffee mugs or chocolate bars because they are now "ours," we certainly are going to like our decisions. Thus, people will stay with their initial decision to join a company because it was *their* choice. Another process: self-enhancement. If we want to feel good about ourselves, we certainly don't want to admit we made a mistake or did something stupid. So that produces another reason people stay in a bad workplace and remain committed to their decision to work in a difficult environment: the reluctance to admit that they made a bad decision. Rather than admitting a mistake or distancing yourself from "your" decision, it is easier to rationalize the initial decision and the ongoing choice to remain. People are great, skilled, indeed consummate rationalizers.

One way of rationalizing commitment to a bad environment entails telling oneself that as bad as the current circumstances are, they aren't going to be forever, and there are other reasons to stay. One finance person noted, "They were paying me crazy money and the job was close to home." A consultant commented that we have it better than our ancestors and not loving one's job is a "total first world problem." I heard rationalizations that tried to make sense of being in harmful work environments, scads of them.

As one executive coach noted about why her clients put in long hours and made so many sacrifices:

> The way most people rationalize it is, "I'm just going to do it a little bit longer." "It's just this one quarter." "It's just this one launch." The truth of it is you can do that for many years. People are not sleeping, they're shaking in meetings, they are

> not aware if they are breathing or not. They're also often very young, so they haven't had the consequences yet.

Commitment also works through people's desire to appear steadfast and consistent. Consistency seems to be valued; the term "flip-flopper" is rarely seen as complimentary. And so, having made a decision, people feel bound to pursue it—including decisions about where to work. People who move too often raise red flags in future employers—what's wrong with the individual that they can't stay at a place? And the push for consistency also increases unwillingness to admit an error. So we believe things will get better, or maybe we are overreacting, or maybe the situation is not as bad or as harmful as it seems. All of which conspire to keep people working in environments that they recognize are unhealthy and harmful to their well-being.

SOCIAL PROOF: WHEN THE TOXIC BECOMES THE NORM

We learn what to expect, what to want, and what is normative by observing others. Psychologists described the concept of informational social influence more than sixty years ago, and it remains a fundamentally important idea.[18] The premise: we are influenced by others because their behavior provides us useful information about what are appropriate attitudes and behaviors—and this is particularly true for others who are socially similar to us. As social psychologist Robert Cialdini has written, relying on social proof—what others do—economizes on cognitive effort.[19] We just have to look at others' behavior. And if we believe that others, the crowds, are wise and have thought things out carefully, relying on others to guide our own attitudes and behavior seems, and often is, sensible. Consider that the word *norm* has the same root as *normative,* and what is a norm and what is normative is, in the end, what most people do and think. In that sense, people collectively come to define a version of reality and certainly what is expected and acceptable.

The influence of others on behavior, with respect to work, is profound. As one high-level accountant who had worked in a financial job noted, "My parents told me to become an accountant and get a good salary and health insurance." Numerous people I interviewed commented how their friends thought they had it made, working at a good job in a prestigious company. So quitting was difficult because it entailed going against the expectations of parents and peers, and telling themselves—and loved ones—that the "wonderful" job they had was actually making them sick.

Social influence is potent. A study of turnover in fast-food restaurants found, in some sense not surprisingly, that turnover was socially contagious.[20] When some people in a facility left, others were much more likely to follow—and conversely, if few to no employees left, their workmates stayed. Even though fast-food work is relatively low paid and not very rewarding, people's response to that work environment, in terms of staying or going, was affected by what their colleagues did. Similarly, people's attitudes toward their jobs—their specific tasks—and their organizations are influenced by their colleagues' reactions.[21] If everyone else thinks a job is interesting and stimulating, then it must be; conversely, if everyone in the workplace thinks the job—and the boss—sucks, they must.

Social influence and the behaviors and beliefs of people in our social network matter. In some sense, no big news there. But the big news is in the implication. Yes, we sort of know that people who want to quit drinking need to stop hanging out with others who drink, and similarly for smoking and taking drugs. And we may have read that even being overweight seems to diffuse through social networks as people come to socially construct and define normative and appropriate eating behavior and weight. These same forces play into how, why, and if we tolerate harmful workplace environments. Surrounded by people who act as if long hours, an absence of job control, and work-family conflict is normal, people come to accept that definition of the situation. They acquiesce and stay, even if deep down they recognize the cost to their well-being and maybe that harmful work environments aren't really "normal."

Unfortunately, in the world of work, long work hours and other aspects of toxic work environments have become the norm in many places. So when people confront such environments, they see nothing unusual. Therefore, people feel odd about complaining about the same work environments their friends and colleagues are experiencing or leaving workplaces where others have chosen to stay. Furthermore, if work practices such as long hours are normative, there would be little prospect of easily finding a more healthful workplace.

Kim was told by one of her Amazon managers that he had worked for plenty of worse companies so, by comparison, Amazon was a great place to be. The executive coach told her clients that everyone was working the same long hours. Long hours, tough environments, are everywhere, and everyone is putting in the hours and putting up with the working conditions. So should you.

In fact, working impossible hours under unrealistic deadlines becomes part of the culture and how people define normality. As the executive coach commented, "When things calm down and people aren't working until 2 a.m. anymore, they will literally say, 'What happened to us? When did we get lazy? When did we stop working?' That's what I mean by 'normalizing'—after a while, there's this indoctrination, this expectation, that this is how you're supposed to work and live." The abnormal and the harmful become defined as normal, acceptable, expected—and even sought as a mark of success and achievement.

ALTERNATIVE NARRATIVES AND SELF-PERCEPTION

Implicit in some of the forgoing, but distinct enough to warrant separate attention, is the idea of the narratives we and others construct about situations (and, for that matter, people). Narratives help us make sense of our environments, and once constructed, we tend to assimilate new information in ways consistent with the narrative and disregard and more readily forget information that doesn't fit the narrative we have developed.

There are two competing narratives about toxic work environments. One is that these environments exist in companies that are competitive, demanding places. Such intense, even stressful workplaces "must" be that way to accomplish the industry disruption and produce the economic achievements that such companies seek. This is the Amazon story told by some, and an account for why ride-sharing company Uber and its controversial ex-CEO, Travis Kalanick, are how they are. As Silicon Valley investor and commentator Jason Calacanis argued, "When you look at technology companies you can count on one or two hands the number of executives who have built a company from five people to five thousand or 50,000. . . . Uber has had to fight to even exist. . . . If you spend all your time fighting, sometimes you get a fighter mentality."[22]

The corollary: people should be happy and proud to work at such places, and be willing to subordinate their own narrow, selfish interests and maybe even their well-being for the growth and success of the collectivity. As the accountant who had worked at One Medical told me:

> I went there and it was just heaven for me because it had a mission. I really truly believed in their mission to make patient care accessible and health care affordable. I believed we were doing good. When I came to this company that was what we all did. They did whatever it took to make it work. We handed over our lives in exchange for this company succeeding. We built this culture of bending over backward . . . but we started to do it without really taking care of ourselves.
>
> What I can say about workplaces and the toxicity of workplaces is that we have traded in the idea of getting a paycheck and the idea of success, a job title, and money for having any

> sort of meaning or any sort of life. . . . Being part of a mission-driven company is one thing. But purpose, like having your own meaning in life, is another. I lost all meaning in life for that other purpose.

This idea of giving oneself over for a cause has the virtue of playing into people's desires to achieve immortality, or a version thereof, by attaching themselves to an institution greater—and longer lived—than themselves.

The counter-narrative is this: some companies are indeed toxic workplaces where human well-being, even human health and life, are subordinated to some leader's ambitions and often to that person's agenda for power, prestige, and wealth, as well as to economic performance measures that do not fully capture, if they capture at all, the human toll. In One Medical, "the leader of the company did not believe in taking care of himself. He really believed in sacrificing his health for the success of the company, and that trickles down." But just because the leader is unbalanced doesn't mean that every employee needs to lose their sense of balance as well. Under this narrative, it is right, indeed self-affirming and a part of people's self-concept, to exercise their right to exit. And by their leaving, people might eventually compel changes to confront high turnover and its associated costs as well as to attract replacements.

The narratives often seem to contrast between selfless sacrifice for the institution and its lofty ambitions and selfish pursuit of individual health and well-being. Let me offer a third narrative, an account that integrates the two and makes taking care of oneself more legitimate: Once you are sick, incapacitated, or even worse, dead from harmful workplace practices, you won't be of much use to the organization or yourself. So if your employer actually was interested in *your* unique and distinct contribution, the place would take better care of you, wouldn't it? If the workplace truly cared about productivity and performance, it just might embrace management practices that produce both well-being and high performance and eschew elements of the work environment that degrade both worker and company well-being. And particularly for companies that tout their environmental or social welfare credentials, those companies might spend more time and effort ensuring that their own human systems, their own workplaces, are sustainable.

HOW PEOPLE FINALLY LEAVE

Notwithstanding the many psychological processes that induce people to stay at toxic workplaces, many do leave. In fact, virtually everyone I interviewed for this book had left a harmful place of employment. People left primarily under three conditions.

First, there might be a precipitating event, the straw the broke the camel's back—an incident so outrageous that it was like a slap in the face that caused the individual to see the reality of their workplace. One person told me about someone she knew who had been called at a friend's funeral to fly home to work. Upon arriving at work the next day, they told her, "Oh, we took care of it." She decided she did not want to spend her life at a place that treated her that way.

Second, family (most often) or friends help people overcome their psychological reluctance to leave and will not countenance their rationalizations any longer. One person, working at a stressful place where they had gained a lot of experience and learning, which had caused them to stay, noted: "The final straw was when I went into work even though I was really sick. My husband basically sat me down and told me that I can't keep going like this. I left as soon as I found another job."

The person from GE went into work to quit one day but came home still working for GE because he was "good enough to be a GE leader." His wife told him that he might be good enough to be a

GE leader, but if he didn't quit, he would not be her husband. That extricated him from the situation.

And third, people leave when they get so psychologically and physically ill that they simply cannot keep going. One person related: "I stayed on Wall Street because I thought I didn't have other options because my skill set was too narrow to transfer and because Wall Street is such a bubble that anything outside it is viewed as 'other.' I eventually left because I couldn't take the soul-crushing environment anymore and had a mental breakdown. I left to protect my sanity."

A person left an electric utility when they went on disability leave with PTSD. Kim left Amazon when she was so exhausted and depressed that she couldn't take it anymore. In that sense, people do leave harmful workplaces. But often only after they have paid a tremendous psychological or physical price.

STOP ACCEPTING THE UNACCEPTABLE

The human capacity to rationalize—it's not so bad, it's only for a while—and to make excuses—it's for a good cause, I'm part of an effort to change the world (*really*, by letting people hook up more easily or have their pictures disappear or by being able to acquire more stuff more quickly)—is enormous. Once individuals have chosen a place to work, once they are surrounded by others putting up with the same insanity and apparently tolerating it, once they are exposed to the narrative that paints them either as loyal, hardworking, successful, or as not good enough, leaving is difficult. And that is true even if people know they are self-medicating, are putting relationships with family and friends at risk, and are ruining their physical and mental health.

So here are a few practical things to do. First, since we are influenced by others, find some people who don't work all the time, who have relationships with their family and friends that extend beyond pictures on screen savers, and who have work that provides a sense of autonomy and control. Then build relationships with those people and spend time with them. They can provide the social information and influence that will help you make better decisions.

Second, recognize and then don't succumb to appeals to ego (*aren't you good enough?*). Be willing to admit that in choosing an employer, as in any other decision you make, it is possible to make a mistake and, once having admitted that mistake, to act to correct it.

Third, understand that, as many people I talked to told me, even after someone leaves a difficult, unhealthy workplace, the effects don't immediately disappear. One person with a background in computer coding as well as consulting described the stress from the internal politics at Hulu. After she left for a new workplace, she still experienced residual stress and the lingering effects of where she had worked before. She commented: "I've discovered there's this thing called baggage in work. It's interesting what you do carry from job to job, so that even if you move to a healthier workplace, you don't completely lose the residue of the bad experiences from the past."

And most important, as you choose a job and evaluate your employer, recognize that in our workplaces, we need to emphasize health and well-being as important outcomes. Work is more than money, and money cannot completely undo damage to relationships or damage to your physical and mental health. Until people take responsibility for finding places where they can thrive, we can't expect our employers to value health, either.

Chapter 8

What Might—and Should—Be Different

BOB CHAPMAN, CEO OF global manufacturer Barry-Wehmiller (and named the number-three CEO in the world in an article in *Inc.* magazine),[1] is right: "I was in front of a thousand CEOs the other day in San Antonio, Texas, and I said, 'You are the cause of the health-care crisis because 74 percent of all illnesses are chronic. The biggest cause of chronic illness is stress, and the biggest cause of stress is work.'"

To reprise the wisdom from the comic strip *Pogo*, "We have met the enemy and he is us." Companies are making their employees sick, governments are not doing much about it, and *everyone* is paying the price.

But it doesn't have to be that way. It is completely possible to save tens of thousands of lives and billions of dollars of health care and other costs annually, all the while making organizations of all sorts more effective and productive. All that companies, public policy, and employees need to do is to understand what I have presented in this book—details about what aspects of the work environment cause the most harm—and then work assiduously to change them, following the lead of some of the positive examples I wrote about.

As places like Barry-Wehmiller, Patagonia, Zillow, Collective Health, Google, and DaVita, among many others, illustrate, it is at once feasible and imperative to create healthy workplaces where human well-being thrives. It is possible and indeed necessary to build work environments that promote, rather than diminish, human sustainability. It is, indeed, good for business.

Many wonderful organizations—albeit not nearly enough—have done so.

Suppose work wasn't a four-letter word, and workplaces were not hazardous to people's physical and mental health. Health-care costs would be lower, both for employers and for society, and productivity and performance would be higher. It shouldn't take data to demonstrate the common-sense idea that physically or psychosocially distressed people don't do their best work, although in Chapter 2 on the toll of workplaces I reviewed evidence and anecdotes consistent with this notion. If we changed workplace practices and environments to reduce stressful conditions, employers would no longer be damaging, even killing, their people. And those people would not have to be "dying for a paycheck."

I have not attempted to compile a comprehensive list of all the ways in which what happens to people at work affects their levels of stress and therefore their health. As such, I have undoubtedly underestimated both the economic and health toll and productivity loss from ill-advised company choices about how to structure work environments.

Other Important Aspects of Work Environments

To take one example of a work environment aspect that is consequential and not considered here, workplace bullying is both widespread and stressful, creating both psychological and physical problems.[2] Abusive behavior at work is shockingly common. One study of nurses working in the National Health Service in the United Kingdom found that 44 percent of the nurses had experienced bullying in the prior twelve months,[3] while a survey of more than 1,100 people reported that more than 50 percent had experienced bullying at work sometime during their careers.[4] Bullying has important consequences for people's well-being. For instance, nurses who experienced bullying reported significantly higher levels of anxiety and psychological depression.[5] A two-year panel study of more than fifty-four hundred hospital employees in Finland reported that even after adjusting for age, gender, and income, bullied employees had two times the likelihood of developing cardiovascular disease and four times the odds of experiencing depression.[6] Although abusive behavior on the part of bosses or coworkers is sometimes seen as an individual behavior not under organizational control, organizations and their leaders can and do decide whether or not to tolerate nasty workplace environments, something my colleague Robert Sutton made clear in his book *The No Asshole Rule*.[7]

Or consider the deleterious impact of discrimination against women, ethnic minorities, or other groups, which not only affects their job prospects and economic security but also their sense of control over their work environment and therefore their levels of stress. A study of 215 Mexican-origin adults found that perceived discrimination was correlated with both depression and poorer general health.[8] A study of 197 African-Americans in Atlanta supported the association between race-based discrimination at work and hypertension, with evidence that the stress of racism raised both systolic and diastolic blood pressure readings.[9] A meta-analysis of 134 samples reported that "perceived discrimination had a significant negative effect on both mental and physical health."[10]

Or take the matter of workplace safety and the physical environment, including factors such as temperature, lighting, and noise, all of which affect health,[11] and all of which were the original focus of occupational safety and health regulations. For instance, a study of 374 automobile plant workers found that wearing hearing protection decreased the adverse effects of noise on blood pressure and heart rate.[12]

The simple fact is that workplaces are important environments for employees. Long-standing research has examined the effects of workplace environments on health—see for instance articles in *The Journal of Occupational Health Psychology*, *The Journal of Occupational and Environmental Medicine*, and numerous articles in many of the medical and public health journals. And yet the management literature, organizational leaders, and public policy practitioners pay astonishingly little attention to the role of workplace environments. When a survey asked respondents what their employers did to alleviate stress in the workplace, 66 percent, almost two-thirds, replied, "nothing."[13]

FIXING THE PROBLEM

Some companies have voluntarily chosen to make employee health and well-being part of their competitive strategy and integral to their culture and values. But many more organizations routinely make decisions that actually kill people or cause them unnecessary physical and mental pain and suffering. Despite an enormous epidemiological literature that speaks to the effects of exposure to toxic organizational practices on health and health-care costs, these decisions and their consequences occur mostly under the radar, invisible to policy makers and even in many cases not noticed by the organizational leaders making them. If we are to reduce the costs to society and companies and eliminate the unnecessary deaths that come from companies' harmful management practices, five things need to occur.

First, we need to measure health and well-being, just as we routinely measure environmental pollution and impact. Second, we need to call out "social polluters" for their toxic practices and workplaces, in the same way we highlight companies that harm the environment. What's more, we need to start celebrating those workplaces that encourage employees to thrive. We can use public admonition and social pressure to produce healthier workplaces. Third, we need policies that reflect the true costs and consequences of management's decisions. This entails having companies pay their share of the costs of ill-health that they create, costs that are now largely externalized and borne by society at large.

Fourth, we must reckon with excuses and false trade-offs—the reality that most companies do *not* confront a difficult trade-off between increasing employee health on the one hand or growing their profits on the other. As we have seen throughout this book, doing things that increase employee health and well-being invariably enhance organizational productivity and profitability, sometimes by a significant amount. As such, the two goals of decreasing health-care costs/increasing employee health and enhancing organizational performance are quite compatible.

Finally, we must insist that organizational leaders and public policy groups prioritize human sustainability and not allow it to be sacrificed at the first sign of economic distress or slighted to increase shareholder return regardless of the social costs. As a civilized society, there ought to be limits on what companies can to do to their people. After all, I don't see people advocating slavery or child labor just because such work arrangements might increase profits. Just as it has become unacceptable for companies to foul the physical environment, through regulation and civic approbation, we should prohibit companies from "fouling the human environment" and creating social pollution. Simply stated, certain dimensions of human well-being should be seen as sacred. I consider each of these recommendations in turn.

MEASURING EMPLOYEE HEALTH AND WELL-BEING

If there is one thing I learned in my research, and I learned a great deal, it is this: there is little to no systematic (or even nonsystematic) attention to measuring employee health and well-being in companies. Self-insured large employers can and often do get, from their health-plan administrators, information on paid claims experience, but that data says nothing about what happened to the people who sought medical services or prescription drugs. Some places, such as Patagonia, measure turnover as a way of ferreting out problems with specific managers or with their ability to retain talent. Patagonia and other companies also rely on exit interviews to surface well-being issues. Some places, like Barry-Wehmiller, DaVita, and Patagonia, measure, either formally or informally, adherence to the company's values. Many, many places measure employee engagement and job satisfaction. Very few companies can or do ignore the online reporting of their work environment presented on websites such as Glassdoor. Human resource professionals, charged with ensuring a healthy company culture and attracting and retaining a talented workforce, certainly spend time talking to people throughout their organizations and worry about work-life balance, work hours, and if their employees are doing well. It's not that there is no concern about employees. There is plenty of concern, at least in some companies, about employee health and well-being. There's just not much systematic data for companies to use.

What is measured gets attention. What is not measured often gets ignored. The aphorism that you can't manage what you don't measure is mostly true. So if we are going to get serious about improving the effects of workplaces on employee health and well-being, we need measures.

Here's the good news: numerous measures are readily available. Many of them are short, and a plethora of measures have been extensively researched to demonstrate validity and reliability. These measures of health and well-being, as well as measures of dimensions of the workplace environment that affect health and well-being, could be implemented with astonishingly little cost or effort.

Employee health is crucial, as a measure of social system functioning and because health has economic consequences. So let's begin with a single-item measure of self-reported health: "How good is your health in general?" Response scales could be: "Excellent, very good, good, fair, or poor," or "Very good, good, fair, bad, or very bad." This single item measure has extremely strong reliability and predictive value.

The Manitoba Longitudinal Study of Aging assessed 3,128 elderly residents of the Canadian province in 1971 using both a self-reported measure of health and objective indicators such as health service utilization and physician-reported medical conditions. The study then followed these respondents, measuring occurrence and date of death over the subsequent six years. Mortality risk was almost three times as large for those self-reporting poor health compared to those saying their health was excellent. Moreover, self-reported health status was a better predictor of whether or not the individual died and how soon the death occurred than the objective measures of health.[14] A study of more than 2,800 people in Finland found that self-reported health was stable over a one-year period (and thus reliable) and was valid in that it prospectively predicted the use of physician services over a one-year period, self-reported physical fitness, and mortality over ten years.[15] Another study of some seven hundred thousand people found that people who reported being in fair or poor health had more than *twice* the risk of subsequent mortality, with the predictive value of self-reported health holding for both genders and all ethnic groups.[16] Moreover, research has begun to understand *why*—the underlying mechanisms that make self-reported health such a useful predictor of mortality.[17]

Other studies have shown that self-reported health status predicts absenteeism caused by sickness.[18] Still other research has shown that self-reported health status measures are valid predictors of subsequent mortality for various subpopulations such as Native Americans, Pacific Islanders, and Hispanics[19] as well as for low-income groups.[20] The studies of the predictive value of self-reported health status span a number of countries. An overview of more than two dozen studies showing the connection between self-reported health status and health outcomes including mortality concluded that "global self-rated health is an independent predictor of mortality in nearly all of the studies, despite the inclusion of numerous specific health status indicators and other relevant covariates known to predict mortality."[21]

The Organisation for Economic Co-operation and Development

(OECD) uses national surveys of self-reported health as one indicator of the health status of nations.[22] Speaking of OECD, their indicators of health measures used to assess the health status of countries could be, in many instances, adapted and applied to smaller populations such as work organizations.

The measurement of well-being is somewhat more complicated but still quite doable. There are more scales to measure people's well-being and mental health at work than there are to measure physical health, and the scales require asking more questions on surveys than a single item.[23] Nonetheless, there is a well-developed research literature on assessing well-being in the workplace that has produced reliable mesures that correlate with important work outcomes such as turnover in predictable ways.

Many if not all the dimensions of work environments that affect health are also readily assessed. For work hours, just ask people how many hours they work a week, and how often they work "off hours" (e.g., nights, weekends, or doing shift work). For access to medical care, a question asking if people have had to postpone seeing a doctor, having some recommended medical procedure, or filling a prescription because of cost considerations is useful. There are well-developed measures of workplace stress,[24] work-family conflict,[25] and job control,[26] which includes the constructs of decision authority and latitude to take decisions. Economic insecurity can be assessed by ecological measures such as the level of unemployment in the local area as well as by individual indicators such as losing a job, having colleagues lose their jobs, and feeling as if one might lose one's job in the near future.[27]

The field of organizational, industrial, and occupational psychology has developed great measures of work environments. Organizations should use those measures—to assess the health of their workplaces, and also to track changes over time as companies intervene to improve employee health and well-being.

HIGHLIGHTING THE "SOCIAL POLLUTERS"

Once we have measures of healthy and unhealthy workplaces, it is useful to publicize that data. In tackling environmental pollution and sustainability more generally, an important assumption has been that publicizing who the polluters are will cause those organizations to curtail their polluting activities to maintain positive brand equity with employees, customers, and suppliers. And publicizing who the most environmentally friendly or "green" companies are will encourage others to emulate those role models and seek to earn comparable recognition.

For instance, the Canadian government has made its data on which companies and other entities pollute not only available to the public but also searchable in an online database. Similarly, awards and lists by organizations such as *Working Mother* magazine[28] and recognition by organizations such as the International Center for Work and Family, operated out of IESE Business School in Barcelona, are designed to encourage companies to adopt policies that make it easier to balance work and family responsibilities. Giving awards on the one hand, and poor scores on the other, encourages organizations and their leaders, who are inherently competitive, to seek to do better. There is no reason to believe that such efforts would be any less successful in the topic domain of employee mental and physical health. What organization would want to be listed as one of the unhealthiest places to work? And conversely, most companies would surely want to be recognized for their positive effects on human well-being.

Two interrelated issues arise in efforts to name and shame companies to do better with respect to their employment practices. First, many of the organizations providing ratings and rankings are commercial entities whose customers are the same organizations as those being rated or ranked. This is true of the for-profit Great Place to Work Institute that sells consulting services to companies even as it ranks them on its ubiquitous best places to work lists. It is true for Glassdoor, which is at once a jobs and recruiting site and also the aggregator of employee ratings of companies and CEOs. Glassdoor sells its job posting and recruiting services to many of the same employers rated on its site. Glassdoor faces the further issue that the reviews it posts are voluntarily submitted, just as reviews are on sites such as Yelp and TripAdvisor. This means that Glassdoor, like those other sites, has to use algorithms (which it does not disclose) to try to detect attempts to game the system. Few to no organizations, Gallup being an exception, use random sampling to provide an objective and unbiased assessment of work environments, and Gallup does not publish data on individual companies.

Second, unlike the case of environmental pollution where governments collect reasonably objective data on discharges, and energy utilization and recycling can be objectively assessed, fewer "independent" entities collect health and well-being information. For the most part, the measures of workplace environments are voluntarily provided, as companies can decide to participate in "best places" contests or not, leaving open the possibility of bias and concerns about the accuracy of measures.

But these difficulties are scarcely insurmountable. The Sustainability Accounting Standards Board, founded in 2011, has worked assiduously to develop objective, auditable standards that companies would report to investors concerning material environmental, social, and governance impacts. Unfortunately, SASB has, for the most part, neglected focusing on human sustainability as it emphasizes issues of environmental impact. But SASB provides a model of what might be attempted in the domain of workplace reporting, if there was sufficient interest in how companies impact the lives and mortality of their workers. In the meantime, lists of places good for working mothers (families) and reviews of workplaces, even if not perfect, are better than nothing in highlighting workplace environments and calling out the best and the worst.

CAPTURING EXTERNALITIES

We need policies that capture the magnitude of externalized costs so that all parties can make better-quality decisions. To take an example, it is both morally wrong and economically inefficient to let me dispose of my garbage by throwing it on my neighbors' property—even though that seemingly helps me and my economic well-being by providing a low-cost way of disposing of my waste. Because I impose a real cost on some other entity that I pass off—externalize—costs to but reduce my own costs, I have few or no incentives to efficiently use resources to reduce the amount of garbage I produce or to figure out ways to dispose of it more effectively. Because my experienced price of "waste" is essentially zero, I overproduce waste and am largely indifferent to how it is managed.

As economists and others well recognize, markets and market pricing are wonderful mechanisms to ensure the efficient allocation and utilization of resources. But market pricing works *only* to the extent that prices reflect to the extent possible full information and actual costs. Distorted prices create distorted incentives that produce distorted and inefficient decisions.

In the case of health-care costs, this issue of the externalization of private costs onto the larger public is far from hypothetical. For example, companies that do not provide health insurance benefits to their (often low-paid) employees leave these employees to fend for themselves and they frequently are uninsured. When the uninsured get sick, they turn to hospital emergency rooms for care. Emergency rooms are extremely cost-inefficient locations to deliver primary care, and often by the time people arrive at the emergency room their health has already deteriorated to a point where treatment requirements and expenses are greater than they would have been with earlier diagnosis and intervention. When the health system has to provide care that is not reimbursed by insurance, the burden falls on health providers. Those providers then either try to recapture these costs by raising the prices paid by employers and employees who are part of the health insurance system, or by seeking public money to reimburse the care provided to those lacking health insurance. In both instances, the costs of health care are borne not by the employers who have shirked their obligations to their workforce but instead by others. For instance, a 2005 study by Families USA estimated that "the average annual health insurance premium was $341 higher for individual coverage and $922 higher for family coverage because of the costs of uncompensated care."[29]

Similarly, once someone is laid off they are no longer the responsibility of the employer but instead the general public. Underpaid people may have to rely on public assistance, so while employers benefit from paying less and reducing their costs, the public has to pay to support working people. The extent and cost of this problem of the shifting of health care and other employment costs is difficult to estimate, but studies suggest that it is significant. One study in California estimated that two million working families—families in which at least one member was in the labor force—received various forms of public assistance in 2002, costing the state some $10 billion. Moreover, almost 46 percent of the families receiving medical services paid for by Medi-Cal were working families.[30] The cost to the state and federal government from providing this health-care assistance was more than $5.7 billion.[31] Furthermore, studies show that these working families receiving health care using federal and state financial resources were not just people employed by the small businesses that are often argued to be less able to bear the burden of health insurance costs. Some 700,000 people enrolled in Medi-Cal were either workers or dependents of workers in companies with 1,000 or more employees, and an additional 440,000 were people working for companies employing between 100 and 1,000 individuals.[32]

Walmart, the largest private-sector employer in the United States, has drawn considerable research attention because even compared to other large retailers, it pays lower wage rates and offers a smaller percentage of its workforce health insurance benefits. Because of various suits against the company, much information has come to light. Briefly summarized, Walmart "spent 38% less on health care per enrolled worker than wholesale/retail stores" and "Walmart's health plans covered a lower percentage of their workers (48% to 61%) than other large retailers in California."[33] Not surprisingly, then, according to Walmart's own data, "24% of its workforce, and 46% of dependent children are either uninsured or enrolled in a public health program,"[34] numbers that are higher than for comparable other large retailers. It is important to note that retail workers earn comparatively less than the average private employee, are more likely to work part-time, and are, therefore, comparatively disadvantaged vis-à-vis most employees, which makes the comparison of Walmart to other large retailers particularly relevant.

The state of Georgia released data on Medicaid enrollment by employees of various employers. "Dependents of Walmart employees accounted for 10,000 of the 166,000 children enrolled in the state's Children's Health Insurance Program (PeachCare) in 2003." Using data on the extent of coverage and amount spent on health insurance costs by Walmart, Ken Jacobs, the chair of the Center for Labor Research at UC Berkeley, estimated that "Medicaid for Walmart employees and their child dependents cost $455 million a year" and that "uncompensated care to Walmart workers adds an additional $220 million in costs shifted to public and private sources."[35]

As the example of Walmart and the evidence from multiple sources, methods, and geographic regions suggests, the issue of externalized costs—costs shifted onto the general public by private employers—for health care specifically but also other aspects of the employment relationship such as low wages that cause people to rely on public assistance, is economically substantial.

Even while cost shifting occurs with respect to health care, other social insurance systems have put policies in place that reduce the ability of companies to completely externalize the costs of their workforce-related decisions, and therefore these policies encourage companies to become more responsible employers. Two relevant examples are the unemployment insurance system and workers' compensation insurance. In both instances, the rates that employers pay per employee to state government or private insurers are adjusted to reflect employer experience.

Just like other insurance systems (such as car insurance), workers' compensation premiums are experience-adjusted for employers' records of compensated workplace injuries—the more workers are injured and the higher the resulting claims, the higher workers' compensation rates get set. This experience-based cost of workers' compensation insurance provides an economic incentive for employers to maintain a safer work environment and thereby save on their premium costs, just as experience-based ratings in auto insurance encourage drivers to do things to avoid accidents and traffic tickets.

Unemployment insurance rates are also typically established to reflect employer experience with firing or laying off employees who then collect such insurance while they are out of a job. Consequently, those employers who have a higher number of ex-employees drawing unemployment benefits pay higher rates to the government to at least partly compensate for this adverse experience and the burden it imposes on governmental budgets.

With respect to physical and mental health, unless and until employers confront the costs of their effects on their employees, they will have neither the data nor the incentive to do a better job at maintaining well-being.

An Example of How to Reduce Cost Shifting

Like all cities in the United States, San Francisco had people who were working but nonetheless uninsured. The city operated a number of health clinics and had a department of public health as well as a hospital, San Francisco General Hospital, where the uninsured received care, paid for by tax dollars. In 2007, then-mayor Gavin Newsom and the board of supervisors passed Healthy San Francisco. One part of the program required employers to spend a minimum of $1.37 per hour per employee on employee health costs. They could do so in one of three ways: purchase private health insurance for their people, contribute to Healthy San Francisco, or pay into a medical reimbursement account for employees who lived outside the city (all health care was delivered by clinics inside the city limits) or earned too much to qualify for the program. "The Health Care Security Ordinance requires businesses with 20 or more workers and nonprofits with 50 or more employees to spend at least $2,849 per year for a full-time employee on health care. For larger employers, the rate is $4,285."[36]

When the program was put in place, the outcry was deafening. The Golden Gate Restaurant Association was just one of many employer groups predicting gloom and doom—that businesses would flee the city because of the incremental wage costs, that attracting other enterprises into the city would be more difficult, and that the system wouldn't work. None of the dire predictions came true—the San Francisco restaurant industry continues to thrive and employment in the city has grown. What did happen is that uninsured fell to only 3 percent of the city's population and that the program "dramatically cut the use of city emergency rooms for routine care by the program's participants," thereby saving money.[37] Some restaurants added a separate line to the bill showing the cost of their employee contribution; others just folded the cost into higher prices. Meanwhile, high-technology companies such as Twitter have continued to locate in the city and the economic climate remains vibrant. Most important, employers cannot shift the cost of medical care from their books to those of the public.

The short but sad story is that cost shifting is not only inherently unfair; it also increases total costs in the system. That's because health care delayed from an absence of insurance and access to doctors often results in greater expenses when people finally do arrive at the health-care system, because their conditions are more advanced and the opportunity to prevent disease or disease progression in the first place has been mostly lost. In San Francisco, "'There were amazing stories early on of people who lived in San Francisco their whole lives and never had access to health care,' Dr. Hali Hammer [medical director of San Francisco General Hospital's Family Health Center] said. People showed up with undiagnosed diabetes, high blood pressure, or even metastatic cancers. Some women had never had a Pap smear."[38] That's why an emphasis on early intervention, both in promoting healthier lifestyles but also healthier work environments, and getting people medical treatment earlier saves money, resulting in fewer hospitalizations and fewer days spent in high-cost delivery settings. Reducing or eliminating cost shifting is not only fairer in that companies become more responsible for the consequences of their workplace decisions, but it also reduces total costs.

What is true for health insurance is also true for other harmful workplace practices. Companies, not having to deal with the costs of laying people off, lay off more people than they would if they had to pay for the adverse health consequences of layoffs. Companies that overwork their employees face no burden when those individuals leave their employer or the labor force if they are too burned out to work—they become society's responsibility. Therefore, there is less incentive than there otherwise would be to manage work hours or other aspects of the work environment more effectively. This socialization or externalization of the private costs of operating unhealthy workplaces is both a serious problem and one that is potentially addressable. If companies were responsible for the social costs of what they do to their employees, they would make better decisions based on the true costs (and benefits) from choices about workplace practices.

NO TRADE-OFF BETWEEN HEALTH AND PROFITS

As we have seen in both the examples and systematic research reviewed throughout this book, inducing companies to concern themselves with employee health does *not* invariably compromise productivity, quality, or profitability. In fact, healthy workplaces are usually more profitable and productive ones. Not only are physically healthy employees more productive and absent less frequently, such employees impose lower costs on employers that offer health insurance or health care.

To take just one example, consider the case of Walmart, which, as already noted, has historically been stingy with its health-care benefits and also has reduced employment, increasing economic insecurity. The company also has paid its people relatively poorly compared to other retailers. As reported by *Bloomberg Businessweek,* between 2008 and 2013 Walmart added 455 stores in the United States, a 13 percent increase, while it reduced its US workforce by about twenty thousand people, or 1.4 percent. The result? For six years in a row, Walmart ranked either last or tied for last place on the American Customer Satisfaction Index's ratings of discount and department stores. Walmart suffered from unstocked shelves as the reduced number of employees per store, from 343 in 2008 to an average of 301 in 2013, left the stores understaffed with long checkout lines and not enough people to restock merchandise.[39] Walmart's same-store sales growth stalled.

MIT management professor Zeynep Ton has argued that higher pay, which improves people's economic security, actually helps retailers by attracting a better workforce and reducing costly turnover.[40] Companies like food purveyor Trader Joe's and Costco, a direct Walmart competitor, pay better, offer better benefits including health insurance, and are able to realize almost twice the sales per employee as Walmart. So even after accounting for the incremental costs, profits per employee are higher.

So if doing things that produce healthier work environments pay off for both employees and employers, why don't more companies do it? Suffice it to say that, for one thing, companies do not invariably implement their knowledge, something my colleague Bob Sutton and I have called the knowing-doing gap.[41] Second, the pull of conventional wisdom is strong, and few companies want to risk being different. Years ago, I commented on the paradox of wanting to earn exceptional returns but to do so by doing what everyone else was doing—something not likely to happen.[42]

Third, there is a time discontinuity. In order to earn a return on investment, it is necessary, by definition, to first make the investment. You cannot earn a return without first doing something. The delay between changing management practices to increase health and well-being and seeing a return is not likely to be that long. But in today's world, anything more than a quarter or two for a publicly traded company may be unacceptable, and the uncertainty of the payoff and timing leaves many leaders pursuing seemingly less risky strategies such as acquisitions—even though these seldom pay off—or relentless cost cutting.

Nonetheless, inducing employers to adopt management practices to enhance employee health is almost certainly the most cost-efficient way to reduce the hundreds of billions of dollars and lives lost because of harmful employer choices. Employers are in the best position to both prevent and remediate employee health issues much more cost-effectively than the government, because employers have both the information and incentives to do so. Walmart, ironically, is already entering aspects of health-care delivery, not just through its pharmacies but also through clinics that give flu shots and do other routine preventive activities in its stores. There is little doubt that Walmart and other employers could both modify their management practices to prevent deleterious health effects in the first place—the most cost-efficient way of providing better health—and also are positioned to recognize health issues earlier and intervene to remedy employee health problems before they become costlier.

MAKING HUMAN HEALTH A PRIORITY

On March 3, 1993, Scott Adams published one of my very favorite *Dilbert* comic strips. In the first frame, the boss says what so many companies ritualistically promulgate: "I've been saying for years that 'employees are our most valuable asset.'" In the second frame, the boss admits that he was wrong, and that "money is our most valuable asset. Employees are ninth." In the final frame, Wally asks what came in eighth? The answer: "Carbon paper."[43]

Sad, but all too true. People and their well-being receive more talk than priority in organizational decisions. Even companies that presumably emphasize health don't invariably implement policies consistent with building a healthy workforce. Consider Aetna. While on the one hand Aetna's CEO is on a health kick and the company has implemented meditation and health promotion policies, Aetna also, virtually every year, engages in downsizing activities in which people are offered early retirement or laid off.[44] We know that layoffs have serious adverse health consequences. Moreover, as a result of the rounds of downsizing, their CEO, Mark Bertolini, noted that "out of 50,000 employees, we probably have less than 1,600 employees who have been with the company longer than 20 years."

Companies are under pressure to make profits and grow stock price, and woe be to employee-centric policies that are perceived as antithetical to those objectives. Whole Foods Market, under the leadership of CEO John Mackey, emphasized values that included taking care of team members. During the 2008 recession, the company laid off fewer than one hundred people, according to a Whole Foods leader in the San Francisco Bay Area. The company's reliance on self-managing teams to make decisions provided people with a sense of job control, and its promotion from within policy made it possible for even individuals without a college degree to advance up the management ranks. The company offered reasonably generous benefits, including "a discount of at least 20 percent on store items, a low-cost health-care plan, and the ability to vote on important benefits."[45] But when its stock price stalled, Whole Foods was besieged by hedge fund investors who eventually forced a sale to Amazon. At a town meeting with employees after the transaction was announced, Mackey, a leader in the conscious capitalism movement, commented that Whole Foods had "a little bit too much team member focus"[46] and talked about taking $300 million out of the company's cost structure.

In response to a growing recognition that measures such as GDP or GDP per capita at a national level, and profits and share price at a company level, may be too narrow as performance indicators, there has been a proliferation of other indicators of social system performance. Starting in 2012, at the urging of the United Nations, there is now a World Happiness Report.[47] The World Economic Forum's Inclusive Development Index (and corresponding report) recognizes the need to measure the extent of participation in and benefits from economic growth—how widely shared prosperity is.[48] The OECD Better Life Index, launched in 2011, seeks to bring together internationally recognized measures of well-being, conceived more broadly. The dimensions of well-being include housing, income, jobs, community (quality of the social support network), education, environmental quality, governance, health, life satisfaction, safety, and work-life balance.[49] At the company level, there is discussion of the triple bottom line, an accounting framework that seeks to go beyond just economic measures such as profits and return on investment to consider environmental and social aspects of performance as well.[50] While all of these efforts, and countless similar others, to expand the dimensions and measurements of performance are well-intentioned, few or no measures have taken narrowly focused economic indicators off center stage. As one person said about the balanced-scorecard movement, although there are multiple measures, there is seldom much balance in that accounting measures of profits and cash flow dominate attention and dominate decision making.

But this needs to change. There are clearly moral limits on what a humane and civilized society permits or at least should permit to occur. Some of those restrictions delimit what employers can do to their workers. For instance, the United Nations charter outlaws slavery, even though slavery might increase profits, as labor costs would be dramatically lower. UN guidelines also prohibit the exploitation of children, and child labor laws exist in virtually all OECD countries including the United States. The underlying idea is that investing in children is good for the larger society and having children get educated rather than spend all day at work builds a country's human capital. Even if children, or employers, want to exploit child labor, it is in a country's collective interest to preclude such behavior. Similarly with workplace safety. Although there obviously are variations in the dangers inherent in different occupations—coal mining is more dangerous than being a university professor, to take one clear example—even in dangerous occupations civilized countries impose regulations that attempt to delimit the harm from engaging in the work. We value human life and try to protect it, at least within reason.

Social psychological research shows that for most people, there are limits to the decisions they will permit market pricing and market exchange to control. As University of Pennsylvania social psychologist Philip Tetlock has summarized:

> On the one hand, as economists frequently remind us, we live in a world of scarce resources in which, like it or not, everything must ultimately take on an implicit or explicit price. . . . On the other hand, sociological observers point out that people often insist with apparently great conviction that certain commitments and relationships are sacred and that even to contemplate trade-offs with the secular values of money or convenience is anathema.[51]

Research shows that people responded to taboo trade-offs with attempts to physically cleanse themselves and with moral outrage.[52]

Of course, what is considered sacred and nonnegotiable depends on the particular time in history and the particular cultural context. Nonetheless, in part because most religious traditions hold human life to be both valuable and sacred, human life and, by extension, human well-being are mostly not exchangeable in markets. The idea of selling body parts for cash appears unseemly to most people, as do conditions that degrade human dignity.

Framed in this way, the cost of 120,000 human lives lost to workplace conditions that are both known and at least to some degree remediable seems inconsistent with fundamental moral precepts and values. Leaving aside the health-care costs of these management practices, it seems taboo and unacceptable to trade people's lives for organizational considerations of cost and efficiency. If this is true, then human health and well-being necessarily should play a much larger role in both organizational and public policy decisions and discussions.

WHAT DO WE VALUE?

In numerous ways, documented throughout this book, we have seen that work organizations have a choice: to create workplaces and implement management practices that create physical and mental ill-health, that literally kill people, and that drive up health-care costs in the process, or to make different choices that result in the exact opposite outcomes. If a society believes that human life is important, indeed, sacred, then it would neither ignore the voluminous research that I have only briefly summarized in this volume about the effects of workplaces on health nor permit unnecessary deaths of human beings to continue. We would worry as much about human health in our economic activities and development as we do now about endangered species and air and water pollution.

And implicitly, employees have some choices to make as well. People choose where they will work. In making that choice, people need to consider the effect of their employer and its workplace practices on their physical and mental well-being and, indeed, on their very life expectancy. Long work hours, an absence of job control, work-family conflict, an absence of social support to cope with stress, the instability created by layoffs, and an absence of health insurance are more than just inconveniences or nuisances. These conditions are, as extensively documented by decades of empirical research, literally a threat to employees' lives. Thus, decisions about where to work should consider the management environment employees are going to face, not just salary and whether or not the job seems interesting. After all, money cannot bring back health or for that matter resurrect people who have lost their lives because of their work environments.

If this book stimulates analysis and interventions that enhance human health and reduce health-care costs, I will be thrilled. If it provokes a deeper discussion of how employers can change their work environments to lower the damage being produced, my research efforts will have paid off. If it actually changes the policy debate to focus on an overlooked but critically important dimension of health and well-being, both the book and I will have achieved a great deal. And maybe, just maybe, some people will live longer and healthier lives.

But I approach this effort with realism about the obstacles. Because I vividly recall a conversation with a religious leader engaged in activities to deliver health care and promote human health.

In July 1999, at a resort in the Florida Keys, I led a board of directors retreat for Holy Cross Hospital of Fort Lauderdale, Florida, to convince the board to follow the wishes of their CEO, John Johnson, and implement a set of high-commitment work practices. At dinner one evening, I was seated to the right of the nun who, at that time, ran the health-care operations of the Sisters of Mercy, the Catholic religious order that sponsored Holy Cross and was a member of the hospital's board. Making conversation, I asked her how she competed in the Washington, DC, policy arena against people from insurance companies and drug companies with lots of campaign contributions to distribute. I don't remember the sister's name, but I will never forget her reply and our interaction:

> "I tell the senators or the representatives that no one is precisely sure what happens when you die, but on the possibility that they will meet their maker and be judged, they should consider the consequences for people and their well-being of the decisions they are making."
>
> "Is that effective?" I asked.
>
> "Jeffrey, can I call you Jeffrey?" she continued. "When our elected representatives have to choose between campaign cash and their immortal souls, I'm sorry to say that most of the time, the cash wins out."

Many times organizational leaders will have to make a similar sort of decision—how much priority to give people's health, lives, and well-being, or how much priority to give to "cash" as those leaders decide about workplace practices and the environment in which people work. I would like to think that the importance and sanctity of human life and welfare will win out. But I do follow the news, as firms like 3G Capital, the highly respected investment firm, lay off ten thousand people, *one-fifth* of the Kraft and Heinz workforce, following Heinz's takeover of Kraft[53]—and earn plaudits rather than opprobrium from the investment community for doing so.

As I think about my conversation with the sister on that long-ago evening in Florida, I wonder what will happen to the souls of people who lead companies in ways that show disdain for the well-being and indeed the lives of their follow human beings. But my nun dinner companion from that evening didn't wonder. She knew.

Acknowledgments

Numerous people contributed in a variety of ways to the development of this book. I am grateful to all of them for the many ways in which each was helpful and supportive.

Nuria Chinchilla, a professor at IESE in Barcelona, helped inspire my initial interest in social pollution (her apt phrase) and the many effects of work environments on people. Her invitation for me to participate in a (never held) conference led to my doing my first writing on the topic of human sustainability. I value my conversations with her and her gracious hospitality and kindnesses during our visits to the school. Over the years, she has become a good friend and has provided much encouragement for this project.

I would have never had the opportunity to meet and interact with Nuria over the years except that the now-former dean of IESE, Jordi Canals, was kind enough to form an ongoing relationship with me out of an early sabbatical visit. Jordi is an extraordinary individual whom I deeply respect. He has talked with me over the years about sustainability and business leaders' broader responsibilities, and he led a school where values infused many aspects of its operations.

And I would have never met Jordi or visited IESE in the first place had it not been for my wonderful friend and colleague, Fabrizio Ferraro. Fabrizio started the Getting Things Done short-focused program during just his second year at IESE, 2006. Each May I have had the privilege of working with him and his colleagues on this program. I have developed many friends at IESE from my visits. Fabrizio was a PhD student in the Management Science and Engineering Department at Stanford and collaborated with Bob Sutton and me on a paper. So in a sense, I met Fabrizio through Bob, who therefore also played a role in the evolution of this research project. I so appreciate Bob's friendship and his being such a great colleague. This story shows how things evolve from small beginnings and meetings in ways that probably no one could have anticipated!

For several years after I became interested in the topic of the effects of the workplace on human health I wanted to obtain an estimate of the aggregate toll of harmful work practices on people and health-care costs. I knew I did not have the modeling and mathematical skills to fully accomplish this. Then, a colleague recommended I talk to Stefanos Zenios in our Operations and Information Technology group at Stanford's GSB. Stefanos told me he was working with a doctoral student, Joel Goh, who might be interested in helping us. Thus began a collaboration that has resulted in several published papers. To describe working with Joel and Stefanos as a privilege and pleasure would be a shockingly huge understatement. I am as proud of the work we did as of anything I have done in my more than forty-year professional career. Brilliant beyond compare and fantastically lovely human beings, Joel and Stefanos have enriched my life and my thinking in many ways.

A large number of people were willing to share their often painful individual stories about the health effects of their workplace with me. I appreciate their time, their candor, and their willingness to reveal very personal aspects of their lives. For obvious reasons, including the fact that many are under nondisparagement agreements, I do not list their names here. Two people were enormously helpful to me in uncovering and making contact with many of the people I talked to. A huge, enormous, special thanks to Amanda Enayati and Christy Johnson. Their unwavering support, substantive help, and enthusiasm for this project has in many ways made the final product possible.

Many individuals were willing to spend time talking with me about what they were doing in their companies to build healthy workplaces where people could thrive. Thanks for the time and wisdom of Dean Carter, Robert Chapman, Andrew Halpert, Corina Kolbe, Lauren Miller, Ben Stewart, and Heather Wasielewski.

The resources, including time and financial support, provided by my employer, the Graduate School of Business at Stanford University, were instrumental in my being able to do the many interviews and having the time to do the writing of this book. I never take that support for granted, and truly appreciate the unique environment in which I work.

My agents, Christy Fletcher and Don Lamm, helped me place the book and think through the trade-offs involved in such a decision. Don provided good advice and many helpful suggestions on an earlier draft of the manuscript. An inveterate editor and good friend, I so appreciate Don's wisdom and support of the project.

My editor, Hollis Heimbouch of HarperCollins, is, in a word, perfect. She "got" what this project was about and did not try to turn the book or me into something that we weren't, even as she provided the editorial support that made the final manuscript more accessible and better in numerous ways. I am blessed to have worked with Hollis on my last two books. She is the best—smart, insightful, and just the perfect balance of supportive and development-oriented.

And always, there is Kathleen. No one, least of all us, could have predicted the consequences of our chance meeting at a party in San Francisco at approximately 10 p.m. on January 19, 1985. In our now thirty-one years of marriage, we have been through a lot together, ranging from the health issues that invariably arise as one ages to traveling to more than forty countries. She is truly my muse. To the best of my knowledge, I have only one life. I am fortunate beyond all belief to be able to spend so much of that one life with the person that friends years ago nicknamed "the Amazing Kathleen." She was, is, and always will be amazing to me.

Jeffrey Pfeffer, August 2017

Notes

Introduction

1. Occupational Safety and Health Administration Commonly Used Statistics, www.osha.gov/oshstats/commonstats.html.
2. "Causes of Stress," WebMD, www.webmd.com/balance/guide/causes-of-stress.
3. "Stress in America," American Psychological Association, February 4, 2015, www.apa.org/news/press/releases/stress/2014/stress-report.pdf.
4. Douglas LaBier, "Another Survey Shows the Continuing Toll of Workplace Stress," *Psychology Today*, April 23, 2014, www.psychologytoday.com/blog/the-new-resilience/201404/another-survey-shows-the-continuing-toll-workplace-stress.
5. Rita Pyrillis, "Employers Missing the Point of Rising Employee Stress," *Workforce*, March/April 2017, 18.
6. LaBier, "Another Survey."
7. See, for instance, J. Combs, Y. Liu, A. Hall, and D. Ketchen, "How Much Do High-Performance Work Practices Matter? A Meta-Analysis of Their Effects on Organizational Performance," *Personnel Psychology, 59* (2006): 501–28; and Jody Hoffer Gittell, Rob Seidner, and Julian Wimbush, "A Relational Model of How High-Performance Work Systems Work," *Organization Science, 21* (2009): 490–506.
8. Jeffrey Pfeffer, *Competitive Advantage Through People* (Boston: Harvard Business School Press, 1994); and Jeffrey Pfeffer, *The Human Equation: Building Profits by Putting People First* (Boston: Harvard Business School Press, 1998).
9. Jeffrey Pfeffer, *Leadership BS: Fixing Workplaces and Careers One Truth at a Time* (New York: HarperCollins, 2015), Introduction.
10. Doug Lederman, "412 Stanford Layoffs," *Inside Higher Ed*, September 3, 2009, www.insidehighered.com/quicktakes/2009/09/03/412-stanford-layoffs.
11. Stanford University Report, letter from Provost John Etchemendy, March 5, 2003, http://news.stanford.edu/news/2003/march5/freezeletter-35.html.
12. "Mausoleum's Heritage Oak Tree to Be Removed in March," Stanford University News Service, News Release, February 23, 1993, http://news.stanford.edu/pr/93/930223Arc3393.html.
13. Eric Van Susteren, "Stanford Cuts Down Oak Tree at Soccer Stadium," August 7, 2013, www.paloaltoonline.com/news/2013/08/07/stanford-cuts-down-oak-tree-at-soccer-stadium.
14. Pfeffer, *The Human Equation*, Introduction.
15. "An Inconvenient Truth," *Wikipedia*, https://en.wikipedia.org/wiki/An_Inconvenient_Truth.
16. Jeffrey Pfeffer, "Building Sustainable Organizations: The Human Factor," *Academy of Management Perspectives, 24* (2010): 34–45.

Chapter 1: Management Decisions and Human Sustainability

1. Carolyn Said, "Suicide of an Uber Engineer: Widow Blames Job Stress," *San Francisco Chronicle*, April 25, 2017, www.sfchronicle.com/business/article/Suicide-of-an-Uber-engineer-widow-blames-job-11095807.php.
2. Caroline O'Donovan and Priya Anand, "How Uber's Hard-Charging Corporate Culture Left Employees Drained," *BuzzFeed*, July 17, 2017, www.buzzfeed.com/carolineodonovan/how-ubers-hard-charging-corporate-culture-left-employees.
3. David Jolly, "Critics Exploit Telecom Suicides, Ex-Executive Says," *New York Times*, April 1, 2010.
4. David Barboza, "String of Suicides Continues at Electronics Supplier in China," *New York Times*, May 25, 2010.
5. "Tom Sykes, "Did Bank of America Merrill Lynch Intern Moritz Erhardt Die of Stress?" *Daily Beast*, November 22, 2013, www.thedailybeast.com/did-bank-of-america-merrill-lynch-intern-moritz-erhardt-die-of-stress.
6. Cara Clegg, "Five Things that Keep Japanese People Chained to Their Jobs," *SoraNews24*, August 26, 2013, http://rocketnews24.com/2013/08/26/five-things-that-keep-japanese-people-chained-to-their-jobs.
7. Akash Kapur, "Letter from India: Agriculture Left to Die at India's Peril," *New York Times*, January 29, 2010.
8. Eve Tahmincioglu, "Workplace Suicides in the U.S. on the Rise," NBCNews.com, June 1, 2010, www/nbcnews.com/id/37402529/ns/buisness-careers/t/workplace-suicides-us-rise/.
9. See, for instance, the studies summarized in J. Paul Leigh, "Raising the Minimum Wage Could Improve Public Health," Economic Policy Institute, July 28, 2016, www.epi.org/blog/raising-the-minimum-wage-could-improve-public-health/.
10. Jeroen Ansink, "C-Suite Suicides: When Exec Life Becomes a Nightmare," *Fortune*, September 10, 2013, http://fortune.com/2013/09/10/c-suite-suicides-when-exec-life-becomes-a-nightmare/.
11. Christine Hauser, "Five Killed in Orlando Workplace Shooting, Officials Say," June 5, 2017, https://nyti.ms/2rL70pX.
12. "Workplace Violence," *Wikipedia*, https://en.wikipedia.org/wiki/Workplace_violence.
13. Ibid.
14. Bryce Covert, "Getting Murdered at Work Is Incredibly Common in the U.S.," *ThinkProgress*, August 26, 2015, http://thinkprogress.org/getting-murdered-at-work-is-incredibly-common-in-the-u-s-4caf76dfe4cb.
15. L. H. Tsoi, S. Y. Ip, and L. K. Poon, "Monday Syndrome: Using Statistical and Mathematical Models to Fine-tune Services in an Emergency Department," *Hong Kong Journal of Emergency Medicine, 18* (2011): 150–54.
16. "Workplace Stress," American Institute of Stress, www.stress.org/workplace-stress/.
17. Sharon Jayson, "Bad Bosses Can Be Bad for Your Health," *USA Today*, August 5, 2012.
18. Annual surveys of stress in Australia are reported by the Australian Psychological Society. See, for instance, "Australians' Stress Levels Remain High, Survey Reveals," https://www.psychology.org/au/inpsych/2014/deceember/npw.

19. Jeff Cottrill, "Putting Stress on Stress," *OHS Canada*, April 22, 2015, www.ohscanada.com/features/putting-stress-on-stress/.
20. www.workstress.net/sites/default/files/stress.pdf.
21. Devin Fidler, "Work, Interrupted: The New Labor Economics of Platforms," Institute for the Future, November 2016. Quote is from p. 4.
22. Erika Fry and Nicolas Rapp, "Sharing Economy: This Is the Average Pay at Lyft, Uber, Airbnb and More," *Fortune*, June 27, 2017, http://fortune.com/2017/06/27/average-pay-lyft-uber-airbnb/.
23. Jia Tolentino, "The Gig Economy Celebrates Working Yourself to Death," *New Yorker*, March 22, 2017, www.newyorker.com/culture/jia-tolentino/the-gig-economy-celebrates-working-yourself-to-death.
24. Michael Quinlan, Claire Mayhew, and Philip Bohle, "The Global Expansion of Precarious Employment, Work Disorganization, and Consequences for Occupational Health: A Review of Recent Research," *Globalization and Occupational Health, 31* (2001): 335–414. Quote is from p. 335.
25. Joel Goh, Jeffrey Pfeffer, and Stefanos A. Zenios, "Workplace Practices and Health Outcomes: Focusing Health Policy on the Workplace," *Behavioral Science and Policy, 1* (2015), 43-52.
26. Personal e-mail from Professor Dame Carol Black, May 4, 2015.
27. Douglas R. Stover and Jade Wood, "Most Company Wellness Programs Are a Bust," *Gallup Business Journal*, February 4, 2015, www.gallup.com/businessjournal/181481/company-wellness-programs-bust.aspx.
28. "Aetna's 'Social Compact' Continues to Support Employees," Aetna News, https://news.aetna.com/2017/01/aetnas-social-compact-continues-support-employees/.
29. David Gelles, "At Aetna, A C.E.O.'s Management by Mantra," *New York Times*, February 27, 2015, https://nyti.ms/1JVrksM.
30. Bob Chapman and Raj Sisodia, *Everybody Matters: The Extraordinary Power of Caring for Your People Like Family* (New York: Portfolio, 2015).
31. See, for instance, John Mackey and Rajendra Sisodia, *Conscious Capitalism: Liberating the Heroic Spirit of Business* (Boston: Harvard Business Review Press, 2013); and Rajendra Sisodia, Jagdish N. Sheth, and David Wolfe, *Firms of Endearment: How World-Class Companies Profit from Passion and Purpose*, 2nd Ed. (New York: Pearson FT Press), 2014.
32. There was extensive media coverage of this dispute because the United States and Asian countries such as China strenuously objected. For one relevant article, see Mark Schapiro, "Green War in the Skies: Can Europe Make U.S. Planes Pay for Pollution?" *Atlantic*, October 5, 2011.
33. http://gmsustainability.com; search done on October 21, 2014.
34. "Sustainability: Enhancing Sustainability of Operations and Global Value Chains," Walmart, http://corporate.walmart.com/global-responsibility/environmental-sustainability.
35. Ibid.
36. Larry W. Beeferman, Director, Pensions and Capital Stewardship Project, Harvard Law School, "Memo RE: Incorporating Labor and Human Rights and Human Capital Risks into Investment Decisions: Conference and Research/Action Agenda," August 12, 2008.
37. www.btplc.com/Responsiblebusiness/ourstory/sustainabilityreport/report/Bbus/G2W/health.aspx.

38. Louise C. O'Keefe, Kathleen C. Brown, and Becky J. Christian, "Policy Perspectives on Occupational Stress," *Workplace Health and Safety, 62* (2014): 432–38.
39. For a review, see Steven L. Sauter, Lawrence R. Murphy, and Joseph J. Hurrell Jr., "Prevention of Work-Related Psychological Disorders: A National Strategy Proposed by the National Institute for Occupational Safety and Health (NIOSH), *American Psychologist, 45 (1990)*: 1146–58.
40. "What Is Total Worker Health?" National Institute for Occupational Safety and Health, www.cdc.gov/niosh/twh/totalhealth.html.
41. O'Keefe, et al., "Policy Perspectives," 432.
42. Personal communication from Professor Dame Carol Black, May 4, 2015.
43. Robert Kerr, Marie McHugh, and Mark McCrory, "HSE Management Standards and Stress-Related Work Outcomes," *Occupational Medicine, 59* (2009): 574–79.
44. Health and Safety Executive, *Annual Statistics Report for Great Britain, 2012-2013.*
45. Jeff Hilgert, "A New Frontier for Industrial Relations: Workplace Health and Safety as a Human Right," in James A. Gross and Lance Compa, eds., *Human Rights in Labor and Employment Relations: International and Domestic Perspectives* (Champaign, IL: Labor and Employment Relations Association, 2009), 43–71.
46. Michael Marmot, *The Status Syndrome: How Social Standing Affects Our Health and Longevity* (London, UK: Bloomsbury Publishing, 2004), p. 247.
47. Amartya Sen, *Development as Freedom* (New York: Knopf, 1999).
48. Ibid., 196. See Chapter 8 for an interesting discussion of this phenomenon.
49. Marmot, *The Status Syndrome*, p. 191.
50. See, for instance, Ed Diener, "Subjective Well-Being: The Science of Happiness and a Proposal for a National Index," *American Psychologist, 55* (2000): 34–43.
51. Noreen E. Mahon, Adela Yarcheski, and Thomas J. Yarcheski, "Happiness as Related to Gender and Health in Early Adolescents," *Clinical Nursing Research, 14* (2005): 175–90.
52. Midge N. Ray, Kenneth G. Saag, and Jeroan J. Allison, "Health and Happiness Among Older Adults: A Community-Based Study," *Journal of Health Psychology, 14* (2009): 503–12.
53. J. F. Helliwell, "How's Life? Combining Individual and National Variations to Explain Subjective Wellbeing," *Economic Modelling, 20* (2003): 331–60.
54. *World Database of Happiness: Archive of Research Findings on Subjective Enjoyment of Life* (Rotterdam, Netherlands: Erasmus University), http://worlddatabaseof happiness.eur.nl.
55. Elena Cottini and Claudio Lucifora, "Mental Health and Working Conditions in Europe," *Industrial and Labor Relations Review, 66* (2014): 958–82. Quote is from p. 958.
56. The World Economic Forum, *Working Towards Wellness: The Business Rationale.*
57. S. Mattke, H. Liu, J. P. Caloyeras, C. Y. Huang, K. R. Van Busum, D. Khodyakov, and V. Shier, "Workplace Wellness Programs Study: Final Report" (Santa Monica, CA: RAND Corporation, 2013).
58. Katie Thomas, "Companies Get Strict on Health of Workers," *New York Times,* March 25, 2013.
59. G. Bensinger, "Corporate Wellness, Safeway Style," *San Francisco Chronicle,* January 4, 2009.

60. There is an enormous literature on the effects of job conditions on individual health-related behaviors. See, for instance, M. Harris and M. Fennell, "A Multivariate Model of Job Stress and Alcohol Consumption," *Sociological Quarterly, 29* (1988): 391–406; A. Kouvonen, M. Kivimaki, M. Virtanen, J. Pentti, and J. Vahtera, "Work Stress, Smoking Status, and Smoking Intensity: An Observational Study of 46,190 Employees," *Journal of Epidemiology and Community Health, 59* (2005): 63–69; and N. Nishitani and H. Sakakibara, "Relationship of Obesity to Job Stress and Eating Behavior in Male Japanese Workers," *International Journal of Obesity, 30* (2006): 528–33.
61. Eilene Zimmerman, "The Lawyer, the Addict," *New York Times*, July 15, 2017, www.nytimes.com/2017/07/15/business/lawyers-addiction-mental-health.html.
62. Richard A. Friedman, "What Cookies and Meth Have in Common," *New York Times*, June 30, 2017, https://nyti.ms/2usEBTH.
63. Watson Wyatt Worldwide, "Building an Effective Health and Productivity Framework: 2007/2008," *Staying@Work Report*.
64. Leonard L. Berry, Ann M. Mirabito, and William B. Baun, "What's the Hard Return on Employee Wellness Programs?" *Harvard Business Review, 88*, no. 12 (2010): 104–12.
65. Douglas R. Stover and Jade Wood, "Most Company Wellness Programs Are a Bust," *Gallup Business Journal*, February 4, 2015, www.gallup.com/businessjournal/181481/company-wellness-programs-bust.aspx.
66. Katherine Baicker, David Cutler, and Zirui Song, "Workplace Wellness Programs Can Generate Savings," *Health Affairs, 29* (2010): 304–11. Quote is from p. 304.
67. Al Lewis, Vik Khanna, and Shana Montrose, "Workplace Wellness Produces No Savings," http://healthaffairs.org/blog/2014/11/25/workplace-wellness-produces-no-savings/.
68. John P. Caloyeras, Hangsheng Liu, Ellen Exum, Megan Broderick, and Soeren Mattke, "Managing Manifest Diseases, But Not Health Risks, Saved PepsiCo Money over Seven Years," *Health Affairs, 33* (2014): 124–31. Quote is from p. 124.
69. Mattke, et al., "Workplace Wellness Programs Study."
70. Ralph L. Keeney, "Personal Decisions Are the Leading Cause of Death," *Operations Research, 56* (2008): 1335–47.
71. The OECD publishes extensive health data that it updates annually and makes statistical tables as well as raw data available on its website, www.oecd.org, *Health at a Glance*, 2015.
72. See, for instance, S. Woolhandler and D. Himmelstein, "The Deteriorating Administrative Efficiency of the US Health Care System," *New England Journal of Medicine, 324* (1991): 1253–58.
73. See, for instance, J. Wennberg, E. Fisher, L. Baker, S. Sharp, and K. Bronner, "Evaluating the Efficiency of California Providers in Caring for Patients with Chronic Illness," *Health Affairs, 24* (2005): 526–43; and Y. Ozcan and R. Luke, "A National Study of the Efficiency of Hospitals in Urban Markets," *Health Services Research, 27* (1993): 719–39.
74. J. Paul Leigh and Juan Du, "Are Low Wages Risk Factors for Hypertension?" *European Journal of Public Health, 22* (2012): 854–59.

Chapter 2: The Enormous Toll of Toxic Workplaces

1. J. Paul Leigh, "Economic Burdens of Occupational Injury and Illness in the United States," *Millbank Quarterly, 89* (2011): 728–72. Quote is from p. 729.
2. Kyle Steenland, Carol Burnett, Nina Lalich, Elizabeth Ward, and Joseph Hurrell, "Dying for Work: The Magnitude of US Mortality from Selected Causes of Death Associated with Occupation," *American Journal of Industrial Medicine, 43* (2009): 461–82.
3. "Psychological Wellbeing Boosts Productivity," *Occupational Health News* (Thomson Reuters), Issue 1088, November 12, 2014.
4. "Demedicalize Disgruntled Worker Claims or They'll Get Worse," *Occupational Health News* (Thomson Reuters), Issue 1089, November 19, 2014.
5. Soeren Mattke, Aruna Balakrishnan, Giacomo Bergamo, and Sydne J. Newberry, "A Review of Methods to Measure Health-related Productivity Loss," *American Journal of Management Care, 13* (2007): 211–17. Quote is from p. 211.
6. "Death from Overwork in China," China Labour Bulletin, August 11, 2006, www.clb.org/hk/en/content/death-overwork-china.
7. Deborah Imel Nelson, Marisol Concha-Barrientos, Timothy Driscoll, Kyle Steenland, Marilyn Fingerhut, Laura Punnett, Annette Pruss-Ustun, James Leigh, and Carlos Corvalan, "The Global Burden of Selected Occupational Diseases and Injury Risks: Methodology and Summary," *American Journal of Industrial Medicine, 48* (2005): 400–418.
8. John Daly, "Stress Accounts for 60% of All Lost Days in the Workplace," *Irish Examiner,* October 9, 2015, www.irishexaminer.com/business/stress-accounts-for-60-of-all-lost-days-in-the-workplace-358497.html.
9. Theodore J. Litman, "The Family as a Basic Unit in Health and Medical Care: A Social Behavioral Overview," *Social Science and Medicine, 8* (1974): 495–519.
10. Stephen Birch, Michael Jerrett, Kathi Wilson, Michael Law, Susan Elliott, and John Eylers, "Heterogeneities in the Production of Health: Smoking, Health Status, and Place," *Health Policy, 72* (2005): 301–10.
11. Christopher R. Browning and Kathleen A. Cagney, "Neighborhood Structural Disadvantage, Collective Efficacy, and Self-Rated Physical Health in an Urban Setting," *Journal of Health and Social Behavior, 43* (2002): 383–99.
12. Nicholas A. Christakis and James H. Fowler, "The Spread of Obesity in a Large Social Network Over 12 Years," *New England Journal of Medicine, 357* (2007): 370–79.
13. Brian Borsari and Kate B. Carey, "Peer Influences on College Drinking: A Review of the Research," *Journal of Substance Abuse, 13* (2001): 391–424.
14. Justin C. Strickland and Mark A. Smith, "The Effects of Social Contact on Drug Use: Behavioral Mechanisms Controlling Drug Intake," *Experimental and Clinical Psychopharmacology, 22* (2014): 23–34. Quote is from p. 23.
15. Ellen Wright Clayton, "Ethical, Legal, and Social Implications of Genomic Medicine," *New England Journal of Medicine, 349* (2003): 562–69.
16. For a recent review of this literature, see Daniel C. Ganster and Christopher C. Rosen, "Work Stress and Employee Health: A Multidisciplinary Review," *Journal of Management, 39* (2013): 1085–122.
17. There are scores of studies on this issue. See, for instance, T. Chandola, E. Brunner, and M. Marmot, "Chronic Stress at Work and the Metabolic Syn-

drome: Prospective Study," *British Medical Journal, 332* (2006): 521–525; and M. Kivimaki, P. Leino-Arjas, R. Luukkonen, H. Riihimai, J. Vahtera, and J. Kirjonen, "Work Stress and Risk of Cardiovascular Mortality: Prospective Cohort Study of Industrial Employees," *British Medical Journal, 325* (2002): 857–60.

18. See Joel Goh, Jeffrey Pfeffer, and Stefanos A. Zenios, "The Relationship Between Workplace Stressors and Mortality and Health Costs in the United States," *Management Science, 62* (2016): 608-628.
19. The results of the meta-analyses described in this chapter have also been published as Joel Goh, Jeffrey Pfeffer, and Stefanos A. Zenios, "Workplace Practices and Health Outcomes: Focusing Health Policy on the Workplace," *Behavioral Science and Policy, 1* (2015): 43-52.
20. See, for instance, M. Sverke, J. Hellgren, and K. Naswall, "No Security: A Meta-Analysis and Review of Job Insecurity and Its Consequences," *Journal of Occupational Health Psychology, 7* (2002): 242–64.
21. See A. Bannai and A. Tamakoshi, "The Association Between Long Working Hours and Health: A Systematic Review of the Epidemiological Evidence," *Scandinavian Journal of Work and Environmental Health, 40* (2014): 5–18; and K. Sparks, C. Cooper, Y. Fried, and A. Shirom, "The Effects of Hours of Work on Health: A Meta-Analytic Review," *Journal of Occupational and Organizational Psychology, 70* (1997): 391–408.
22. C. Viswesvaran, J. Sanchez, and J. Fisher, "The Role of Social Support in the Process of Work Stress: A Meta-Analysis," *Journal of Vocational Behavior, 54* (1999): 314–34.
23. See, for instance, M. Kivimaki, S. T. Nyberg, G. D. Batty, E. I. Fransson, K. Heikkila, I. Alfredsson, and T. Theorell, "Job Strain as a Risk Factor for Coronary Heart Disease: A Collaborative Meta-Analysis of Individual Participant Data," *Lancet, 380* (2012): 1491–97.
24. E. L. Idler and Y. Benyamini, "Self-Rated Health and Mortality: A Review of Twenty-seven Community Studies," *Journal of Health and Social Behavior, 38* (1997): 21–37.
25. For instance, see S. Miilunpalo, I. Vuon, P. Oja, M. Pasanen, and H. Urponen, "Self-Rated Health Status as a Health Measure: The Predictive Value of Self-reported Health Status on the Use of Physician Services and on Mortality in the Working-Age Population," *Journal of Clinical Epidemiology, 50* (1997): 517–28; and D. L. McGee, Y. Liao, G. Cao, and R. S. Cooper, "Self-Reported Health Status and Mortality in a Multiethnic US Cohort," *American Journal of Epidemiology, 149* (1999): 41–46.
26. For an explanation of the calculation and interpretation of odds ratios, see www.biochemia-medica.com/content/odds-ratio-calculation-usage-and-interpretation.
27. Joel Goh, Jeffrey Pfeffer, and Stefanos A. Zenios, "Workplace Stressors and Health Outcomes: Health Policy for the Workplace," *Behavioral Science and Policy, 1* (2015): 33–42.
28. "Deaths and Mortality," Centers for Disease Control and Prevention," www.cdc.gov/nchs/fastats/deaths.htm.
29. Much of this research is summarized in Michael Marmot, *The Status Syndrome: How Social Standing Affects Our Health and Longevity* (London, UK: Bloomsbury Publishing, 2004).

30. A. Wilper, S. Woolhandler, K. Lasser, D. McCormich, D. Bor, and D. Himmelstein, "Health Insurance and Mortality in U.S. Adults," *American Journal of Public Health, 99* (2009): 2289–95.
31. Ralph L. Keeney, "Personal Decisions Are the Leading Cause of Death," *Operations Research, 56* (2008): 1335–47.
32. Paul A. Schulte, Gregory R. Wagner, Aleck Ostry, Laura A. Blanciforti, Robert G. Cutlip, Kristine M. Krajnak, Michael Luster, Albert E. Munson, James P. O'Callaghan, Christine G. Parks, Petia P. Simeonova, and Diane B. Miller, "Work, Obesity, and Occupational Safety and Health," *American Journal of Public Health, 97* (2007): 428–36.
33. Michael R. Frone, "Work Stress and Alcohol Use," *Alcohol Research and Health, 23* (1999): 284–91.
34. Anne Kouvonen, Mika Kivimaki, Marianna Virtanen, Jaana Pentti, and Jussi Vahtera, "Work Stress, Smoking Status, and Smoking Intensity: An Observational Study of 46,190 Employees," *Journal of Epidemiology and Community Health, 59* (2005): 63–69.
35. Rajita Sinha, "Chronic Stress, Drug Use, and Vulnerability to Addiction," *Annals of the New York Academy of Sciences, 1141* (2008): 105–30.
36. "Prolonged Exposure to Work-Related Stress Thought to Be Related to Certain Cancers," *ScienceDaily*, January 17, 2017, www.sciencedaily.com/releases/2017/01/170117105044.htm.
37. Jeffrey Pfeffer and Dana Carney, "The Economic Evaluation of Time May Cause Stress," *Academy of Management Discoveries* (in press).
38. See, for instance, S. S. Dickerson and M. E. Kemeny, "Acute Stressors and Cortisol Responses: A Theoretical Integration and Synthesis of Laboratory Research," *Psychological Bulletin, 130* (2004): 355–91; R. G. Reed and C. L. Raison, "Stress and the Immune System," in C. Esser, ed., *Environmental Influences on the Immune System* (New York: Springer, 2016), 97–126; and S. E. Segerstrom and G. E. Miller, "Psychological Stress and the Human Immune System: A Meta-Analytic Study of 30 Years of Inquiry," *Psychological Bulletin, 130* (2004): 601–30.
39. Marmot, *The Status Syndrome*.
40. S. Jay Olshansky, Toni Antonucci, Lisa Berkman, Robert H. Binstock, Axel Boersch-Supan, John T. Cacioppo, Bruce A. Carnes, Laura L. Carstensen, Linda P. Fried, Dana P. Goldman, James Jackson, Martin Kohli, John Rother, Yuhui Zheng, and John Rowe, "Differences in Life Expectancy Due to Race and Educational Differences are Widening, and Many May Not Catch Up," *Health Affairs, 8* (2012): 1803–13.
41. Michael Marmot, "Social Determinants of Health Inequalities," *Lancet, 365* (2005): 1099–104.
42. Marmot, *The Status Syndrome*.
43. S. Anand, "The Concern for Equity in Health," *Journal of Epidemiological and Community Health, 56* (2002): 485–87.
44. E. E. Gakidou, C. J. L. Murray, and J. Frenk, "Defining and Measuring Health Inequality: An Approach Based on the Distribution of Health Expectancy," *Bulletin of the World Health Organization, 78* (2000): 42–54. Quote is from p. 42.
45. See, for instance, Amy M. Christie and Julian Barling, "Disentangling the Indirect Links Between Socioeconomic Status and Health: The Dynamic Roles of

Work Stressors and Personal Control," *Journal of Applied Psychology, 94* (2009): 1466–78.

46. Jane C. Clougherty, Kerry Souza, and Mark R. Cullen, "Work and Its Role in Shaping the Social Gradient in Health," *Annals of the New York Academy of Sciences, 1186* (2010): 102–24. Quote is from p. 102.
47. Joel Goh, Jeffrey Pfeffer, and Stefanos A. Zenios, "How Differences in Work Environments Help Account for Inequality in Lifespans," *Health Affairs, 34* (2015): 1761–68.
48. L. T. Yen, D. W. Edington, and P. Witting, "Associations Between Health Risk Appraisal Scores and Employee Medical Claims Costs in a Manufacturing Company," *American Journal of Health Promotion, 6* (1991): 46–54.
49. Dee Edington, "Helping Employees Stay Healthy Is a Good Investment," Society for Human Resource Management, February 10, 2014, www.shrm.org/resourcesandtools/hr-topics/benefits/pages/dee-edington.aspx.
50. Alicia A. Grandey and Russell Cropanzano, "The Conservation of Resources Model Applied to Work-Family Conflict and Strain," *Journal of Vocational Behavior, 54* (1999): 350–70.
51. Antonio Chirumbolo and Johnny Hellgren, "Individual and Organizational Consequences of Job Insecurity: A European Study," *Economic and Industrial Democracy, 24* (2003): 217–40.
52. Shirley Musich, Deborah Napier, and D. W. Edington, "The Association of Health Risks with Workers' Compensation Costs," *Journal of Occupational and Environmental Medicine, 43* (2001): 534–41.
53. W. N. Burton, D. J. Conti, C. Y. Chen, A. B. Schultz, and D. W. Edington, "The Role of Health Risk Factors and Disease on Worker Productivity," *Journal of Occupational and Environmental Medicine, 41* (1999): 863–77.
54. Wayne N. Burton, Glenn Pransky, Daniel J. Conti, Cin-Yu Chen, and Dee W. Edington, "The Association of Medical Conditions and Presenteeism," *Journal of Occupational and Environmental Medicine, 46* (2004): S38–S45.
55. Alyssa B. Schultz and Dee W. Edington, "Employee Health and Presenteeism: A Systematic Review," *Journal of Occupational Rehabilitation, 17* (2007): 547–79.

Chapter 3: Layoffs and Economic Insecurity

1. Michael Luo, "For Workers at Closing Plant, Ordeal Included Heart Attacks," *New York Times*, February 25, 2010.
2. Michael Winerip, "Set Back by Recession, and Shut Out of Rebound, Older Workers Find Age Bias at Each Turn," *New York Times*, August 27, 2013, B1.
3. James A. Evans, Gideon Kunda, and Stephen R. Barley, "Beach Time, Bridge Time, and Billable Hours: The Temporal Structure of Technical Contracting," *Administrative Science Quarterly, 49* (2004): 1–38.
4. Lawrence F. Katz and Alan B. Krueger, "The Rise and Nature of Alternative Work Arrangements in the United States, 1995–2015," Working Paper #603 (Princeton University, Industrial Relations Section), September 2016. Quote is from p. 7.
5. Bryce Covert, "How Unpredictable Hours Are Screwing Up People's Lives," *ThinkProgress*, September 11, 2014, https://thinkprogress.org/how-unpredictable-hours-are-screwing-up-peoples-lives-6ebd2d393662.

6. Jonathan Rauch, "The Conservative Case for Unions," *Atlantic,* July/August 2017, 15.
7. Lydia DePillis, "The Next Labor Fight Is over When You Work, Not How Much You Make," *Washington Post,* May 9, 2015.
8. Christopher Nohe, Alexandra Michel, and Karlheinz Sonntag, "Family-Work Conflict and Job Performance: A Diary Study of Boundary Conditions and Mechanisms," *Journal of Organizational Behavior, 35* (2014): 339–57. Quote is from p. 339.
9. Joel Goh, Jeffrey Pfeffer, and Stefanos A. Zenios, "The Relationship Between Workplace Stressors and Mortality and Health Costs in the United States," *Management Science, 62* (2016): 608–28.
10. Arne L. Kalleberg, *Good Jobs, Bad Jobs* (New York: Russell Sage Foundation, 2011). Quote is from p. 85.
11. Ibid., 100.
12. Louis Uchitelle, *The Disposable American: Layoffs and Their Consequences* (New York: Knopf, 2006).
13. Deepak K. Datta, James P. Guthrie, Dynah Basuil, and Alankrita Pandey, "Causes and Effects of Employee Downsizing: A Review and Synthesis," *Journal of Management, 36* (2010): 281–348.
14. Peter Cappelli, *The New Deal at Work: Managing the Market-Driven Workforce* (Boston: Harvard Business School Press, 1999).
15. www.wecglobal.org/.
16. World Employment Confederation, *The Future of Work: White Paper from the Employment Industry* (Brussels, Belgium: September 2016).
17. P. Virtanen, U. Janiert, and A. Hammarstrom, "Exposure to Temporary Employment and Job Insecurity: A Longitudinal Study of Health Effects," *Occupational and Environmental Medicine, 68* (2011): 570–74. Quote is from p. 570.
18. Anna-Karin Waenerlund, Pekke Virtanen, and Anne Hammarstrom, "Is Temporary Employment Related to Health Status? Analysis of the Northern Swedish Cohort," *Scandinavian Journal of Public Health, 39* (2011): 533–39.
19. Minsoo Jung, "Health Disparities Among Wage Workers Driven by Employment Instability in the Republic of Korea," *International Journal of Health Services, 43* (2013): 483–98.
20. Magnus Sverke, Johnny Hellgren, and Katharina Naswall, "No Security: A Meta-Analysis and Review of Job Insecurity and Its Consequences," *Journal of Occupational Health Psychology, 7* (2002): 242–64.
21. Mel Bartley, "Job Insecurity and Its Effect on Health," *Journal of Epidemiology and Community Health, 59* (2005): 718–19. Quote is from p. 719.
22. Eileen Y. Chou, Bidhan L. Parmar, and Adam D. Galinsky, "Economic Insecurity Increases Physical Pain," *Psychological Science, 27* (2016): 443–54.
23. Sepideh Modrek and Mark R. Cullen, "Job Insecurity During Recessions: Effects on Survivors' Work Stress," *BMC Public Health,* October 6, 2013, https://bmcpublichealth.biomedcentral.com/articles/10.1186/1471-2458-13-929.
24. See, for instance, Mohamad Alameddine, Andrea Baumann, Audrey Laporte, and Raisa Deber, "A Narrative Review on the Effect of Economic Downturns on the Nursing Labour Market: Implications for Policy and Planning," *Human Resources for Health, 10* (2012), https://human-resources-health.biomedcentral.com/articles/10.1186/1478-4491-10-23.

25. Ralph Catalano, Sidra Goldman-Mellor, Katherine Saxton, Claire Margerison-Zildo, Meenakshi Subbaraman, Kaja LeWinn, and Elizabeth Anderson, "The Health Effects of Economic Decline," *Annual Review of Public Health, 32* (2011): 431–50. Quote is from p. 432.
26. Ibid., 431.
27. Jane E. Ferrie, Hugo Westerlund, Marianna Virtanen, Jussi Vahtera, and Mika Kivimaki, "Flexible Labor Markets and Employee Health," *Scandinavian Journal of Work, Environment, and Health, 34* (2008): 98–110.
28. Vera Keefe, Papaarangi Reid, Clint Ormsby, Bridget Robson, Gordon Purdie, Joanne Baxter, and Ngati Kahungunu Iwi Incorporated, "Serious Health Events Following Involuntary Job Loss in New Zealand Meat Processing Workers," *International Journal of Epidemiology, 31* (2002): 1155–61.
29. Marcus Eliason and Donald Storrie, "Does Job Loss Shorten Life?" *Journal of Human Resources, 44* (2009): 277–301.
30. Margit Kriegbaum, Ulla Christensen, Rikke Lund, and Merete Osler, "Job Losses and Accumulated Number of Broken Partnerships Increase Risk of Premature Mortality in Danish Men Born in 1953," *Journal of Occupational and Environmental Medicine, 51* (2009): 708–13.
31. Daniel Sullivan and Till von Wachter, "Mortality, Mass-Layoffs, and Career Outcomes: An Analysis Using Administrative Data," Cambridge, MA: National Bureau of Economic Research, Working Paper 13626, November 2007.
32. Kate W. Strully, "Job Loss and Health in the U.S. Labor Market," *Demography, 46* (2009): 221–46. Quote is from p. 233.
33. Ibid., 240.
34. Matthew E. Dupre, Linda K. George, Guangya Liu, and Eric D. Peterson, "The Cumulative Effect of Unemployment on Risks for Acute Myocardial Infarction," *Archives of Internal Medicine, 172* (2012): 1731–37.
35. Mika Kivimaki, Jussi Vahtera, Jaana Pentti, and Jane E. Ferrie, "Factors Underlying the Effect of Organisational Downsizing on Health of Employees: Longitudinal Cohort Study," *British Medical Journal, 320* (2000): 971–75.
36. Leon Grunberg, Sarah Moore, and Edward S. Greenberg, "Managers' Reactions to Implementing Layoffs: Relationship to Health Problems and Withdrawal Behaviors," *Human Resource Management, 45* (2006): 159–78.
37. Matthew B. Stannard and Rachel Gordon, "2 Men, Woman Slain in Mountain View," *San Francisco Chronicle*, November 15, 2008.
38. Joseph A. Kinney and Dennis L. Johnson, *Breaking Point: The Workplace Violence Epidemic and What to Do About It* (Charlotte, NC: National Safe Workplace Institute, 1993).
39. "Workplace Violence—Is It Getting Worse?" www.dailyhrtips.com/2010/10/01/hr-blog-workplace-violence/.
40. Ralph Catalano, Raymond W. Novaco, and William McConnell, "Layoffs and Violence Revisited," *Aggressive Behavior, 28* (2002): 233–47. Quote is from p. 235. The quote refers to an earlier study, R. Catalano, D. Dooley, R. Novaco, G. Wilson, and R. Hough, "Using ECA Survey Data to Examine the Effect of Job Layoffs on Violent Behavior," *Hospital and Community Psychiatry, 44* (1993): 874–78.
41. Ibid.
42. Ibid., 435.

43. U. Janlert and A. Hammarstrom, "Alcohol Consumption Among Unemployed Youths: Results from a Prospective Study," *British Journal of Addiction, 87* (1992): 703–14.
44. A. Hammarstrom, "Health Consequences of Youth Unemployment," *Public Health, 108* (1994): 403–12.
45. A. C. Merline, P. M. O'Malley, J. E. Schulenberg, J. G. Bachman, and L. D. Johnston, "Substance Use Among Adults 35 Years of Age: Prevalence, Adulthood Predictors, and Impact of Adolescent Substance Abuse," *American Journal of Public Health, 94* (2004): 96–102.
46. Janlert and Hammatstrom, "Alcohol Consumption."
47. D. Dooley and J. Prause, "Underemployment and Alcohol Misuse in the National Longitudinal Survey of Youth," *Journal of Studies of Alcohol, 59* (1998): 669–80.
48. Wayne F. Cascio, *Responsible Restructuring* (San Francisco, CA: Berrett-Koehler, 2002).
49. Art Budros, "The New Capitalism and Organizational Rationality: The Adoption of Downsizing Programs, 1979–1994," *Social Forces, 76* (1997): 229–50.
50. Art Budros, "Organizational Types and Organizational Innovation: Downsizing Among Industrial, Financial and Utility Firms," *Sociological Forum, 17* (2000): 307–42; and Art Budros, "Causes of Early and Later Organizational Adoption: The Case of Corporate Downsizing," *Sociological Inquiry, 74* (2004): 355–80.
51. See, for instance, C. L. Ahmadjian and P. Robinson, "Safety in Numbers: Downsizing and the Deinstitutionalization of Permanent Employment in Japan," *Administrative Science Quarterly, 46* (2001): 622–54; and C. Tsai, S. Wuy, H. Wang, and I. Huang, "An Empirical Research on the Institutional Theory of Downsizing: Evidence from MNC's Subsidiary Companies in Taiwan," *Total Quality Management & Business Excellence, 17* (2006): 633–54.
52. Dan L. Worrell, Wallace N. Davidson III, and Varinder M. Sharma, "Layoff Announcements and Stockholder Wealth," *Academy of Management Journal, 34* (1991): 662–78.
53. Robert D. Nixon, Michaell A. Hitt, Ho-uk Lee, and Eui Jeong, "Market Reactions to Announcements of Corporate Downsizing Actions and Implementation Strategies," *Strategic Management Journal, 25* (2004): 1121–29.
54. Peggy M. Lee, "A Comparative Analysis of Layoff Announcements and Stock Price Reactions in the United States and Japan," *Strategic Management Journal, 18* (1997): 879–94.
55. Morley Gunderson, Anil Verma, and Savita Verma, "Impact of Layoff Announcements on the Market Value of the Firm," *Relations Industrielles/Industrial Relations, 52* (1997): 364–81.
56. Datta, et al., "Causes and Effects of Employee Downsizing," 335.
57. Oded Palmon, Huey-Lian Sun, and Alex P. Tang, "Layoff Announcements: Stock Market Impact and Financial Performance," *Financial Management, 26* (1997): 54–68.
58. James P. Guthrie and Deepak K. Datta, "Dumb and Dumber: The Impact of Downsizing on Firm Performance as Moderated by Industry Conditions," *Organization Science, 19* (2008): 108–23.
59. "1994 AMA Survey on Downsizing: Summary of Key Findings" (New York: American Management Association).
60. Ibid.

61. Martin Neil Baily, Eric J. Bartelsman, and John Haltiwanger, "Downsizing and Productivity Growth: Myth and Reality," Working Paper No. 4741 (Cambridge, MA: National Bureau of Economic Research), May 1994.
62. Peter Cappelli, "Examining the Influence of Downsizing and Its Effect on Establishment Performance," Working Paper No. 7742 (Cambridge, MA: National Bureau of Economic Research), June 2000.
63. Cited in Louis Uchitelle, "More Downsized Workers are Returning as Rentals," *New York Times*, December 8, 1996, 22.
64. Tania Marques, Isabel Suarez-Gonzalez, Pedro Pinheiro da Cruz, and Manuel Portugal Ferreira, "The Downsizing Effect on Survivors: A Structural Equation Modeling Analysis," *Management Research: The Journal of the Iberoamerican Academy of Management, 9* (2011): 174–91.
65. Teresa M. Amabile and Regina Conti, "Changes in the Work Environment for Creativity During Downsizing," *Academy of Management Journal, 42* (1999): 630–40.
66. Datta, et al., "Causes and Effects of Employee Downsizing," 309, 321.
67. David Cote, "Honeywell's CEO on How He Avoided Layoffs," *Harvard Business Review*, June 2013, 45.
68. Kevin F. Hallock, "Layoffs, Top Executive Pay, and Firm Performance," *American Economic Review, 88* (1998): 711–23.
69. Matt Glynn, "Ex-Southwest CEO Offers Lessons in Leadership from Post-9/11 Crisis," *Buffalo News*, May 19, 2014, www.buffalonews.com/business/ex-southwest-airlines-ceo-offers-lessons-in-leadership-from-post-911-crisis-20140519.
70. Erik Schonfeld, "The Silicon Chameleon," *Business 2.0*, September 2003, 84–85.
71. Frank Koller, *Spark: How Old-Fashioned Values Drive a Twenty-First-Century Corporation* (New York: Public Affairs Books, 2010).
72. See, for instance, Stephen Nickell, "Unemployment and Labor Market Rigidities: Europe versus North America," *Journal of Economic Perspectives, 11* (1997): 55–74; and Vicente Navarro, "Neoliberalism, 'Globalization,' Unemployment, Inequalities, and the Welfare State," *International Journal of Health Services, 28* (1998): 607–82.

Chapter 4: No Health Insurance, No Health

1. Eduardo Porter, "When Cutting Access to Health Care, There's a Price to Pay," *New York Times*, June 27, 2017, https://nyti.ms/2tfOWoM.
2. Andrew Dugan, "Cost Still Delays Healthcare for About One in Three in U.S.," *Gallup*, November 30, 2015, www.gallup.com/poll/187190/cost-delays-healthcare-one-three.aspx.
3. Andrew P. Wilper, Steffie Woolhandler, Karen E. Lasser, Danny McCormick, David H. Bor, and David U. Himmelstein, "Health Insurance and Mortality in US Adults," *American Journal of Public Health, 99* (2009): 2289–95.
4. See, for instance, J. Appleby and S. Carty, "Ailing GM Looks to Scale Back Generous Health Benefits," *USA Today*, June 23, 2005; and D. P. Levine, "GM Orders Staff to Pay Part of Health-Care Cost," *New York Times*, August 26, 1992.
5. Because once people turn sixty-five they are covered by Medicare, most analyses of an absence of health insurance and its consequences focus on individuals younger than sixty-five, typically referred to as the nonelderly.

6. The Kaiser Family Foundation is one of the leading resources for data and discussion of health insurance issues. John Holahan and Vicki Chen, "Changes in Health Insurance Coverage in the Great Recession, 2007–2009," Kaiser Commission on Medicaid and the Uninsured, December 2011; available at www.kff.org.
7. "The Uninsured: A Primer: Key Facts About Americans Without Health Insurance," Kaiser Commission on Medicaid and the Uninsured, October 2011; available at www.kff.org.
8. "Key Facts about the Uninsured Population," KFF.org, September 29, 2016, http://kff.org/uninsured/fact-sheet/key-facts-about-the-uninsured-population/.
9. "2015 Employer Health Benefits Survey," KFF.org, September 22, 2015, http://kff.org/report-section/ehbs-2015-summary-of-findings/.
10. "Health, United States, 2015," U.S. Department of Health and Human Services, Centers for Disease Control and Prevention, www.cdc.gov/nchs/data/hus/hus15.pdf#063.
11. Robert Kuttner, "The American Health Care System: Health Insurance Coverage," *New England Journal of Medicine, 340* (1999): 163–68.
12. Ibid., 16.
13. Marsha Lillie-Blanton and Catherine Hoffman, "The Role of Health Insurance Coverage in Reducing Racial/Ethnic Disparities in Health Care," *Health Affairs, 24* (2005): 398–408.
14. Hugh Walters, Laura Steinhardt, Thomas R. Oliver, and Alice Burton, "The Costs of Non-Insurance in Maryland," *Journal of Health Care for the Poor and Underserved, 18* (2007): 139–51.
15. Institute of Medicine, *Care Without Coverage: Too Little, Too Late* (Washington, DC: National Academy Press, 2002).
16. Stan Dorn, *Uninsured and Dying Because of It: Updating the Institute of Medicine Analysis on the Impact of Uninsurance on Mortality* (Washington, DC: The Urban Institute, January 2008).
17. J. Hadley and T. Waidmann, "Health Insurance and Health at Age 65: Implications for Medical Care Spending on New Medicare Beneficiaries," *Health Services Research, 41* (2006): 429–51.
18. Steffie Woolhandler and David U. Himmelstein, "The Relationship of Health Insurance and Mortality: Is Lack of Insurance Deadly?" *Annals of Internal Medicine*, http://annals.org/aim/article/2635326. Quote is from p. 6 of the online version.
19. Ibid., 5.
20. Wilper, et al., "Health Insurance and Mortality in US Adults."
21. J. R. Curtis, W. Burke, A. W. Kassner, and M. L. Aitken, "Absence of Health Insurance Is Associated with Decreased Life Expectancy in Patients with Cystic Fibrosis," *American Journal of Respiratory and Critical Care Medicine, 155* (1997): 1921–24.
22. Nicholas Bakalar, "Canadians with Cystic Fibrosis Live 10 Years Longer than Americans with the Disease," *New York Times*, March 15, 2017, https://nyti.ms/2mJWbA2.
23. John Z. Ayanian, Betsy A. Kohler, Toshi Abe, and Arnold M. Epstein, "The Relation Between Health Insurance Coverage and Clinical Outcomes Among

Women with Breast Cancer," *New England Journal of Medicine, 329* (1993): 326–31.

24. Stacey A. Fedewa, Vilma Cokkinides, Katherine S. Virgo, Priti Bandi, Debbie Saslow, and Elizabeth M. Ward, "Association of Insurance Status and Age with Cervical Cancer Stage at Diagnosis: National Cancer Database, 2000–2007," *American Journal of Public Health, 102* (2012): 1782–90.
25. J. J. Shen and E. L. Washington, "Disparities in Outcomes Among Patients with Stroke Associated with Insurance Status," *Stroke, 38* (2007): 1010–16.
26. Joseph J. Sudano Jr. and David W. Baker, "Intermittent Lack of Health Insurance Coverage and Use of Preventive Services," *American Journal of Public Health, 93* (2000): 130–37. Quote is from p. 130.
27. Ibid.
28. Ibid., 11.
29. Jack Hadley, "Insurance Coverage, Medical Care Use, and Short-Term Health Changes Following an Unintentional Injury or the Onset of a Chronic Condition," *Journal of the American Medical Association, 297* (2007): 1073–84.
30. David Card, Carlos Dobkin, and Nicole Maestas, "Does Medicare Save Lives?" *Quarterly Journal of Economics* (2009): 124597–636.
31. Bejamin D. Sommers, Katherine Baicker, and Arnold M. Epstein, "Mortality and Access to Care Among Adults after State Medicaid Expansions," *New England Journal of Medicine, 367* (2012): 1025–34.
32. The Henry J. Kaiser Family Foundation, "Key Facts About the Uninsured Population," http://kff.org/uninsured/fact-sheet/key-facts-about-the-uninsured-population/.
33. There is an enormous literature demonstrating this relationship. See, for instance, T. Chandola, E. Brunner, and M. Marmot, "Chronic Stress at Work and the Metabolic Syndrome: Prospective Study," *British Medical Journal, 332* (2006): 521–25; and M. Kivimaki, P. Leino-Arjas, R. Luukkonen, H. Riihimai, J. Vahtera, and J. Kirjonen, "Work Stress and Risk of Cardiovascular Mortality: Prospective Cohort Study of Industrial Employees," *British Medical Journal, 325* (2002): 857–60.
34. See, for instance, H. Harris and M. Fennell, "A Multivariate Model of Job Stress and Alcohol Consumption," *Sociological Quarterly, 29* (1988): 391–406; A. Kouvonen, M. Kivimaki, M. Virtanen, J. Pentti, and J. Vahtera, "Work Stress, Smoking Status, and Smoking Intensity: An Observational Study of 46,190 Employees," *Journal of Epidemiology and Community Health, 59* (2005): 63–69; and P. Piazza and M. Le Moal, "The Role of Stress in Drug Self-Administration," *Trends in Pharmaceutical Science, 19* (1998): 67–74.
35. David U. Himmelstein, Elizabeth Warren, Deborah Thorne, and Steffie Woolhandler, "Illness and Injury as Contributors to Bankruptcy," *Health Affairs, 24*: W5-63–W5-73.
36. K. Cook, D. Dranove, and A. Sfekas, "Does Major Illness Cause Financial Catastrophe?" *Health Services Research, 45* (2010): 418–36.
37. Robert W. Seifert and Mark Rukavina, "Bankruptcy Is the Tip of a Medical-Debt Iceberg," *Health Affairs, 25* (2006): W89–W92. Quote is from p. 90.
38. Thomas C. Buchmueller and Robert G. Valletta, "The Effects of Employer-Provided Health Insurance on Worker Mobility," *Industrial and Labor Relations Review, 49* (1996): 439–55. Quote is from p. 440.

39. Alan C. Monheit and Philip F. Cooper, "Health Insurance and Job Mobility: Theory and Evidence," *Industrial and Labor Relations Review, 48* (1994): 68–85. Quote is from p. 68.
40. Buchmueller and Valletta, "The Effects of Employer-Provided Health Insurance on Worker Mobility."
41. Brigitte C. Madrian, "Employment-Based Health Insurance and Job Mobility: Is There Evidence of Job-Lock?" *Quarterly Journal of Economics, 109* (1994): 27–54.
42. Kevin T. Stroupe, Eleanor D. Kinney, and Thomas J. J. Kneisner, "Chronic Illness and Health-Insurance-Related Job Lock," *Journal of Policy Analysis and Management, 20* (2001): 525–44.
43. Jonathan Gruber and Brigitte C. Madrian, "Health Insurance and Job Mobility: The Effects of Public Policy on Job-Lock," *Industrial and Labor Relations Review, 48* (1994): 86–102.
44. Victor Y. Haines III, Patrice Jalette, and Karine Larose, "The Influence of Human Resource Management Practices on Employee Voluntary Turnover Rates in the Canadian Non-Governmental Sector," *Industrial and Labor Relations Review, 63* (2010): 228–46.
45. Steffie Woolhandler and David U. Himmelstein, "The Deteriorating Administrative Efficiency of the US Health Care System," *New England Journal of Medicine, 324* (1991): 1253–58.
46. See, for instance, Louis Tze-ching Yen, Dee W. Edington, and Pam Witting, "Associations Between Health Risk Appraisal Scores and Employee Medical Claims Costs in a Manufacturing Company," *American Journal of Health Promotion, 6* (1991): 46–54.
47. John Carroll, "Companies Switching to On-Site Medical Clinics," www.louisianamedicalnews.com/companies-switching-to-on-site-medical-clinics.
48. On-Site Health Centers: Policies to Preserve and Promote an Effective Employer solution. (Washington, DC: National Business Group on Health), September 2011, 15.
49. Christopher Sears, "Is There a Doctor in the House?" December 31, 2008, www.lorman.com/resources/is-there-a-doctor-in-the-house-15257.
50. Sam Black, "Smaller Firms Now Offering On-Site Medical Clinics,"*Minneapolis/St. Paul Business Journal,* April 15, 2011.

Chapter 5: Health Effects of Long Work Hours and Work-Family Conflict

1. Catherine Makino, "Death from Overwork Persists Amid Economic Crunch," *Inter Press Service,* October 28, 2009, www.ipsnews.net/2009/10/japan-death-from-overwork-persists-amid-economic-crunch/.
2. Jonathan Soble, "Chief of Dentsu, Japanese Ad Agency, to Resign Over Employee's Suicide," *New York Times,* December 28, 2016, http://nyti.ms/2iEMLCA.
3. "In China, Office Work Can Be Deadly," *Bloomberg Businessweek,* July 7–13, 2014.
4. Zaria Gorvett, "Can You Work Yourself to Death?" BBC online, September 13, 2016, www.bbc.com/capital/story/20160912-is-there-such-thing-as-death-from-overwork.
5. Soble, "Chief of Dentsu, Japanese Ad Agency, to Resign."
6. Katsuo Nishiyama and Jeffrey V. Johnson, "Karoshi—Death from Overwork:

Occupational Health Consequences of Japanese Production Management," *International Journal of Health Services, 27* (1997): 625–41.

7. "In China, Office Work Can Be Deadly."
8. Ibid.
9. Paul Gallagher, "Slavery in the City: Death of a 21-year-old Intern Moritz Erhardt at Merrill Lynch Sparks Furor over Long Hours and Macho Culture at Banks," *Independent,* August 20, 2013, www.independent.co.uk/news/uk/home-news/slavery-in-the-city-death-of-21-year-old-intern-moritz-erhardt-at-merrill-lynch-sparks-furor-over-8775917.html.
10. Eilene Zimmerman, "The Lawyer, the Addict," *New York Times,* July 15, 2017, https://nyti.ms/2voimyC.
11. Jeffrey M. O'Brien, "Is Silicon Valley Bad for Your Health?" *Fortune,* November 1, 2015, 156.
12. Ibid.
13. Ibid., 157.
14. Mike Kivimaki, G. David Batty, Mark Hamer, Jane E. Ferrie, Jussi Vahtera, Marianna Virtanen, Michael G. Marmot, Archana Singh-Manoux, and Martin J. Shipley, "Using Additional Information on Working Hours to Predict Coronary Heart Disease," *Annals of Internal Medicine, 154* (2011): 457–63.
15. Brigid Schulte, "Beyond Inbox Zero: The Science of Work-Life Balance," *New American Weekly,* Edition 144, December 1, 2016, www.newamerica.org/weekly/edition-144/beyond-inbox-zero/.
16. Daniel S. Hamermesh and Elena Stancanelli, "Long Workweeks and Strange Hours," National Bureau of Economic Research, Working Paper No. 20449, September 2014, www.nber.org/papers/w20449.
17. David Kelleher, "Survey: 81% of U.S. Employees Check Their Work Mail outside Work Hours," *TechTalk,* May 20, 2013, https://techtalk.gfi.com/survey-81-of-u-s-employees-check-their-work-mail-outside-work-hours/.
18. Zimmerman, "The Lawyer, the Addict."
19. Caroline O'Donovan and Priya Anand, "How Uber's Hard-Charging Corporate Culture Left Employees Drained," July 17, 2017, *BuzzFeed,* www.buzzfeed.com/carolineodonovan/how-ubers-hard-charging-corporate-culture-left-employees.
20. Alissa J. Rubin, "'Right to Disconnect' from Work Email and Other Laws Go into Effect in France," *New York Times,* January 3, 2017, A6.
21. "After-Hours Email Expectations Negatively Impact Employee Well-Being," *ScienceDaily,* July 27, 2016, www.sciencedaily.com/releases/2016/07/160727110906.htm.
22. Justin McCarthy and Alyssa Brown, "Getting More Sleep Linked to Higher Well-Being," *Gallup,* March 2, 2105, www.gallup.com/poll/181583/getting-sleep-liniked-higher.aspx.
23. Alina Tugend, "Vacations Are Good for You, Medically Speaking," *New York Times,* June 7, 2008, www.nytimes.com/2008/06/07/business/yourmoney/07shortcuts.html.
24. Kathryn Vasel, "Half of American Workers Aren't Using All Their Vacation Days," *CNN Money,* December 10, 2016, http://moneyi.cnn.com/2016/12/19/pf/employees-unused-paid-vacation-dyas/index.html.
25. Rebecca Ray and John Schmitt, "No-Vacation Nation," Washington, DC: Center

for Economic and Policy Research, May 2007, http://cepr.net/publications/reports/no-vacation-nation.

26. Brian Wheeler, "Why Americans Don't Take Sick Days," *BBC News*, September 14, 2016, www.bbc.com/news/world-us-canada-37353742.
27. "Survey Shows Workers Often Go to Work Sick," Cision PR Newswire, January 12, 2016, www.prnewswire.com/news-releases/survey-shows-workers-often-go-to-work-sick-300202979.html.
28. Wheeler, "Why Americans Don't Take Sick Days."
29. Anders Knutsson, Bjorn G. Jonsson, Torbjom Akerstedt, and Kristina Orth-Gomer, "Increased Risk of Ischaemic Heart Disease in Shift Workers," *Lancet*, *338* (1986): 89–92.
30. Mark. L. Bryan, "Workers, Workplaces, and Working Hours," *British Journal of Industrial Relations*, *45* (December 2007): 735–59. Quote is from p. 735.
31. Richard Newton, "Dublin Goes Dark: Google's Experiments with Employee Wellbeing," March 21, 2015, www.virgin.com/disruptors/dublin-goes-dark-googles-experiments-employee-wellbeing.
32. Schulte, "Beyond Inbox Zero."
33. Sylvia Ann Hewlett and Carolyn Buck Luce, "Extreme Jobs: The Dangerous Allure of the 70-Hour Workweek," *Harvard Business Review*, *84* (2006, Issue 12): 49–59.
34. Drake Baer, "When Did Busy Become Cool?" *Thrive Global*, May 23, 2017, https://journal.thriveglobal.com/when-did-busy-become-cool-8ca13f5f54f9.
35. Olivia A. O'Neill and Charles A. O'Reilly, "Careers as Tournaments: The Impact of Sex and Gendered Organizational Culture Preferences on MBA's Income Attainment," *Journal of Organizational Behavior*, *31* (2010): 856–76.
36. Ken Belson, "At I.B.M., a Vacation Anytime, or Maybe None," *New York Times*, August 31, 2007.
37. J-P. Chaput, A. M. Sjodin, A. Astrup, J-P. Despres, C. Bouchard, and A. Tremblay, "Risk Factors for Adult Overweight and Obesity: The Importance of Looking Beyond the 'Big Two'," *Obesity Facts*, *3* (2010): 320–27.
38. G. Copinschi, "Metabolic and Endocrine Effects of Sleep Deprivation," *Essential Pharmacology*, *6* (2005): 341–47.
39. www.drugabuse.gov/publications/drugfacts/cocaine.
40. Alan Schwarz, "Workers Seeking Productivity in a Pill are Abusing A.D.H.D. Drugs," *New York Times*, April 18, 2015, https://nytimes.com/2015/04/19/us/workers-seeking-productivity-in-a-pill-are-abusing-adhd-drugs.html.
41. P. Buell and L. Breslow, "Mortality from Coronary Heart Disease in California Men Who Work Long Hours," *Journal of Chronic Diseases*, *11* (1960): 615–26.
42. Haiou Yang, Peter L. Schnall, Maritza Jauregui, Tai-Chen Su, and Dean Baker, "Work Hours and Self-Reported Hypertension among Working People in California," *Hypertension*, *48* (2006): 744–50.
43. A. Shimazu and B. Schaufeli, "Is Workaholism Good or Bad for Employee Well-Being? The Disincentiveness of Workaholism and Work Engagement Among Japanese Employees," *Industrial Health*, *47* (2009): 495–502.
44. Kate Sparks, Carry Cooper, Yitzhad Fried, and Arie Shirom, "The Effects of Hours of Work on Health: A Meta-Analytic Review," *Journal of Occupational and Organizational Psychology*, *70* (1997): 391–408.
45. Claire C. Caruso, Edward M. Hitchcock, Robert B. Dick, John M. Russo, and

Jennifer M. Schmit, National Institute for Occupational Safety and Health, "*Overtime and Extended Work Shifts: Recent Findings on Illnesses, Injuries, and Health Behaviors*, Washington, DC: National Institute for Occupational Safety and Health, April 2004.

46. Jeanne Geiger-Brown, Carles Muntaner, Jane Lipscomb, and Alison Trinkoff, "Demanding Work Schedules and Mental Health in Nursing Assistants Working in Nursing Homes," *Work and Stress, 18* (2004): 292–304.
47. Elizabeth Kleppa, Bjarte Sanne, and Grethe S. Tell, "Working Overtime Is Associated with Anxiety and Depression: The Hordaland Health Study," *Journal of Occupational and Environmental Medicine, 50* (2008): 658–66.
48. O'Donovan and Anand, "Uber's Hard-Charging Corporate Culture."
49. Emma Luxton, "Does Working Fewer Hours Make You More Productive?" World Economic Forum, March 4, 2016, www.weforum.org/agenda/2016/03/does-working-fewer-hours-make-you-more-productive.
50. Ibid.
51. Lonnie Golden, "The Effects of Working Time on Productivity and Firm Performance: A Research Synthesis Paper," (Geneva, Switzerland: International Labour Organization, 2012).
52. E. Shepard and T. Clifton, "Are Longer Hours Reducing Productivity in Manufacturing?" *International Journal of Manpower, 21* (2000): 540–53.
53. G. Cette, S. Change, and M. Konte, "The Decreasing Returns on Working Time: An Empirical Analysis on Panel Country Data," *Applied Economics Letters, 18* (2011): 1677–82.
54. M. White, *Working Hours: Assessing the Potential for Reduction* (Geneva, Switzerland: International Labour Organization, 1987).
55. E. E. Kossek and M. D. Lee, "Implementing a Reduced-Workload Arrangement to Retain High Talent: A Case Study," *Psychologist-Manager Journal, 43* (2008): 49–64.
56. Ulrica von Thiele Schwarz and Henna Hasson, "Employee Self-Rated Productivity and Objective Organizational Production Levels: Effects of Worksite Health Interventions Involving Reduced Work Hours and Physical Exercise," *Journal of Occupational and Environmental Medicine, 53* (2011): 838–44.
57. See, for instance, Jeffrey H. Greenhaus and Nicholas J. Beutell, "Sources of Conflict Between Work and Family Roles," *Academy of Management Review, 10* (1985): 76–88; and Tammy D. Allen, David E. L. Herst, Carly S. Bruck, and Martha Sutton, "Consequences Associated with Work-to-Family Conflict: A Review and Agenda for Future Research," *Journal of Occupational Health Psychology, 5* (2000): 278–308.
58. Michael H. Frone, Marcia Russell, and Grace M. Barnes, "Work-Family Conflict, Gender, and Health-Related Outcomes: A Study of Employed Parents in Two Community Samples," *Journal of Occupational Health Psychology, 1* (1996): 57–69.
59. Michael R. Frone, "Work-Family Conflict and Employee Psychiatric Disorders: The National Comorbidity Survey," *Journal of Applied Psychology, 85* (2000): 888–95.
60. Michael R. Frone, Marcia Russell, and M. Lynne Cooper, "Relation of Work-Family Conflict to Health Outcomes: A Four-Year Longitudinal Study of Employed Parents," *Journal of Occupational and Organizational Psychology, 70* (1997): 325–35.

61. Karyl E. Macewen, Julian Barling, and E. Kevin Kelloway, "Effects of Short-Term Role Overload on Marital Interactions," *Work and Stress, 6* (1992): 117–26.
62. Shelly Coverman, "Role Overload, Role Conflict, and Stress: Addressing Consequences of Multiple Role Demands," *Social Forces, 67* (1989): 965–82.
63. Steven L. Grover and Chun Hui, "The Influence of Role Conflict and Self-Interest on Lying in Organizations, *Journal of Business Ethics, 13* (1994): 295–303.
64. N. W. H. Jansen, I. J. Kant, L. G. P. M. van Amelsvaart, T. S. Kristensen, G. M. H. Swaen, and F. J. N. Nijhuis, "Work-Family Conflict as a Risk Factor for Sickness Absence," *Occupational and Environmental Medicine, 63* (2006): 488–94.
65. Jennifer Paterson, "Employee Benefits Live: Google Focuses on Emotional Wellbeing to Make Staff Healthiest on the Planet, September 27, 2011, www.employeebenefits.co.uk/issues/september-2011-online/employee-benefits-life-google-focuses-on-emotional-wellbeing-to-make-staff-healthiest-on-the-planet/.
66. http://reviews.greatplacetowork.com/whole-foods-market.
67. Ariane Hegewisch and Janet C. Gornick, "Statutory Routes to Workplace Flexibility in Cross-National Perspective," Washington, DC: Institute for Women's Policy Research, 2008, vii.
68. Ibid., 2.

Chapter 6: Two Critical Elements of a Healthy Workplace

1. "Does Silicon Valley Have a Perks Problem?" *Rocketrip*, February 1, 2016, http://blog.rocketrip.com/silicon-valley-have-a-perks-problem.
2. Maarit A-L Vartia, "Consequences of Workplace Bullying with Respect to the Well-Being of Its Targets and the Observers of Bullying," *Scandinavian Journal of Work, Environment & Health, 27* (2011): 63–69.
3. Francesco Gamberale, Anders Kjellberg, Torbjom Akerstedt, and Gunn Johansson, "Behavioral and Psychophysiological Effects of the Physical Work Environment: Research Strategies and Measurement Methods," *Scandinavian Journal of Work, Environment & Health, 16*, Supplement 1 (1990): 5–16.
4. M. G. Marmot, G. Rose, M. Shipley, and P. J. S. Hamilton, "Employment Grade and Coronary Heart Disease in British Civil Servants," *Journal of Epidemiology and Community Health, 32* (1978): 244–49.
5. M. G. Marmot, H. Bosma, H. Hemingway, E. Brunner, and S. Stansfeld, "Contribution of Job Control and Other Risk Factors to Social Variations in Coronary Heart Disease Incidence," *Lancet, 350* (1997): 235–39. Quote is from p. 235.
6. Michael Marmot, Amanda Feeney, Martin Shipley, Fiona North, and S. I. Syme, "Sickness Absence as a Measure of Health Status and Functioning from the UK Whitehall II Study," *Journal of Epidemiology and Community Health, 49* (1995): 124–30.
7. Tarani Chandola, Eric Brunner, and Michael Marmot, "Chronic Stress at Work and the Metabolic Syndrome: Prospective Study," *British Medical Journal, 332* (2005): 521–25.
8. John Robert Warren, Pascale Carayon, and Peter Hoonakker, "Changes in Health Between Ages 54 and 65: The Role of Job Characteristics and Socioeconomic Status," *Research on Aging, 30* (2008): 672–700.
9. Tjasa Pisijar, Tanja van der Lippe, and Laura den Dulk, "Health Among Hospi-

tal Employees in Europe: A Cross-National Study of the Impact of Work Stress and Work Control," *Social Science and Medicine, 72* (2011): 899–906.

10. Robert Karasek, "Lower Health Risk with Increased Job Control among White Collar Workers," *Journal of Organizational Behaviour, 11* (1990): 171–85.
11. "Worked to Death? IU Study Says Lack of Control over High-stress Jobs Leads to Early Grave," *EurekAlert!*, October 17, 2016, https://www.eurekalert.org/pub_releases/2016-10/iu-wtd101416.php.
12. Chester S. Spell and Todd Arnold, "An Appraisal of Justice, Structure, and Job Control as Antecedents of Psychological Distress," *Journal of Organizational Behavior, 28* (2007): 729–51.
13. Martin E. P. Seligman, "Learned Helplessness," *Annual Review of Medicine, 23* (1972): 407.
14. Steven F. Maier and Martin E. P. Seligman, "Learned Helplessness: Theory and Evidence," *Journal of Experimental Psychology: General, 105* (1976): 3–46.
15. Ibid., 13.
16. Philip M. Boffey, "Satisfaction on the Job: Autonomy Ranks First," *New York Times*, May 28, 1985.
17. Frederick P. Morgeson, Kelly Delaney-Klinger, and Monica A. Hemingway, "The Importance of Job Autonomy, Cognitive Ability, and Job-Related Skill for Predicting Role Breadth and Job Performance," *Journal of Applied Psychology, 90* (2005): 399–406.
18. "Netherlands: Steady Decline in Job Autonomy," European Foundation for the Improvement of Living and Working Conditions (Eurofound), May 6, 2015. The report notes that "Job autonomy . . . has been declining for decades in much of Europe." This site has a great deal of information about workplace conditions and their effects.
19. Ellen J. Langer, "The Illusion of Control," *Journal of Personality and Social Psychology, 32* (1975): 311–28.
20. Jeffrey Pfeffer, Robert B. Cialdini, Benjamin Hanna, and Kathleen Knopoff, "Faith in Supervision and the Self-Enhancement Bias: Why Managers Don't Empower Workers," *Basic and Applied Social Psychology, 20* (1998): 313–21.
21. W. Eugene Broadhead, Berton H. Kaplan, Sherman A. James, Edward H. Wagner, Victor J. Schoenbach, Roger Grimson, Siegfried Heyden, Gosta Tibblin, and Stephen H. Gehrlach, "The Epidemiological Evidence for a Relationship Between Social Support and Health," *American Journal of Epidemiology, 117* (1983): 521–37.
22. Markham Heid, "You Asked: How Many Friends Do I Need?" *Time Health*, March 18, 2015, http://time.com/3748090/friends-social-health/.
23. Bert N. Uchino, "Social Support and Health: A Review of Physiological Processes Potentially Underlying Links to Disease Outcomes," *Journal of Behavioral Medicine, 29* (2006): 377–87. Quotes are from p. 377.
24. Steve Crabtree, "Social Support Linked to Health Satisfaction Worldwide," *Gallup*, February 17, 2012, www.gallup.com/poll/152738/social-support-linked-health-satisfaction-worldwide.aspx.
25. James M. LaRocco, James S. House, and John R. P. French Jr., "Social Support, Occupational Stress, and Health," *Journal of Health and Social Behavior, 21* (1980): 202–18.
26. Chockalingam Viswesvaran, Juan I. Sanchez, and Jeffrey Fisher, "The Role of

Social Support in the Process of Work Stress: A Meta-Analysis," *Journal of Vocational Behavior, 54* (1999): 314–34.

27. Sheldon Cohen and Thomas Ashby Wills, "Stress, Social Support, and the Buffering Hypothesis," *Psychological Bulletin, 98* (1985): 310–57.
28. Uchino, "Social Support and Health," 377.
29. Roy F. Baumeister and Mark R. Leary, "The Need to Belong: Desire for Interpersonal Attachments as a Fundamental Human Motivation," *Psychological Bulletin, 117* (1995): 497–529. Quote is from p. 497.
30. Andrew Hill, "Forced Ranking Is a Relic of an HR Tool," *Financial Times*, July 16, 2012, www.ft.com/content/0243818e-cd09-11e1-92c1-00144feabdc0.
31. "It's Official: Forced Ranking Is Dead," *Wall Street Journal*, http://deloitte.wsj.com/cio/2014/06/10/its-official-forced-ranking-is-dead/.
32. Alison Griswold, "Uber Is Designed So That for One Employee to Get Ahead, Another Must Fail," *Quartz*, February 27, 2017, https://qz.com/918582/uber-is-designed-so-that-for-one-employee-to-succeed-another-must-fail.
33. "SAS Institute (B): The Decision to Go Public," Stanford, CA: Graduate School of Business Case #HR-6B, September 16, 2003.
34. "Gary's Greeting: Taking Care of Each Other," https:.//issuu.com/southwestmag/docs/02_february_2016/18.
35. DaVita Reports on 2015 Corporate Social Responsibility and Innovation, Bridge of Life, April 18, 2016, www.bridgeoflifeinternational.org/davita-reports-on-2015-corporate-social-responsibility-and-innovation/.
36. "Trilogy of Care II: A Day in the Life of a Dialysis Healthcare Administrator," February 5, 2014, http://careers.davita.com/our-story/blogs/trilogy-care-ii.
37. Laszlo Bock, *Work Rules!* (New York: Hachette Group, 2015), 278.
38. Ibid.
39. Ibid., 279.
40. Ibid., 263.
41. D. Byrne, "Interpersonal Attraction and Attitude Similarity," *Journal of Abnormal and Social Psychology, 62* (1961): 713–15.
42. Jerry M. Burger, Nicole Messian, Shebani Patel, Alicia del Prado, and Carmen Anderson, "What a Coincidence! The Effects of Incidental Similarity on Compliance," *Personality and Social Psychology Bulletin, 30* (2004): 35–43.
43. UnitedHealth Group, "Doing Good Is Good for You: 2013 Health and Volunteering Study," Minnetonka, MN: UnitedHealth Group, 2013.
44. www.southwest.com/html/about-southwest/careers/benefits.html.

Chapter 7: Why People Stay in Toxic Workplaces

1. Jodi Kantor and David Streitfeld, "Inside Amazon: Wrestling Big Ideas in a Bruising Workplace," *New York Times*, August 16, 2015, http://nyti.ms/1TFqcOG.
2. Mike Pare, "Inside the Deal that Lured Amazon to Chattanooga," *Chattanooga Times Free Press*, December 26, 2010, www.timesfreepress.com/news/news/story/2010/dec/26/inside-the-deal-that-lured-amazon/37827/.
3. Larry Gigerich, "Siting a Contact Center or Data Center Requires Supreme Diligence," *Trade and Industry Development*, June 30, 2012.
4. Eilene Zimmerman, "The Lawyer, the Addict," *New York Times*, July 15, 2017, https://nyti.ms/2voimyC.

5. Paul A. Samuelson, "Consumption Theory in Terms of Revealed Preference," *Economica, 15* (1948): 243–53.
6. Amartya K. Sen, "Rational Fools: A Critique of the Behavioral Foundation of Economic Theory," *Philosophy and Public Affairs, 6* (1977): 322.
7. Sherwin Rosen, "The Theory of Equalizing Differentials," *Handbook of Labor Economics, 1* (1986): 641–92.
8. See, for instance, Randall W. Eberts and Joe A. Stone, "Wages, Fringe Benefits, and Working Conditions: An Analysis of Compensating Differentials," *Southern Economic Journal, 52* (1985): 274–80; and Stephanie Bonhomme, "The Pervasive Absence of Compensating Differentials," *Journal of Applied Econometrics, 24* (2009): 763–95.
9. See, for instance, Dan Ariely, *Predictably Irrational: The Hidden Forces That Shape Our Decisions* (New York: HarperCollins, 2008).
10. Kantor and Streitfeld, "Inside Amazon."
11. Ibid.
12. Ibid.
13. Vera Hoorens, "Self-Enhancement and Superiority Biases in Social Comparison," *European Review of Social Psychology, 4* (1993). 113–39.
14. Zlatan Krizan and Jerry Suls, "Losing Sight of Oneself in the Above-Average Effect: When Egocentrism, Focalism, and Group Diffuseness Collide," *Journal of Experimental Social Psychology, 44* (2008): 929–42.
15. Leaf Van Boven, David Dunning, and George Loewenstein, "Egocentric Empathy Gaps between Owners and Buyers: Misperceptions of the Endowment Effect," *Journal of Personality and Social Psychology, 79* (2000): 66–76.
16. Kantor and Streitfeld, "Inside Amazon."
17. The literature on commitment is vast. See, for instance, Robert B. Cialdini and Noah J. Goldstein, "Social Influence: Compliance and Conformity," *Annual Review of Psychology, 55* (2004): 591–621; and Gerald R. Salancik, "Commitment Is Too Easy!" *Organizational Dynamics, 6* (1977): 62–80.
18. See, for instance, Leon Festinger, "A Theory of Social Comparison Processes," *Human Relations, 7* (1954): 117–40; and Morton Deutsch and Harold B. Gerard, "A Study of Normative and Informational Social Influences Upon Individual Judgment," *Journal of Abnormal and Social Psychology, 5* (1955): 629–36.
19. Robert B. Cialdini, *Influence: The Psychology of Persuasion* (New York: HarperCollins, 2009).
20. David Krackhardt and Lyman W. Porter, "The Snowball Effect: Turnover Embedded in Communications Networks," *Journal of Applied Psychology, 71* (1986): 50–55.
21. Gerald R. Salancik and Jeffrey Pfeffer, "A Social Information Processing Approach to Job Attitudes and Task Design," *Administrative Science Quarterly, 23* (1978): 224–53.
22. Harriet Taylor, "Travis Kalanick Will Be 'Legendary' Like Bill Gates, Says Uber Investor," CNBC, March 1, 2017, www.cnbc.com/2017/03/01/uber-ceo-travis-kalanick-needs-to-stop-self-inflicted-wounds-jason-calacanis.html.

Chapter 8: What Might—and Should—Be Different

1. Barry-Wehmiller website, www.barrywehmiller.com/our-business/leadership-team/bob-chapman.

2. See, for instance, Robert I. Sutton, *The No Asshole Rule: Building a Civilized Workplace and Surviving One That Isn't* (New York: Hachette, 2007).
3. Lyn Quine, "Workplace Bullying in Nurses," *Journal of Health Psychology, 6* (2001): 73–84.
4. Charlotte Rayner, "The Incidence of Workplace Bullying," *Journal of Community and Applied Social Psychology, 7* (1997): 199–208.
5. Quine, "Workplace Bullying in Nurses."
6. M. Kivimaki, M. Virtanen, M. Vartia, M. Elovainio, J. Vahtera, and L. Keltikangas-Jarvinen, "Workplace Bullying and the Risk of Cardiovascular Disease and Depression," *Occupational and Environmental Medicine, 60* (2003): 779–83.
7. Sutton, *The No Asshole Rule.*
8. Elena Flores, Jeanne M. Tschann, Juanita M. Dimas, Elizabeth A. Bachen, Lauri A. Pasch, and Cynthia L. de Groat, "Perceived Discrimination, Perceived Stress, and Mental and Physical Health Among Mexican-Origin Adults," *Hispanic Journal of Behavioral Sciences, 30* (2008): 401–24.
9. Rebecca Din-Dzietham, Wendy N. Nembhard, Rakale Collins, and Sharon K. Davis, "Perceived Stress Following Race-Based Discrimination at Work Is Associated with Hypertension in African-Americans: The Metro Atlanta Heart Disease Study, 1999–2001," *Social Science and Medicine, 58* (2004): 449–61.
10. Elizabeth A. Pascoe and Laura Smart Richman, "Perceived Discrimination and Health: A Meta-Analytic Review, *Psychological Bulletin, 135* (2009): 531–554. Quote is from p. 531.
11. Judith H. Heerwagen, Janet G. Heubach, Joseph Montgomery, and Wally C. Weimer, "Environmental Design, Work, and Well-Being: Managing Occupational Stress through Changes in the Workplace Environment, *AAOHN Journal, 43* (1995): 458–68.
12. Sally L. Lusk, Bonnie M. Hagerty, Brenda Gillespie, and Claire C. Caruso, "Chronic Effects of Workplace Noise on Blood Pressure and Heart Rate," *Archives of Environmental Health: An International Journal, 57* (2002): 273–81.
13. Douglas LaBier, "Another Survey Shows the Continuing Toll of Workplace Stress, *Psychology Today,* April 23, 2014, www.psychologytoday.com/blog/the-new-resilience/201404/another-survey-shows-the-continuing-toll-workplace-stress.
14. J. M. Mossey and E. Shapiro, "Self-Rated Health: A Predictor of Mortality Among the Elderly," *American Journal of Public Health, 72* (1982): 800–808.
15. Seppo Miilunpalo, Ilkka Vuori, Pekka Oja, Matti Pasanen, and Helka Urponen, "Self-Rated Health Status as a Health Measure: The Predictive Value of Self-Reported Health Status on the Use of Physician Services and on Mortality in the Working-Age Population," *Journal of Clinical Epidemiology, 50* (1997): 517–28.
16. Daniel L. McGee, Youlian Liao, Guichan Cao, and Richard S. Cooper, "Self-Reported Health Status and Mortality in a Multiethnic US Cohort," *American Journal of Epidemiology, 149* (1999): 41–46.
17. Marja Jylha, "What Is Self-Rated Health and Why Does It Predict Mortality? Towards a Unified Conceptual Model," *Social Science and Medicine, 69* (2009): 307–16.
18. M. Marmot, A. Feeney, M. Shipley, F. North, and S. L. Syme, "Sickness Absence as a Measure of Health Status and Functioning: From the UK Whitehall II Study," *Journal of Epidemiology and Community Health, 49* (1995): 124–30.

19. Daniel L. McGee, Youlian Liao, Guichan Cao, and Richard S. Cooper, "Self-Reported Health Status and Mortality in a Multiethnic US Cohort," *American Journal of Epidemiology, 149* (1999): 41–46.
20. Elizabeth Frankenberg and Nathan R. Jones, "Self-Rated Health and Mortality: Does the Relationship Extend to a Low Income Setting?" *Journal of Health and Social Behavior, 45* (2004): 441–52.
21. Ellen L. Idler and Yael Benyamini, "Self-Rated Health and Mortality: A Review of Twenty-Seven Community Studies," *Journal of Health and Social Behavior, 38* (1997): 21–37. Quote is from p. 21.
22. OECD Health Statistics 2017, www.oecd.org/els/health-systems/health-data.htm.
23. See, for instance, Kevin Daniels, "Measures of Five Aspects of Affective Well-Being at Work," *Human Relations, 53* (2000): 275–94; and Peter Warr, "The Measurement of Well-being and Other Aspects of Mental Health," *Journal of Occupational and Organizational Psychology, 63* (1990): 193–210.
24. Peter R. Vagg and Charles D. Spielberger, "Occupational Stress: Measuring Job Pressure and Organizational Support in the Workplace," *Journal of Occupational Health Psychology, 3* (1998): 294–305; and Paul E. Spector and Steve M. Jex, "Development of Four Self-Report Measures of Job Stressors and Strain: Interpersonal Conflict at Work Scale, Organizational Constraints Scale, Quantitative Workload Inventory, and Physical Symptoms Inventory," *Journal of Occupational Health Psychology, 3* (1998): 356–67.
25. Dawn S. Carlson, K. Michele Kacmar, and Larry J. Williams, "Construction and Validation of a Multidimensional Measure of Work-Family Conflict," *Journal of Vocational Behavior, 56* (2000): 249–76.
26. M. G. Marmot, H. Bosma, H. Hemingway, E. Brunner, and S. Stansfeld, "Contribution of Job Control and Other Risk Factors to Social Variations in Coronary Heart Disease Incidence," *Lancet, 350* (1997): 235–39.
27. Ralph Catalano, "The Health Effects of Economic Insecurity," *American Journal of Public Health, 81* (1991): 1148–52.
28. 2016 *Working Mother* 100 Best Companies, www.workingmother.com/2016-Working-Mother-100-Best-Companies.
29. Ken Jacobs, "The Hidden Cost of Jobs Without Health Care Benefits," *Perspectives on Work, 11* (Winter 2007): 14.
30. Carol Zabin, Arindrajit Dube, and Ken Jacobs, "The Hidden Public Costs of Low-Wage Jobs in California," Berkeley, CA: University of California Institute for Labor and Employment, 2004, http://escholarship.org/uc/item/9hb1k75c.
31. Jacobs, "The Hidden Cost," 15.
32. Ibid.
33. Arindrajit Dube and Steve Wertheim, "Wal-Mart and Job Quality—What Do We Know, and Should We Care," Paper prepared for Presentation at the Center for American Progress, October 16, 2005. Berkeley, CA: Institute of Industrial Relations, University of California.
34. Ibid.
35. Jacobs, "The Hidden Cost," 16.
36. Barbara Grady, "Healthy San Francisco, City's Universal Health Plan, Rests on Unstable Funding," *Huffington Post San Francisco,* November 19, 2011, www.huffingtonpost.com/2011/11/19/healthy-san-francisco_n_1102978.html.
37. Ibid.

38. "Aspiring to Universal Access: Healthy San Francisco Opens Up Care," http://www.amednews.com/article/10530/government/305309949/4/.
39. Renee Dudley, "Walmart Faces the Cost of Cost-Cutting: Empty Shelves," *BusinessWeek*, March 28, 2013, www.bloomberg.com/news/articles/2013-03-28/walmart-faces-the-cost-of-cost-cutting-empty-shelves.
40. Zeynep Ton, "Why 'Good Jobs' are Good for Retailers," *Harvard Business Review*, January–February 2012, http://hbr.org/2012/01/why-good-jobs-are-good-for-retailers.
41. Jeffrey Pfeffer and Robert I. Sutton, *The Knowing-Doing Gap: How Smart Companies Turn Knowledge into Action* (Boston: Harvard Business School Press, 2000).
42. Jeffrey Pfeffer, *The Human Equation: Building Profits by Putting People First* (Boston: Harvard Business School Press, 1998), Chapter 5.
43. Scott Adams, Dilbert cartoon, September 10, 2017, http://dilbert.com/strip/1993-03-03.
44. Mara Lee, "Aetna to Cut Workforce, Reduce Work-at-Home Policy," *Hartford Courant*, October 11, 2016, www.courant.com/business/hc-aetna-work-at-home-20161010-story.html.
45. Jena McGregor, "Five Telling Things the Whole Foods CEO Said About the Amazon Deal in an Employee Town Hall," *Washington Post*, June 20, 2017.
46. Rick Wartzman, "Amazon and Whole Foods Are Headed for a Culture Clash," *Fortune*, June 26, 2017, http://fortune.com/2017/06/26/amazon-whole-foods-corporate-culture-clash-jeff-bezos-john-mackey/.
47. "World Happiness Report," *Wikipedia*, https://en.wikipedia.org/wiki/World_Happiness_Report.
48. www.weforum.org/reports/the-inclusive-growth-and-development-report-2017.
49. "OECD Better-Life Index," *Wikipedia*, https://en.wikipedia.org/wiki/OECD_Better-Life_Index.
50. Timothy F. Slaper and Tanya J. Hall, "The Triple Bottom Line: What Is It and How Does It Work?" *Indiana Business Review*, *86* (2011): 4–8. www.ibrc.indiana.edu/ibr/2011/spring/article2.html.
51. Philip E. Tetlock, "Thinking the Unthinkable: Sacred Values and Taboo Cognitions," *Trends in Cognitive Sciences*, *7* (2003): 320–24. Quote is from p. 320.
52. See, for instance, Philip E. Tetlock, Orie V. Kristel, S. Beth Elson, Melanie C. Green, and Jennifer S. Lerner, "The Psychology of the Unthinkable: Taboo Trade-offs, Forbidden Base Rates, and Heretical Counterfactuals," *Journal of Personality and Social Psychology*, *78* (2000): 853–70.
53. Scheherazade Daneshkhu, Lindsay Whipp, and James Fontanella-Kahn, "The Lean and Mean Approach of 3G Capital," *Financial Times*, May 7, 2017.

Index

Note: Page numbers followed by "*f*" indicate a figure; "*t*" indicates a table.

About the Author

JEFFREY PFEFFER is the Thomas D. Dee II Professor of Organizational Behavior at the Graduate School of Business, Stanford University, where he has taught since 1979. He is the author or coauthor of fifteen books, including *Leadership B.S., Power, The Human Equation, Managing with Power, Hidden Value, Hard Facts, Dangerous Half-Truths, and Total Nonsense,* and *The Knowing-Doing Gap.* From 2003 to 2007, Pfeffer wrote a monthly column, "The Human Factor," for *Business 2.0.* Pfeffer has presented seminars in thirty-nine countries throughout the world and provides consulting and executive education for numerous companies, associations, and universities in the United States. He won the Richard D. Irwin Award for scholarly contributions to management and has been listed in the top twenty-five management thinkers by Thinkers50 and as one of the HR Most Influential Thinkers by *HR Magazine.* In 2011, Pfeffer received an honorary doctorate from Tilburg University in the Netherlands.